MONEY
&
WEALTH

IN THE NEW MILLENNIUM

A Prophetic Guide to the New World Economic Order

NORM FRANZ

Dedication

This book is dedicated to you, the reader, and all the nations of the earth who have been taken captive by the world's debt-based financial system.

My prayer is that God anoints you with the wisdom of the sons of Issachar, who understood the times and had knowledge of what to do (1 CHRONICLES 12:32).

In God's Love,

Norm Franz
A Messenger of the Covenant

TABLE OF CONTENTS

CHAPTER 4
Debt Makes the World Go Round

CHAPTER 5
It Sounds Like a Plan

CHAPTER 6
Modus Operandi

CHAPTER 11
Worldwide Financial Collapse

CHAPTER 12
Debt-for-Equity Swaps

CHAPTER 16

God's Ways of Prosperity

CHAPTER 17

When Money Ends and Wealth Begins

Additional Insights

Acknowledgments

My first devotion of thanks is to the Lord Jesus Christ, who has granted me life and is the source of all that I am or ever hope to be. It is only by His grace that I have been able to bring forth the revelation recorded in this book.

To my Dad and Mom, Norman Sr. and Gloria Franz, who taught me the principle of hard work at an early age.

To Dr. Larry Bates who mentored me concerning the secret ways of the U.S. Federal Reserve. His knowledge of fractional reserve banking gave me the necessary understanding of the monetary system without which this book could never have been written.

To Simon Pang and the leaders in Singapore, who confronted Asia with the truth behind its financial crisis even when it was not popular. Their commitment to God's truth concerning the use of unjust scales in the financial markets has played a major role in taking the message in this book to the nations.

To Ivy Ho, David Ong, Y C Lee and their families at Genesis One Media Pte Ltd, who labored endlessly to complete this work.

And last but not least, to Warren and Margo Schoder, Mark and Connie Gotschall, Norma Pecora, and the faithful of Ascension Ministries, who were there for me during the dark night of my soul. Without your un-wavering love and support, I could not have continued.

Introduction

Ever since the early 1980s, I have felt a calling on my life to help people in the area of finance and investments. My heartfelt goal has always been to help families build businesses and plan their financial future, so they could leave an inheritance to their children's children.

Early on, I was taught that helping people financially meant getting them the money they needed to buy all the material goods they wanted. As a result, I entered the field of finance, where I put together millions of dollars in consumer loan packages. I helped hundreds of people obtain the things they wanted through the magical banking phenomenon called credit.

Unfortunately, I also saw many go bankrupt as they lost control of their credit lines or a personal financial shaking broke their payment cycle. All the things they thought they owned were actually the property of the financial institution they borrowed the money from. Overnight, I saw people go from having an abundance of material possessions to having virtually nothing. I saw families break up because debt had consumed their future, and their children ultimately suffered the consequences.

At that point, I began to ask myself if it was pleasing to the Lord for me to help people go into debt. When I read the Bible where God says that His people are to be lenders and not borrowers, I justified my actions because I was doing the lending. However, it was harder to justify putting people in debt to a heartless credit system that enslaved its debtors.

Then a rapidly expanding Christian investment firm recruited me for their business development and finance department. I advanced quickly and within 18 months I became president and chief operation officer of one of three sister companies.

Everything was going along great until the 1986 Tax Reform Act knocked the guts out of limited partnerships. Investments that were considered almost foolproof, became all but worthless overnight. I was personally grieved for my clients, because I saw them lose their investments and there was nothing I could do for them. This was the first time I saw how Washington could devastate the financial future of its citizens with a stroke of its pen.

The next blow came during the October 19, 1987 stock market crash, when programmed trading began to liquidate an early form of derivatives called "portfolio insurance." It was called "Black Monday," and the financial effects were devastating. I saw investors lose large sums of money, which destroyed a lot of people's plans for retirement. Many investors like myself had to virtually start over, and some even went bankrupt.

The final blow came shortly after the crash, when I was let go from my position during the company's restructuring program. This blew me out of the water, because I had accumulated a mountain of debt to finance the image of prosperity that I presented to potential clients. When I couldn't make the payments, my creditors rose up against me and I became their slave.

At this point I began to seek the Lord for answers. The primary question on my heart was: "If You are the Lord of heaven and earth, why would you allow these financial catastrophes to come upon all these good people—including Christians?" It seemed to me that if God was in charge, then the financial markets should not be going through cycles of booms and busts, where the rich get richer at the expense of the small investor.

This is when the Lord started opening my eyes to the fact that He was not the author of the current world system. That's when He planted a question in my heart that asked: "Why do you think it's called the *world system*?" At that moment, all of my understanding and experience in business development, finance and investments came crashing into the revelation that the world financial system had not been designed by the God of Heaven, but by the "god of this world."

Suddenly, I could see how debt was used to manipulate the economic and investment behavior of whole nations. I understood that "Commercial Babylon" was a global system of dishonest scales that feeds man's root sin—the love of money.

From there, the Lord took me on a fourteen-year travel study through the world's debt-based financial system, where He taught me how to identify and come out of my bondage to it. This book, MONEY AND WEALTH IN THE NEW MILLENNIUM, is the essence of that journey, and it is written in a manner that will help you to come out also.

Chapter 1

THE ROOT OF ALL EVIL

"For the love of money is the root of all evil."
1 TIMOTHY 6:10, KJV

The essence of original sin is hotly debated throughout religious circles today, and greater theologians than I have generated a host of convincing studies in support of their theses. However, if we hold to the biblical truth that the love of money is the root of all evil, then the first and original sin ever committed in God's Kingdom must have been associated with the quest for riches.

The love of money is simply the lust for material possessions, which money is used to obtain. It lives and breeds in the business arena and has been the root source of evil from the first time that unrighteousness was found among the heavenly host.

This takes us back to when and why sin was first found in Lucifer. The prophet Isaiah describes Lucifer as being so filled with pride that he attempted to raise himself above the stars of heaven and become "like" (equal with) God (ISAIAH 14:12–14). This produced his violent attempt to overthrow God's throne, which cost him his position as the covering cherub (guardian angel) of the garden and resulted in his fall.

This act of pride is what established the biblical principle that "pride goes before destruction" (PROVERBS 16:18) and has become what some consider to be Satan's original sin. However, I submit to you that if the love of money is the root of all evil, then there had to be an earlier root sin in Satan, more vile than his pride, that manifested as an unrighteous desire to accumulate riches.

Lucifer's Original Sin

The prophet Ezekiel explains how Lucifer's abundance of trade caused iniquity to be found in him, which led him to commit the first sin:

> "You [Lucifer] were in Eden, the garden of God ... You were the anointed cherub [archangel] who covers, and I [God] placed you there ... . You were blameless in your ways from the day you were created, *until unrighteousness was found in you. By the abundance of your trade [merchandise and business] you were internally filled with violence, and you sinned ...*"
> (EZEKIEL 28:13, 14–16)

There are a lot of things happening in this passage of Scripture. First, it would appear that before his attempted coup against Jehovah (YHVH), Lucifer was involved in an abundance of business and trade that was being transacted in the Kingdom of Heaven.

Second, it would also appear that *original sin* was birthed in Lucifer while he was in the midst of those business activities. This abundant volume of trade filled Lucifer with so much violence that he actually launched a frontal assault against Jehovah to get more. Can you imagine anyone trying anything so foolish? This appears to be the first example of how the lust for money and material possession can drive anyone to believe that they don't have to obey God's Word.

Vanity and Pride Enter Lucifer

Ezekiel goes on to point out how Lucifer's lust for financial abundance, combined with his physical beauty, produced a vanity that corrupted his God-given wisdom:

> "Your heart was lifted up [in pride] because of your beauty; you corrupted your wisdom by reason of your splendor ... ." (v 17)

Lucifer's financial prowess caused him to focus on his own beauty instead of the beauty of the Lord. This produced vanity in him, which seduced him into believing that he was even more beautiful than God. This is why the world refers to the wicked rich as "the beautiful people," whether they are or not.

At this point, *by reason of his splendor*, Lucifer became wise in his own eyes and the sin of pride manifested in him. Pride has always been the danger surrounding the deceitfulness of riches. The richer people become, the more pride rises up and causes them to think that they are the source of their wealth instead of Jehovah God.

Moses points out that when this happens, they become delusional to the point where they walk away from obeying God's commandments:

"When you have eaten and are satisfied, you shall bless the Lord your God for the good land which He has given you. Beware lest you forget the Lord your God by not keeping His commandments and His ordinances and His statutes which I am commanding you today; lest, when you have eaten and are satisfied, and have built good houses and lived in them, and when your herds and your flocks multiply, and your silver and gold multiply, and all that you have multiplies, *then your heart becomes proud*, and you forget the Lord your God who brought you out from the land of Egypt [saved you], out of the house of slavery [prospered you]." (DEUTERONOMY 8:10–14)

This is exactly what happened to Lucifer. His love for, and accumulation of, material possessions caused vanity and pride to rise up in him. The combination of abundant wealth, vanity and pride deceived Lucifer into believing that he was like (equal with) God, which deceived him into believing that he could conduct business contrary to the laws of God.

Unrighteous Trade

Once Lucifer came to believe that he was Jehovah's equal, he lost his submission to God and began to make up his own rules. It was here that he began to operate according to his own unrighteous standards when conducting his business affairs. Ezekiel goes on to say:

"By the multitude of your iniquities, in the *unrighteousness of your trade*, you profaned your sanctuaries …" (EZEKIEL 28:18)

Lucifer's abundant trade produced the root sin of lust to obtain wealth faster than righteous trading would allow. So he began to implement dishonest business practices that he used to cheat his trading partners. This ended his ministry as the covering cherub, and God expelled him from the Kingdom, thus excluding him from its business affairs. In doing so, Jehovah clearly established that dishonest trade would not be tolerated anywhere in His Kingdom.

At this point, Lucifer became his own god, who is now Satan, "the god of this world" (2 CORINTHIANS 4:4). As Satan, he began to follow the leading of his own spirit, which is "the spirit of the world" (1 CORINTHIANS 2:12), and started building his own kingdom, which is "the kingdom of this world" (MATTHEW 4:8; REVELATION 11:15).

God's Enterprising Nature

To some, the thought that there were business activities in God's Kingdom before the fall is unsettling. However, it is important for us to understand that God's very nature is about creating wealth through enterprise. His best example of this is in creation itself, where He built His greatest enterprise ever. Within that labor, God made man in His own image and likeness, imparting to man His own work ethic of honesty and integrity.

Then, He put man in the garden where he could exercise that work ethic:

> "The Lord God took the man and put him in the Garden of Eden to *work* it and take care of it." (GENESIS 2:15, NIV)

It is also important to note that Jehovah rested on the seventh day, which set the heavenly pattern of six days "on" and one day "off" that creation still follows down to this very day.

Since *wealth is created when man applies labor to natural resources*, Adam's work in the garden was actually man's first wealth- producing enterprise on the earth. In that sense, the garden became man's first marketplace, which God created to operate according to the righteous standards of His Kingdom; standards that reflected His very image and character.

God's character, in this pure and undefiled marketplace, was one of servanthood. It was a place where true service to one another was the only motivation for being in business. This produced a continuous flow of wealth because it required wealth to serve your neighbor.

As Adam worked the garden, it was God who gave him "the power to create wealth" (DEUTERONOMY 8:18). He prospered through the work of his hands to the Lord's delight, because "God delights in the prosperity of His servants" (PSALMS 35:27). It was heaven on earth, especially as it related to business endeavors.

Man's Original Sin

Tragically, Adam and Eve allowed themselves to be seduced by the god of this world. It was clear that Satan's plan was to tempt Adam and Eve with the same sin that had so easily beset him. After all, if it worked on him, it was sure to work on them:

> "And when the woman saw that the tree was good for food, and that it was pleasant to the eyes, and a tree to be desired to make one wise, she took of the fruit

thereof, and did eat, and gave also unto her husband with her; and he did eat." (GENESIS 3:6, KJV)

Here, we see that the same three things that seduced Lucifer also seduced Adam and Eve:

1 *The lust of the flesh*: They saw that the abundant fruit of the tree of the knowledge of good and evil was good for food—i.e., it produced a lust in their flesh for more than what God provided.

2 *The lust of the eyes*: It was pleasant to their eyes, which produced a lust in their eyes that only having more of its fruit would satisfy. This is known in God's Kingdom as having an "evil eye." (PROVERBS 28:22)

3 *The pride of life*: This lust caused them to become wise in their own eyes, which produced a pride that led them to believe they could become like (equal with) God.

Man's Fallen Nature

When this happened, there was an infusion of the root of all evil that caused man's love for God to be replaced with a love for money, riches and the things of this world. This produced a painful change in man's very nature, and he went from being an uncorrupted and imperishable man to a corrupt and perishable sinner. He went from being filled with God's Holy Spirit, to being filled with Satan's "spirit of the world."

This began the war between the Kingdom of Heaven led by God, and the kingdom of this world led by Satan. One conducts its business affairs according to God's nature of righteousness, while the other conducts its business affairs according to Satan's nature of unrighteousness. It is the age-old battle between good and evil, and the largest battlefield is the marketplace of money and trade. And just like in the garden, man is still right in the middle of it, trying to decide which tree to eat from.

The apostle John puts it all together, when he warns us not to follow the lusts that are in the world:

> "Do not love the world, nor the things in the world. If anyone loves the world, the love of the father is not in him. For all that is in the world, *the lust of the flesh and the lust of the eyes and the boastful pride of life*, is not from the Father, but is from the world." (1 JOHN 2:15–16)

Unfortunately, this warning has gone largely unheeded by Adam's descendants, and unregenerate man continues to be seduced by the same love of money and riches that Lucifer seduced him with in the garden. As a result, Satan has been able to systematically lead modern man into establishing an international financial network that conducts his brand of unrighteous trade through a worldwide system of dishonest scales.

Chapter 2

DISHONEST SCALES

"Do not use dishonest standards when measuring
length, weight or quantity. Use honest scales
and honest weights, an honest ephah
[bushel] and an honest hin [gallon]."
LEVITICUS 19:35–36, NIV

Lucifer's unrighteous trade obviously transgressed the righteous
trade laws of God's Kingdom. These dishonest business endeavors
ran contrary to the nature and character of God, which everything
in His Kingdom is built upon. Since God desires that His "will
be done, on earth as it is in heaven" (MATTHEW 6:10), we must
assume that the same standards of righteous trade, which He spells
out in Scripture, apply to us today.

The use of honest standards is God's cornerstone for conducting
righteous trade on earth as it is also conducted in heaven. God
takes the principles behind His commandments not to lie, steal or
covet anything that belongs to our neighbor, and applies them to
His laws, which govern business and trade. His primary ordinance
for conducting business transactions is that we not use dishonest
standards of any kind (scales, weights, or measures).

Dishonest Weights

Lucifer's lust for riches led him to conduct unrighteous trade by using the full array of dishonest standards. His love of money focused primarily on his use of dishonest scales and the weights they used for measuring goods and services. The terms "dishonest weights," "dishonest scales," "false balances," "unjust scales," and "unjust gain" are used synonymously in the Bible (AMOS 8:4–5; PROVERBS 11:1; HOSEA 12:7, NIV; PROVERBS 28:8, KJV). As a result, the use of dishonest weights is the primary scheme that incites the love of money (1 TIMOTHY 6:9–10). It is also why the use of dishonest scales is the only unrighteous business practice that God calls an abomination (PROVERBS 11:1).

Moses reiterates this commandment when he prophesies:

> "You shall not have in your bag differing weights, a large and a small. You shall not have in your house differing measures, a large and a small. You shall have a full and just weight; you shall have a full and just measure …" (DEUTERONOMY 25:13–14)

The use of dishonest scales and weights is the predominant cause of all man's financial woes, and the love of money is its root. Once Satan contaminated Adam and Eve with his fallen nature, man's labor became cursed (GENESIS 3:17–19). The work of his hands lost its joy and became a painful experience against which his flesh rebelled.

As a result, man began to manifest the same unrighteous trading practices that Lucifer used among the heavenly host. Simply put, man's newly acquired love for riches led him to develop unrighteous trading schemes, whereby he could get rich quicker than righteous trade would allow.

The apostle Paul points this truth out when he says:

> "But people who long to be rich soon begin to do all kinds of wrong things [unrighteous schemes] to get money." (1 TIMOTHY 6:9, LB)

Dishonest Merchants

These unrighteous schemes allow dishonest merchants to live and consume off the labor of others, which is the origin of plunder. Throughout history, this plunder has been acquired primarily by the use of dishonest weights within a nation's system of scales for measuring the value of money (currency).

For example, suppose I were a dishonest merchant in the marketplace during ancient times, buying from the farmers and selling to the general public. As a dishonest merchant, I would have bags containing differing weights and measures (large and small) that I would use to plunder my fellow man.

When I purchased wheat from a farmer, I would use my set of large (heavy) weights, which included a "50-pound" weight that actually weighed 60 pounds. During the trade, I would use the heavy "50-pound" weight to dishonestly measure out 60 pounds worth of wheat, but I would pay him for only 50 pounds. In other words, during this unrighteous trade, I created (multiplied) for myself 10 pounds of wealth (in the form of wheat) out of nothing, through the use of my dishonest "50-pound" weight.

Now when I sold this wheat to the average housewife, I would use a set of small (light) weights, which included a "50-pound" weight that weighed only 40 pounds. During this transaction, I would use the light "50-pound" weight to weigh out 40 pounds of wheat, but I would charge her for 50 pounds. Here again,

I created wealth for myself, from nothing, through the use of dishonest weights.[†]

The Bible refers to this form of creating or multiplying wealth out of nothing as "unjust gain" (PROVERBS 28:8, KJV). It is the Hebrew word *tarbiyth* from the root word *rawbaw*, which means "to increase in whatever respect, enlarge, make to multiply."[1] It pertains to more than just usury. It implies the use of an unrighteous sleight-of-hand that allows one man to "make to multiply" his wealth by unjustly transferring it from his trading partners to himself.

Honest Money

When King Solomon said, "A false balance is an abomination to the Lord, but a just weight is His delight"(PROVERBS 11:1), he was referring to the righteous versus the unrighteous use of money when trading in the marketplace.

In ancient times money was not used to produce wealth. As I stated earlier, *wealth is created when man applies labor to natural resources*. Money was originally designed to be a standardized store of value that was used as a medium of exchange to transfer wealth. Although wealth and money are different in a technical sense, they work hand-in-hand to produce, store, and transfer man's financial assets from place to place.

God designed money to be of unchanging value that man could use to trade with instead of being forced to use *product barter*. For example, if I had a cow and my neighbor had corn, we could *product barter* an equal value of corn for the cow. However, if

† See Financial Seminar DVDs for visual aid on this process.

my neighbor with the corn wanted a cow, but I wanted wheat, money provided the standard value that he would pay me with, so I could then purchase the same value of wheat somewhere else.

When we look to the Scriptures for what God has established as honest money, we see that gold and silver are the only monetary assets ever ordained by the Lord. That's because precious metals are honest weights that have a tangible value attached to them. That value is based on their scarcity, consistency, durability, divisibility and transportability.

Many believe that God put gold in the land of Havilah before He put Adam in the garden, because gold was intended to be used as the money of the garden economy (GENESIS 2:11–12, 15). Silver was the most popular form of money that was used for everyday purchases. In fact, the Hebrew word for *money* is *keceph*, which is translated "silver."[2]

Webster's Twentieth Century Dictionary concurs with God's design for a righteous monetary system by defining money as:

> "Standard pieces of gold, silver, copper, nickel, etc., stamped by government authority and used as a medium of exchange and a store of value."

Dishonest Money Produces Inflation

In ancient Israel, the shekel was a gold or silver weight (about 0.533 of an ounce). This not only allowed the shekel weight to be used as a standard when measuring products on a set of scales, but it also served as money in payment for goods and services.

One of ancient Israel's great sins was not only the use of unjust weights and measures within the standard scale system, but also the practice of diluting the silver shekels as a method of unjust gain. The prophet Isaiah points this out when he prophesies:

> "How the faithful city has become a harlot, she who was full of justice! Righteousness once lodged in her, but now murderers. *Your silver has become dross, your drink diluted with water.*" (ISAIAH 1:21)

Creating a dishonest hin of wine is easy—you just add water. However, creating a dishonest silver shekel weight was a lot more complicated. Dishonest merchants and government officials in Israel would (1) melt down the silver shekels, (2) add a dross metal, (3) re-mint the coins, and (4) spend them back out into circulation. Although adding the dross metal increased the money supply, the dross was cheaper and lighter than the silver, which made the new shekel worth less than an honest silver shekel weight.

The decrease in silver content, combined with the increase in the number of coins, caused the value (purchasing power) of each coin to decrease—i.e., the money was devalued. Consequently, it took more of the devalued money to buy the same amount of goods and services. This is known as "debauching the currency," and it always produces inflation.

Webster's Twentieth Century Dictionary defines "inflation" as:

> "The increase in the quantity of money or credit or both that causes a sharp and sudden drop in its value and a rise in prices."

The prophet Amos clearly exposed Israel's inflation-producing use of dishonest scales when he prophesied:

"Hear this, you who trample the needy, to do away with the humble of the land, saying, 'When will the new moon be over, so that we may buy grain, and the Sabbath, that we may open the wheat market, *to make the bushel smaller and the shekel bigger, and to cheat with dishonest scales ...*'" (AMOS 8:4–5)

Here, the prophet provides us with an ancient description of how dishonest scales were used to debauch the currency and produce inflation. When Israel added dross to the shekel, it increased the money supply, which Amos describes as *making the shekel bigger*. This devalued the shekel so that it bought less grain, which he describes as *making the bushel smaller*. This type of debauchery produces inflation in any monetary system during any age and is the major cause of the world's financial woes today.

Credit and Inflation

Webster's Dictionary also says that *credit* can be used to increase the money supply, which further contributes to inflation. This takes us from ancient Israel to Europe during the Middle Ages, when people began to leave their gold on deposit with the goldsmith for safekeeping. This was the first form of modern day banking, whereby the goldsmith would issue depositor's paper receipts for their gold. These receipts were called gold notes, which served as IOUs for the gold, and they could be redeemed by whoever presented the note.

People soon discovered they could use the gold notes like money when purchasing goods and services in the local stores. This was great until the goldsmith realized that people had become so accustomed to trading with their gold notes that they seldom withdrew the actual gold. This is when the goldsmith began using the principle of dishonest scales to go into the loan business. He did this by simply writing out (printing up) more gold notes, which he then loaned out as new money. Without a gold reserve to back up these new gold notes, he was actually creating money out of nothing and loaning it out in the form of debt and credit.

At this point, all the new money became debt that the goldsmith/banker could never pay back. He further oppressed the consumers by charging them interest on the money/loans that he created out of nothing. This fulfilled the words of the prophet Hosea who said:

> "A merchant, in whose hands are false balances, he loves to oppress." (HOSEA 12:7)

In other words, the goldsmith combined his unjust gain (creating money out of nothing) with usury (charging interest on the loan) to increase his wealth. Although this type of unrighteous trade prospers the dishonest merchant for a time, King Solomon warns that God will avenge the innocent:

> "He that by usury [interest] and unjust gain [dishonest scales] increaseth his substance, he shall gather it for him that will pity the poor."(PROVERBS 28:8, KJV)

As the amount of loans increased, the marketplace was flooded with new money in the form of gold notes. This reduced their purchasing power, and the devalued gold notes became worth less and less. This drove people to begin redeeming them for the actual gold at the goldsmith's. Since the goldsmith only had a *fraction* of gold on deposit for the amount of gold notes in circulation, he quickly ran out of gold, and the people at the back of the line were stuck with worthless paper IOUs.

This example of dishonest weights produced (1) a debauching of the currency, which (2) devalued its purchasing power that (3) produced inflation so bad, it (4) caused a run on the bank. It was only when the bank run started that unsuspecting consumers came to the horrifying realization that their paper wealth was actually a debt that could never be paid back. Unfortunately, by that time, it was too late.

The Love of Money

Everyone, on both sides of the issue, was caught up in the love of money. The goldsmith obviously printed the unrighteous gold notes for gain, and the people borrowed them in order to obtain the riches (material possessions) that they could not otherwise afford. The principle of dishonest weights that the goldsmith used to produce the unrighteous loans fed everyone's love of money and haste for riches.

This type of unrighteous trade was considered such a serious crime that the people took the dishonest goldsmith out and hanged him! However, hanging the goldsmith did nothing to restore their wealth. Their unfaithfulness to obey God's Word caused them to suffer punishment just as King Solomon had warned:

> "A faithful man will abound with blessings, but he who makes haste to be rich will not go unpunished." (PROVERBS 28:20)

Unfortunately, the use of dishonest weights did not stop in the Middle Ages when they hanged the goldsmiths. Unrepentant man has simply repackaged new schemes of unjust scales within the different monetary systems that have evolved over the centuries down to the present day.

The Ultimate Abomination

When the love of money entered Lucifer, it became the root of all evil. As a result, he began the practice of unrighteous trade, which undoubtedly resulted in his use of dishonest scales. This is the heart of original sin, which God has established as the ultimate and eternal abomination. Therefore, when man emulates Lucifer's unrighteous trade through the use of dishonest scales and weights, he's not just *practicing* an abomination, but God says he *becomes* an abomination to Him.

God clearly points this out through the prophet Moses:

> "You shall not have in your bag differing weights, a large and a small. You shall not have in your house differing measures, a large and a small. You shall have a full and just weight; you shall have a full and just measure ... *For everyone who does these things, everyone who acts unjustly is an abomination to the Lord your God.*" (DEUTERONOMY 25:13–16)

Unrighteous trade, through the use of dishonest scales, has fueled man's love of money and corruption from the beginning. To that end, he has built a worldwide financial system that operates according to an integrated network of dishonest scales known as "Commercial Babylon."

Chapter 3

THE MYSTERY OF COMMERCIAL BABYLON

"And the angel said to me, 'Why do you wonder?
I shall tell you of the mystery of the woman
and the beast that carries her which has the
seven heads and ten horns ....'"
REVELATION 17:7

As the monetary systems of the world evolved and became more and more sophisticated, so did man's use of dishonest scales. The continuous implementation of scheme after scheme, building one on top of another, has produced a worldwide financial system that many refer to as "Commercial Babylon."

Although the term "Commercial Babylon" is not found in the Scriptures, the book of Revelation refers to "Mystery Babylon" (REVELATION 17:5, KJV). The apostle John goes on to describe Mystery Babylon as a symbiotic relationship between a woman and a beast. He further identifies this relationship as a demonic blend of economics, politics and religion that come together to form the last world empire of the antichrist (REVELATION 17 & 18).

Therefore, Commercial Babylon is simply the economic and financial side of "Mystery Babylon." This financial mystery centers around man's love of money and his use of dishonest scales to obtain it.

History of the Mystery

History shows that most national monetary systems started out with gold and silver serving as the actual currency. Like Israel's ancient shekel, America's currency also started out as a gold and/or silver weight known as a "dollar." The Coinage Act of 1792 established that a dollar was 412.5 grains of silver or 1/42 ounce of gold.

This is why Congress could "not make anything but gold and silver coin a tender in payment of debts."[3] It was set up this way because many of the founding fathers understood the disastrous history of dishonest weights used by the private banks of Europe since the goldsmiths of the Middle Ages.

America's monetary system was also originally set up so that only "Congress shall have the power to coin Money, regulate the value thereof, and of foreign Coin, and *fix the standard of weights and measures*."[4] America realized the need to keep its money supply in the hands of Congress and out of the hands of the international bankers. The goal was to protect the country and its citizens from the financial aspirations of men like central banker Nathan Mayer de Rothschild who said:

> "Give me control of a nation's monetary system, and
> I care not who writes their laws."[5]

Unfortunately, the Federal Reserve Act of 1913 handed control of our nation's money supply over to the bankers, who then created America's privately owned central bank of the Federal Reserve Bank (the Fed). That's right, the Fed is a privately held corporation with the majority of Fed stock being held by national and international member banks from around the world.[6] As a result, since 1913, the Fed, not Congress, has had control of America's monetary system.

Soon after it came into being, the Fed began to print paper money called gold and silver certificates. Like the notes our goldsmith issued in the Middle Ages, these certificates were IOUs that were redeemable in gold and silver coin that was actually on deposit in the U.S. Treasury. This was still legitimate, because the Fed could not print any more paper certificates (money) than there was gold and silver to redeem them.

However, as the decades passed, central bankers worked with ignorant and/or corrupt legislators to systematically replace the dollar's redeemable gold and silver weight with an unredeemable "promise to pay" called Federal Reserve Notes (FRNs). And like our goldsmith, the Fed now uses the same principles of dishonest scales to create debt from nothing and loan it into existence as money.

Dishonest Scales of Fractional Reserve Banking

Once the Fed eliminated the gold and silver backing of the nation's currency, they began to manipulate the flow of money through what is known as Fractional Reserve Banking (FRB). It is an unrighteous sleight-of-hand that every central bank around the world uses today.

Except for its dishonest accounting methods (dishonest scales), a bank is like any other corporation. It has ASSETS, LIABILITIES and NET WORTH. Its ASSETS consist mainly of "Cash and Reserves," "Investment Securities," and "Loans." Its LIABILITIES consist mainly of "Deposits," which means that all bank deposits are actually loans made to the bank by depositors. The bank even pays them interest on those deposits/loans. So, in reality, depositors are actually creditors of the bank. But the terms have been changed to keep the public off balance and in submission to the banking system.

With this in mind, let's take a closer look at the bank's loan process under the FRB system. When an individual deposits (loans) $100,000 into a bank, the banker credits "Deposits" on the LIABILITIES side of the bank's ledger, and debits "Cash and Reserve" on the ASSETS side of the ledger. Since FRB only requires the bank to keep a *fraction* of that deposit on reserve (today it's roughly 10% or $10,000 in this example), the bank is free to loan out the remaining $90,000 to its other customers.

This is where the dishonest accounting (scales) comes into play. In this loan transaction, the bank transfers $90,000 of the "Cash and Reserve" to "Loans" on the ASSETS side of the ledger, and then deposits the $90,000 loan into the borrowers account by crediting a new "Deposit" on the LIABILITIES side of the ledger. This $90,000 loan is now a fresh new deposit of money, which requires a corresponding $90,000 entry in "Cash and Reserves" on the ASSETS side of the ledger.

In other words, through the FRB process, the bank has created $90,000 of new money out of nothing in the form of computerized ledger book debt. When this newly created debt is deposited into the customer's account as money, the size of the bank is immediately increased by $90,000. This is what opponents of Fractional Reserve Banking call PFA (Pluck From Air) banking.

Since the bank only has to keep 10% ($9,000) of the new deposit in "Cash and Reserves," it can lend the remaining $81,000 out as more "new" money, thus repeating the cycle over and over again. Without going into the complications of the formula, a reserve requirement of 10% allows the bank to multiply the original $100,000 deposit up to ten times.[7] This allows the creation of $1 million of new money in the form of computerized ledger book debit and extended credit such as loans, lines of credit, credit card money, etc.[†]

All Money is Debt

The bank's ability to create debt in the form of ledger book deposit entries and then lend them out as money means that all money is debt. That's why America's currency is called Federal Reserve Notes (FRNs). As a former consumer loan officer and investment company president, I can tell you that a "note" is considered "debt." It is an IOU that promises to repay the borrowed money according to the terms of the note.

However, if you take any FRN out of your wallet and look at it, you will see that there is no promise to pay you anything. In other words, a FRN is an "IOU nothing." And like my friend Dr. Larry

---

† See Financial Seminar DVDs for visual aid on this process.

Bates says, "When they start to issue the new global currency, it will be a 'who owes you nothing,' because you won't know who it is that owes you nothing."

In contrast, a one-dollar "Silver Certificate" (1935 series) clearly spelled out the terms of the contract by stating: "THIS CERTIFIES THAT THERE IS ON DEPOSIT IN THE TREASURY OF THE UNITED STATES OF AMERICA ONE DOLLAR IN SILVER PAYABLE TO THE BEARER ON DEMAND" (see Figure 1).

Figure 1: *Silver Certificate*

In 1935, a dollar was an honest weight of tangible redeemable silver. But today, the only thing that gives the FRN any value is the reassuring babble in the upper left hand portion of the note, which states: "THIS NOTE IS LEGAL TENDER FOR ALL DEBTS, PUBLIC AND PRIVATE" (see Figure 2).

Since a "note" is debt, the FRN is actually saying, "THIS DEBT IS LEGAL TENDER FOR ALL DEBTS, PUBLIC AND PRIVATE." In other words, our entire monetary system uses debt for the payment of debt, as well as the purchase of goods and services. It is a debt-based monetary system, where all money is loaned into existence as debt through the dishonest scales of Fractional Reserve Banking.

Figure 2: *Current FRN*

A View From the Inside

Academic insider Carroll Quigley (1910–1977) was professor of history at the Foreign Services School of Georgetown University, and also taught at Princeton and Harvard. In his highly respected tell-all book, *Tragedy and Hope: The History of the World in Our Time*, Quigley describes the fractional reserve process as follows:

> "In effect, this creation of paper claims greater than the reserves available means that *bankers were creating money out of nothing*. ... Deposit bankers discovered that orders and checks drawn against DEPOSITS by depositors and given to a third person were often not cashed by the latter but were deposited to their own accounts. Thus there were no actual movements of funds, and payments were made simply by book-keeping transactions on the accounts."

"Accordingly, it was necessary for the banker to keep on hand in actual money (gold, certificates, and notes) no more than the FRACTION of deposits likely to be drawn upon and cashed; the rest could be used for loans, and if these loans were made by creating a deposit [account] for the borrower, who in turn would draw checks upon it rather than withdraw it in money, such 'created deposits' or loans could also be covered adequately by retaining reserves to only a FRACTION of their value. *Such created deposits also were a creation of money out of nothing*, although bankers usually refused to express their actions, either note issuing or deposit lending, in these terms."[8]

The dishonest accounting methods used in FRB are clearly the modern day equivalent of the ancient dishonest scales referred to in the Bible. They have been legalized by dishonest and corrupt men, who were seduced by the same iniquity and root sin that seduced Lucifer while he was trading among the heavenly hosts.

Sir Josiah Stamp, former president of the bank of England and fellow insider, clearly disclosed the origin of FRB when he said:

"The [FRB] process is perhaps the most astounding piece of sleight of hand ever invented. *Banking was conceived in iniquity and born in sin.* The bankers own the earth; take it away from them, but leave them the power to create deposits and with the flick of a pen they will create enough deposits to buy it back again. However, take it away from them and all the great fortunes like mine will disappear, and they ought to disappear, for this would be a happier world to live in. *But if you wish to remain the slaves to bankers and pay the cost of your own slavery, let them continue to create deposits.*"[9]

Interest Compounds Man's Slavery

When Sir Josiah says that we will pay the cost of our own slavery, he is referring to the interest payments on the debt. In fact, the most horrifying thing about the FRB process is that, after the banks create the loans (money) out of nothing, they further enslave the borrowers by charging them interest on top of it.

William Patterson, who first obtained the charter for the Bank of England in 1694, boasted of this abomination, saying:

> "The bank hath benefit of interest on all moneys which it creates out of nothing."[10]

The Hebrew word for interest and usury is *neshek* from the root word *neshak*, and it means:

> "To strike with a sting as a serpent; (figuratively) to oppress with interest on a loan."[11]

In other words, FRB combines its unjust gain (creating money for loans out of nothing) with usury (charging interest on the loan) to increase its wealth and compound man's slavery to the financial system.

This fulfills the words of the prophet Hosea who said:

> "A merchant, in whose hands are false balances, he loves to oppress." (HOSEA 12:7)

Seduced by the Love of Money

Whenever I share the truth about FRB at meetings and conferences, there are always some people who get upset with their bankers. The natural tendency is to go down and lay hands on their bankers (usually around the neck). But I always have to remind them that, even though FRB is an abomination, nobody forced them to borrow any money.

Their real problem is not the banker or FRB. Their real problem is the lust of their own flesh and the lust of their own eyes and their own boastful pride of life (1 JOHN 2:15) that borrowed money enables them to satisfy. In other words, they lusted after that car, house, boat, furniture, clothes, business opportunity, etc. But instead of trusting God to supply by His hand, they went to the altar of the loan window at the bank to get the money (debt) they needed to live beyond their means.

The material possessions they acquire with the loans only give them the image of prosperity, because they don't actually own those possessions—the lender does. All they really own is the debt. At this point, they not only become a servant (slave) to the lender, but their interest payments make them a servant to the money (mammon) itself.

In essence, they are serving the god of mammon, and the interest payments have become a tithe to the world's financial system. In many cases, their monthly debt payments are so large that they cannot afford to pay their tithes to the Lord, which doubles their bondage to mammon and the curse that goes with it (MALACHI 3:8–9).

My Personal Revelation of Commercial Babylon

This was much my situation during the 1987 stock market crash, when God first opened my eyes to the debt system of Commercial Babylon. I was president and chief operations officer of a financial services and investment firm that was leveraged to the hilt. I was also leveraged personally, with over $110,000 of debt, including a mortgage, cars, clothes, furniture, and credit cards.

When the company's debt bubble popped during the crash, I was let go in the restructuring. With the loss of my job, I couldn't make my loan payments, my credit cards were maxed out, and I couldn't qualify for any additional loans without a comparable job. Lenders started repossessing things, which brought my whole financial world crashing down around me. I know now that this was God's way of allowing me to experience what it was like to become a slave to my lenders.

In the depth of my financial bondage, God showed me how I had been using loan after loan to satisfy my love of money. Unfortunately, there was never enough, and I went deeper and deeper into debt until the system owned me. My constant battle of trying to scrape together another payment for my creditors kept me from fulfilling the work that God was calling me to. It was here, in the pit of debt, that I truly realized that, "you cannot serve God and mammon"(MATTHEW 6:24).

Here is where God also revealed to me that the mystery of Commercial Babylon was the world's debt-based monetary system. Many prophecy teachers have tried to identify Commercial Babylon as the United States, but this is not the case. Commercial Babylon is a sophisticated global system of dishonest scales called Fractional Reserve Banking, which exploits man's love of money through easy credit, and brings him under slavery to debt.

With this revelation, I cried out to Jesus and said, "O God, deliver me from this Babylonian system." Immediately, He spoke to my heart and said, "Norm, I can't take you out of Babylon until I take Babylon out of you." At that point, I cut up the credit cards and covenanted with God to trust Him for My provision rather than the debt system of Commercial Babylon. I immediately began to live within my means, and today I'm debt-free and serving God in an international ministry.[12]

The Ultimate Graven Image

Fractional reserve debt is the ultimate graven image, because it feeds man's root sin of the love of money. It is an unrighteous monetary system that continuously draws man back into the temple of the banks, where he willingly bows down at the altar of the loan window and worships the god of mammon, i.e., debt.

At first, FRB seems like a good system for supplying easy money for the global economy. However, it has brought the people and the nations of the world into slavery to the lenders. In the end, debt is a graven image that makes the world go round.

Chapter 4

DEBT MAKES THE WORLD GO ROUND

"Men prepare a meal for enjoyment, and
wine makes life merry, and money
is the answer to all things."
ECCLESIASTES 10:19

In September 1998, I was invited to meet with a high-ranking government official in Singapore. He had seen a video that I did on Fractional Reserve Banking (FRB) and wanted to discuss its effects on Asia's financial crisis.

As we examined the FRB process together, he understood that it was the use of dishonest scales. However, he also understood that the world's financial system would immediately collapse without the ability to create additional money in the form of debt and extended credit.

We joked about the old saying that "money makes the world go round," but there was a sense of foreboding as everyone in the meeting came to the horrible realization that, since all money is debt, it is actually debt that makes the world go round.

Anatomy of the World's Financial System

The world's financial system is made up of three interconnecting systems (see Figure 3 below). On one side, there is the economic system, which is simply trade and commerce relating to the development, production, distribution, and consumption of goods and services. Economics is simply the science of measuring and reporting trade and commerce.[13]

On the other side, there is the investment system, which consists of both real and paper assets. Real assets are natural resources such as precious metals, agricultural products, petroleum products, timber, real estate, etc. In contrast, paper assets consist of stocks, bonds, mutual funds, insurance products, futures, options, derivatives, etc.

In the middle of all this lies the monetary (money) system, which is the engine that makes it all run. Without money, no one has the power to purchase either consumer goods or investments. However, since all money is FRB debt, it is actually the ever increasing debt bubble that keeps the economy and investment markets going.

Figure 3: *World Financial System*

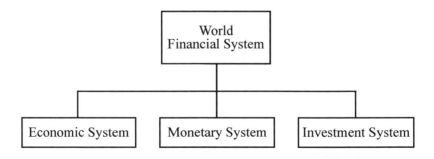

Debt and the Economy

When banks create debt and loan it out as money, the borrower uses it to purchase goods and services. As the consumer's passion for material possessions continues to grow beyond his paycheck, so does his need (love) for more money. This results in additional loans, which he spends into the economy as money, thereby increasing the demand for more products. The demand for more products creates a need for more businesses to meet that demand. Therefore, additional debt is created and loaned into existence as money to expand business production.

This injection of new money stimulates other sectors of the economy such as construction, communication, manufacturing and labor. The labor pool is paid with money that is generally loaned back to the banking system when workers deposit their paychecks into their bank accounts. This continues to feed the banking system, which drives the debt machine.

Since the amount of new loans largely determines the amount of money released into the economy, the economy generally grows in proportion to the amount of new consumer and business debt. If the banking system ever stopped creating money in the form of loans, the whole world's financial system (economy, money and investments) would collapse.

Therefore, the financial system is in a continuous posture of having to create new money in the form of debt. This is one reason why the system in America will lend money to almost anyone for any reason. They simply have to make loans in order to keep the economy going.

However, as the debt bubble grows so does the amount of interest due, which creates a demand for even more money. As a result, both consumers and businesses are forced into refinancing their loans in order to stay afloat. Soon they find themselves awash in debt that they cannot repay without more debt, and so the vicious cycle goes on.

The reality is that FRB has produced the ultimate tail-eating dragon that won't stop until it consumes itself.

Debt Controls Consumer Prices

When interest rates are low, people can more readily afford to borrow and spend money, which grows the economy. However, as money supply increases, inflation (the increase in the supply of money or credit causing higher prices) also grows. The more money that is loaned into the economy, the less each currency unit is worth. As a result, the currency is devalued and it takes more currency units to buy the same amount of goods and services. To the consumer, it appears as though prices have risen, but in reality, the currency has simply lost its purchasing power.

As inflation rises, central banks raise interest. As a result, consumers borrow and spend less money, which slows the economy down, and prices fall. Unfortunately, the slower demand for goods means that less workers are needed for production, and people lose their jobs. The country goes into a recession, which affects everything, from consumer prices to investment values. Recession and bankruptcy flush out all the mal-investment, and we start the process all over again.[†]

---

† See Financial Seminar DVDs for visual aid on this process.

What I am saying is that the ups and downs and the booms and busts of our economic cycles are not a phenomenon of nature. Instead, they are the direct result of deliberate action taken by those who control monetary policy. In effect, they control the price of everything, from your car to your house, and even determine whether you have a job or not. This is the total control that Nathan Mayer Rothschild was referring to when he said, "Give me control of a nation's monetary system, and I care not who writes their laws."

Two Types of Investments

As the dishonest scales of Fractional Reserve Banking (FRB) moved through both the monetary and economic systems, it gave birth to a debt-based investment system. Money that is not spent into the economy is generally used to purchase investments. Investments fall into one of two categories of assets—they are either *ownership assets,* which are equity-based, or *loanership assets,* which are debt-based.

Ownership assets are real (tangible) assets an investor can take possession of. These include precious and industrial metals, agricultural products, petroleum products, timber and real estate. Paper equities (stocks) are also considered *ownership assets,* because they represent real ownership in a company. *Ownership assets* may also include antiques, collectibles, and other tangibles that can appreciate in value. We will deal with *ownership assets* later.

Loanership assets are the paper receipts (IOUs) an investor receives when he loans his money out to the system at interest. Money markets, passbook savings, CDs, Treasury securities (bonds, notes and bills), corporate bonds, municipal bonds, and cash value insurance products all represent money that the investor has loaned to the institution that issued the debt.

It is hard to comprehend that when we deposit money into our bank account we are not really depositors, as we have been led to believe, but creditors. We are creditors because we have loaned them our money at interest. Unfortunately, we have been duped into believing that the receipt (IOU) we got in return is an investment, when all it really is, is someone else's debt.

These debt receipts we call investments stipulate the conditions and payback of the loan, if any. They are recorded as an asset (accounts receivable) on our balance sheets, and show up as both a liability and an asset on the balance sheet of those we loaned our money to. With this in mind, let's explore how debt is used to perpetuate the investment system.

Debt Pyramid Investing

In 1993, while I was serving as senior economist at First American Monetary Consultants, Dr. Larry Bates gave me an assignment to trace where an investor's money went after having been deposited into a particular money market. Through the use of investment prospectuses, I traced the flow of money, and discovered that the original investment was loaned out over and over again.

The money actually ended up flowing to hundreds of different investments, but to keep it simple and understandable, I have limited this example to just one $10,000 stream of money as follows:

1 When the original investor deposited $10,000 into the money market he actually loaned his money to that money market at interest. The money market issued the investor an IOU in the form of a paper statement describing the terms of the transaction, complete with the balance owed him. This debt-based investment was listed as an asset on the investor's balance sheet.

2 The money market had to invest that money at a higher rate of interest in order to pay the original investor his interest and earn a profit for the money market at the same time. So, it loaned the original $10,000 to a corporation through the purchase of a corporate bond issue that paid a higher rate of interest. In other words, the money market re-loaned the original $10,000 to a corporation.

3 The corporation deposited that money into their bank account. By doing this, the corporation re-loaned the original $10,000 to the bank in the form of a bank deposit.

4 From that bank account, the corporation spent most of the money into the economy to pay for an expansion. However, the balance that remained in the bank, above the reserve requirement, was either multiplied ten times through FRB and loaned out as new money, or it was re-loaned directly to the government through the bank's purchase of a Treasury security (T-bill, note, or bond).

In this mild case of *Debt Pyramid Investing*, the investor's original $10,000 was loaned and then re-loaned a total of four times, which created a $40,000 debt pyramid. By re-loaning the $40,000 back into four institutions created by the system, it is easy to see how debt has become the lifeblood of the money market, the corporation, the bank, and the government.

The Insurance Debt Pyramid

As a former insurance broker, I can tell you that cash value insurance products (annuities, whole life, universal life, etc.) rely on the same type of debt pyramid scheme described above. Insurance premiums are simply loans made to the insurance company, which are re-loaned over and over again into the debt-based investment world of passbook savings, bank CDs, bonds, government securities, real estate mortgages, etc.

Each loan is recorded on its respective balance sheet as both a liability and an asset. The only problem is that those assets are actually someone else's liability (debt). The Debt Pyramid Investing scheme makes everyone dependent on obtaining more debt to survive.

Remember that, in a debt-based financial system, you pay your debts with debt. And since all money is debt, this keeps the banking system in a continuous posture of having to create more new money in the form of debt, that is also loaned out at interest to pay back the debt that is already loaned out at interest. And so the cycle goes on. Unfortunately, this means that there is a lot more debt out there than there is money to pay it off with.

Debt and Government Deficits

Debt is also the driving force behind a big government's deficit spending. When a government spends more than it takes in, politicians make up the difference in one of three ways—they either tax the money, borrow the money, or print the money. The lack of economic production leaves them no other way to finance their deficits.

Tax the money. Tax money is not new money, but simply the redistribution of money that is already in circulation. Higher taxes reduce available money for consumer spending, thus causing the economy to stagnate or even decline. Governments can only raise taxes so much, before the economy suffers a slow-down.

Borrow the money. The government borrows money by issuing Treasury securities (T-bills, notes and bonds) that investors buy in the credit markets. Issuing treasury securities does not increase the money supply. It simply borrows from the net national savings of the people, which is limited. If too much demand to borrow from the national savings develops, interest rates will skyrocket and the economy will collapse.

For example, the U.S. government has borrowed $5.6 trillion,[14] which makes it the largest debtor nation in the world. It could never borrow all this from national savings, so it had to sell much of its debt in the international credit markets. Therefore, our creditors include individuals, businesses, governments and central banks from around the world.

The real problem is that every other country in the world is doing the same thing in order to lessen demand on their national savings, and keep their interest rates low. This has created international currency wars that have exacerbated and led to the collapse of financial systems throughout entire regions of the world.

With over a trillion dollars in annual interest due on worldwide government debt, taxing and borrowing the amount from current global savings is impossible. This leaves them with only one alternative.

Print the money. The only thing left to do is print the money, which is where the country's central bank comes in. A country's central bank is to a government what a commercial bank is to an individual or business. When that government cannot raise the necessary funds by taxing its citizens or borrowing from the credit markets, it borrows directly from their central bank.

The central bank buys the government's debt (T-bills, notes, and bonds) by drawing a check on itself and depositing it into the government's national account. This is known as monetizing the debt, which means the Fed is simply printing the money as needed to keep the government afloat.

A 10% reserve requirement limits the amount of money (debt) the banking system can create. However, the Monetary Control Act of 1980 gave the Fed unlimited lending ability by authorizing it to lower the reserve requirement to *zero* if needed.[15] In other words, if there is no requirement to maintain any cash reserves, the Fed is free to print as much money as it needs to keep the government going.[†]

Lenders Control Business and Governments

As you can see, debt does make the world go round. But at what price? Like it or not, the world's financial system has been designed so that both private enterprise and governments eventually become slaves to the debt-based monetary system and its lenders.

At this point, most honest people are wondering why anyone would devise and implement such a lewd and oppressive scheme

---

[†] See *Monetary Control Act of 1980* on page 219.

to defraud the nations of the world. This is where globalist and fellow insider, Carroll Quigley, best describes the overall plan behind the FRB system:

> "In time they [the financial elite] brought into their financial network the provincial banking centers, organized as commercial banks and savings banks, as well as insurance companies, *to form all of these into a single financial system on an international scale which manipulated the quantity and flow of money so that they were able to influence, if not control, governments on one side and industries on the other*. The men who did this ... aspired to establish dynasties of inter-national bankers and were at least as successful at this as were many of the dynastic political rulers."[16]

If you're saying to yourself, "It sounds like a plan," you're right! Quigley is making a clear reference to an international conspiracy that seeks to establish a one-world financial system. The plan is to control both industry and government by manipulating the quantity and flow of money through debt. It is the ultimate conspiracy that exploits man's root sin of the love of money, to take him captive under slavery to FRB debt and the men who control it.

Chapter 5

It Sounds Like a Plan

"The wicked plots against the righteous,
and gnashes at him with his teeth."
Psalms 37:12

The next step to understanding money and wealth in the new millennium is the high level of manipulation that takes place in the investment markets every day. However, to properly comprehend this, we must first gain a reasonable grasp of the conspiratorial plans of the wicked.

In the above Scripture verse, King David points out a universal truth that wicked men passionately conspire against righteous men. These are the wicked elite (kings and rulers), who are actively carrying out conspiratorial plans to establishing a "new world order" (NWO) under draconian rule.

As you are about to see, it is not a communist conspiracy or even a Jewish conspiracy, but a Satanic conspiracy that has been in operation from the beginning of time. This truth makes it imperative for the body of Christ to understand not only the origins of this conspiracy, but also the part that it plays in Bible prophecy as it relates to the end of the age and the return of Jesus Christ.

The Master Conspirator

In his delusion of greed and pride, even after he had been expelled from God's Kingdom, Lucifer continued his plan to ascend to heaven and become like the Most High. His first act was to conspire with one-third of the angelic hosts in a rebellion against Jehovah. He most likely enticed them with promises of riches, position, power, and eventual Godhood once they conquered the Kingdom of heaven. The seductive power that works through the promise of wealth and position is an overpowering force that cannot be underestimated.

His next target was mankind, who had been created in the image and likeness of God. There, in the garden, Satan conspired with Adam and Eve to break God's commandment not to eat of the tree of the knowledge of good and evil. True to his pattern, he seduced them with the same financial 'carrot' and promise of Godhood that we have already identified as the lust of the flesh, the lust of the eyes, and the boastful pride of life.

By joining in this conspiracy, man lost the image of Jehovah and took on the fallen nature of Satan. As a result, man forfeited his authority over the earth to Satan, who became the "god of this world." From there, Satan set out to implement his plan for building the "kingdom of this world," which is a one-world political, financial and religious system under his rule. The apostle John referred to it as "Mystery Babylon," which has surfaced in these last days under the term New World Order.

Mystery Babylon and the New World Order

Throughout the ages, Satan has conspired with unrighteous men to build his New World Order (NWO), which functions in complete opposition to God's heavenly order. Today's NWO plan is called "globalism," which was birthed in GENESIS 11:4 on the plains of Shinar, when Nimrod and his army of Babylonian masons joined their voices together, saying:

> "Come, let us build for ourselves a city, and a tower whose top will reach into heaven, and let us make for ourselves a name ... ." (GENESIS 11:4)

Even though this initial plan was foiled when Jehovah confused their language, Satan's plan to finish building his great city of Babylon—also known as "Mystery Babylon"—has always been his intended goal (REVELATION 17:1–3). This plan has been kept alive and perpetuated by the "spirit of the world," which leads Satan's unrighteous servants to build the "kingdom of this world" in much the same manner that the "Spirit of God" leads His righteous servants to build the "Kingdom of heaven" (1 CORINTHIANS 2:12).

The "spirit of the world" leads wicked man to conspire with one another against God's plan to restore fallen man back into His Kingdom through Jesus Christ. King David speaks about this aspect of the conspiracy when he says:

> "Why are the nations in an uproar, and the peoples devising a vain thing? The kings of the earth take their stand, and the rulers take counsel [conspire] together against the Lord and against His Anointed." (PSALMS 2:1–2; see also ACTS 4:25–26)

Satan's plans for his NWO have been passed down from empire to empire throughout the history of man. From Nimrod's Babylon it went to the Pharaohs of Egypt. From there it went back to Nebuchadnezzar's Babylon, then on to Persia, Greece, and Rome. Although these world empires did not encompass the whole geographical world, their progressive efforts at world domination have provided the foundational pattern for building today's NWO.

After Rome fell, this spirit moved out into the rest of the world and manifested as the struggle between kingdoms trying to dominate one another politically, economically, religiously and militarily. However, in the 1700s, this plan began to take shape as a multinational conspiracy among the political and financial elite (kings and rulers) of the world.

Adam Weishaupt and the Illuminati

The most notable conspirator of this millennium was Professor Adam Weishaupt (1748–1811), who formally established the Illuminati on May 1, 1776 in Ingolstadt Bavaria (Germany).[17] Also referred to as the "Order," Weishaupt's Illuminati is based on the ancient Babylonian doctrine of Illuminism, which promises that its followers will attain the mystical knowledge of Lucifer, who they promote as the light-bearing god of this world.

When Jehovah dispersed Nimrod's Babylon, the spirit and teachings of Illuminism were carefully passed down through a multitude of secret societies within the successive empires of the world. However, in 1776, Weishaupt became Lucifer's agent and began to bring them all back together under a single world order according to the original plan that was set down through

Nimrod's Babylon.

Weishaupt's philosophy of establishing a one-world empire is clearly in line with Lucifer's plan to rule the earth. This goal is well-documented in Weishaupt's teachings, where he emphatically states:

> "It is necessary to establish a universal regime and empire over the whole world."[18]

In 1785, the Bavarian government discovered the Illuminati's conspiracy and exposed its plans to overthrow society. The government conducted an investigation into its purpose and published a report entitled *"Original Writings of the Order of the Illuminati."*[19] It found the Illuminati to be anti-Christian and concluded that:

> "... the expressed aim of this Order was to abolish Christianity, and overthrow all civil government."[20]

Their findings are also well documented in *The Encyclopaedia Britannica*, which describes the Illuminati as a political movement:

> "... founded as a secret society in 1776 in Bavaria by Adam Weishaupt, professor of canon law at the University of Ingolstadt and a former Jesuit. Its aim was to replace Christianity by a religion of reason. It was banned by the Bavarian government in 1785."[21]

Unfortunately, the Bavarian government mistakenly concluded that the Illuminati died when they outlawed it in 1785. Illuminism is empowered by Lucifer, which means that it does not die when men die or governments ban its practice. It is driven by the *spirit* and *god of this world*, and it transfers from one man to another, from generation to generation, and from kingdom to kingdom.

From Bavaria, it spread like a cancer among the nations, seducing its followers with the same Satanic promise of position, money, and power that it has used since the garden. Weishaupt was keenly aware of this attraction and used it to lure would-be followers into joining the Order:

> "The pupils [members of the Illuminati] are convinced that the Order will rule the world. *Every member therefore becomes a ruler.* We all think of ourselves as qualified to rule. It is therefore an alluring thought both to good and bad men. *By this lure the Order will spread.*"[22]

In 1920, before he became Prime Minister of England, Winston Churchill, wrote with perfect clarity about what he had discovered concerning the Illuminati's continuing worldwide conspiracy to overthrow civilization:

> "From the days of Spartacus-Weishaupt to those of Karl Marx, to those of Trotsky, Bela Kun, Rosa Luxembourg, and Emma Goldman, this *worldwide conspiracy for the overthrow of civilization and the reconstitution of society* on the basis of arrested development, of envious malevolence and impossible equality, has been steadily growing.
>
> "It played a definitely recognizable role in the tragedy of the French Revolution. It has been the mainspring of every subversive movement during the nineteenth century, and now at last this band of extraordinary personalities from the underworld of the great cities in Europe and America have gripped the Russian people by the hair of their heads, and

have become practically the undisputed masters of that enormous empire."[23]

Spartacus was the code name for Adam Weishaupt, which was used inside the Order to identify him in conversation. The French Revolution of 1789 was a conspiracy by the Illuminati to put their fellow Illuminist, the Duc d'Orleans, on the throne of France. Karl Marx was the "father of communism," and Leon Trotsky, Bela Kun, Rosa Luxembourg, and Emma Goldman were all revolutionaries involved in the communist overthrow of Russia in 1917.

In other words, by linking Weishaupt's Illuminati of 1776 to the French Revolution of 1789, Karl Marx of 1848, and the communist revolution of 1917, Churchill identified the Illuminati as a subversive global conspiracy that was at least 140 years old and growing.

Secrecy

Weishaupt taught his followers that secrecy must be maintained if the Order was to be successful in establishing their NWO. In fact, he felt that misdirection and outright deceit would provide the necessary zeal to keep the Order fresh and on its toes:

> "Secrecy gives greater zest to the whole ... the slightest observation shows that nothing will so much contribute to increase the zeal of the members as secret union. *The great strength of our Order lies in its conceal-ment:* let it never appear in its own name, but always covered by another name, and another occupation."[24]

This secrecy included taking secret "antique" names to protect themselves from being discovered, as they had been in Bavaria. I have already noted that Weishaupt went by the name of Spartacus, the greatest of all Roman gladiators, who led the slaves in an insurrection against Rome for three years. Other key Illuminists also had code-names—Baron von Knigge took the name Philo, Herr von Zwack became Cato, Marquis di Contanza was Diomede, and so on.[25]

Professor Quigley also notes that the conspirators wished to keep their operations secret from the general populace when he said:

> "I have no aversion to [the Order] or to most of its aims and have, for much of my life, been close to it and to many of its instruments. I have objected, both in the past and recently, to a few of its policies ... but in general my chief difference of opinion is that *it wishes to remain unknown,* and I believe its role in history is significant enough to be known."[26]

Keeping the Order a secret was about the only disagreement Quigley had with them. In fact, he felt that it was a *tragedy* that they kept their plans for a NWO secret, because he believed a NWO was the only *hope* for mankind. Thus, the name of his book: *Tragedy and Hope.*

Round Table Groups

Never letting the Order appear in its own name, but always in another name and/or occupation gave rise to other secret societies throughout the world. Weishaupt put forth the mandate that, if the Order was to be successful in establishing their NWO, they would have to branch out into a network of secret organizations. In a letter to a fellow Illuminist, he wrote:

> "Nothing can bring this [NWO] about but hidden societies. Hidden schools of wisdom are the means which will one day free men from their bonds. Princes and nations shall vanish from the earth."[27]

As the Order implemented this mandate, it formed a growing network of political and financial organizations, whose goals were to infiltrate and influence other segments of society into adopting the policies of their NWO. Professor Quigley describes this network best when he emphatically states:

> "There does exist, and has existed for a generation, an international Anglophile network which operates, to some extent, in the way the radical right believes the Communists act. In fact, this network, which we may identify as the *Round Table Groups*, has no aversion to cooperating with the Communists, or any other groups, and frequently does so.
>
> *"I know of the operations of this network because I have studied it for twenty years* and was permitted for two years, in the early 1960s, to examine its papers and secret records."[28]

Rhodes Scholarship Trust

Cecil Rhodes (1853–1902) was the first Illuminist to really give the Round Table Groups (RTG) some teeth, when he formally established the secret inner circle of his RTG on February 5,

1891. Known as the "Association of Helpers," Rhodes dedicated his life and his money (Rhodes Scholarship Trust at Oxford) to educating potential college initiates in the ways and purposes of the Illuminati. Members included Lord Alfred Milner, Alfred Beit, Lord Arthur Balfour, Lord Albert Grey, Lord Rothschild, along with scions of the Morgan, Carnegie, and Rockefeller families.[29]

By 1915, money from the Rhodes Scholarship Trust had established RTGs in seven countries, including England, South Africa, Canada, Australia, New Zealand, India, and the United States.[30] In 1920–21, England's *Royal Institute of International Affairs* (RIIA) and America's *Council on Foreign Relations* (CFR) emerged as the two predominant global RTGs.[31]

Royal Institute of International Affairs and the Council on Foreign Relations

On May 30, 1919, under the direction of Baron Edmond Rothschild of France, select members from the delegations to the Paris Peace Conference met and established the Royal Institute of International Affairs (RIIA). Their purpose was to become an international organization that would advise world governments on international affairs.[32]

On June 5, 1919, they decided to establish two separate groups that would work in concert with each other toward the same goal. The Royal Institute of International Affairs (RIIA), also known as the Chatham House Study Group, was established in England to advise the British government. Its sister organization, the Council on Foreign Relations (CFR), was established on July 29, 1921, to advise the U.S. government toward a NWO.[33]

Subsidiary groups such as the Centre d'Etudes de Politique Etrangere, the Institute für Auswartige Politik and the Institute of Pacific Relations were set up to influence the French, German and Far Eastern governments respectively.[34] In addition to influencing world governments, they purposed to expand the number of RTGs, which eventually produced the Bilderbergs (1954), the Club of Rome (1968), and the Trilateral Commission (1973).[35]

The Bilderbergs

The Bilderberg Group, for example, was birthed as an annual planning conference called by the global establishment. The first conference was convened by Prince Bernard during May 1954. They met at the Bilderberg Hotel in Oosterbeek, Netherlands; hence the name "Bilderbergs."[36]

Since then, they have held their annual meetings in different places all over the world. These are secret invitation-only meetings that are restricted to about 100 Illuminists from the international banking dynasties, international business corporations, global media enterprises, American tax-exempt foundations, and high-ranking government officials.[37]

Club of Rome

Aurelio Peccei, a wealthy Italian industrialist, organized the Club of Rome (CR) in April 1968.[38] Its stated goal is to promote global government and oversee the regionalization of the world—EU, NAFTA, ASEAN, etc. The CR's goal of dividing the world up into ten regional governments was published in a study done by two of its members in a book *Mankind at the Turning Point*.[39] More on this in chapter ten.

Trilateral Commission

The Trilateral Commission was formed in 1973 by David Rockefeller and numerous members from other RTGs. Membership is limited to 325 members from the trilateral countries of North America (98 members), Europe (146 members) and Japan (81 members). Its goal is to harness the economic resources of these three regions and use them to finance the establishment of a completely interdependent financial system.

This system redistributes the wealth of the richer nations to the poorer nations. It promotes a world currency and global taxation as part of its plan for a NWO.[40] The history of these men and their secret RTGs clearly show that their intended goal is to integrate the economic and political powers of the earth into one giant monolith of global power which transcends all others, even communism.

Communism and the New World Order

Many have tried to connect this global conspiracy to the communist conspiracy, but they were all aiming below the target. For example, the global establishment discredited Senator Joseph McCarthy's accusations of a communist conspiracy within the U.S. government because he could never actually connect all the dots back to the Kremlin.

The July 30, 1953 Senate Judiciary Committee report *Interlocking Subversion In Government Departments*—also known as the Jenner report—conclusively proved there was interconnecting conspiratorial subversion at the highest levels of the U.S. government. However, it failed to place the head of the conspiracy in Moscow, Peking or anywhere else.[41] The reason Senators McCarthy, Jenner and others have failed to prove that the communist conspiracy was the head of the dragon was because the NWO conspiracy is bigger than communism.

Dr. Bella Dodd, a former member of the National Committee of the U.S. Communist Party, confirmed this thesis when she said:

> "I think the communist conspiracy is merely a branch of a much bigger conspiracy."[42]

Right after World War II, Dodd said that she became aware of a mysterious "super leadership" that transcended communism. She noted there were a number of times that the Party had difficulty getting direction from Moscow on some vital matters that needed immediate action. Moscow told the hierarchy of the U.S. Communist Party that for those types of emergencies, they were to contact one of three men located at the Waldorf Towers. Dodd was quick to point out that none of them were Russians or even communists, but wealthy American capitalists. To this she replied, "I would certainly like to find out who is really running things."[43]

Professor Quigley answers Dodd's question by identifying those who are really running things:

"It was this group of people, whose wealth and influence so exceeded their experience and understanding, who provided much of the framework of the influence which the Communist sympathizers and fellow travelers took over in the United States in the 1930s. It must be recognized that the power that these energetic left wingers exercised was *never their own power or communist power* but was ultimately the power of the international financial coterie ..."[44]

In 1956, the House Committee on Un-American Activities conducted a study, *The Communist Conspiracy: Strategy and Tactics of World Communism*. In this study, J. Edgar Hoover says of the confrontation with communism that:

"... the individual is handicapped by coming face to face with a conspiracy so monstrous he cannot believe it exists."[45]

Hoover was not referring to the communist conspiracy, but to the NWO conspiracy that dominates every government in the world, including communism. With this understanding, we can now explore the Order's modus operandi.

Chapter 6

Modus Operandi

"Transgression speaks to the ungodly within his
heart … The words of his mouth are wickedness
and deceit … He plans wickedness upon his bed;
he sets himself on a path that is not good;
he does not despise evil."
Psalms 36:1, 4

A lot can be learned about a person or a group based on their
"modus operandi" or method of operation. In John 10:10, Jesus
taught us how to distinguish between the methods of the Kingdom
of heaven and the kingdom of this world when He said:

"The thief comes only to steal, and kill, and destroy;
I came that they might have life, and might have it
abundantly." (John 10:10)

The Lord's Kingdom brings salvation, healing and life, while
Satan's kingdom brings damnation, destruction and death.
Weishaupt brought Satan's "modus operandi" into the Order and
taught that it was to be brutal and without conscience, destroying
everything in its path while remaining hidden. Weishaupt said:

"The true purpose of the Order was to rule the world. To achieve this it was necessary for the Order to destroy all religions, overthrow all governments and abolish all private property rights."[46]

As stated earlier, conducting this chaos in secret is eminently part of the Order's method. King David understood the secret ways of political conspirators and exposed their methods for destroying the righteous when he prayed for protection from them:

"Hide me from the *secret* counsel of evildoers, from the tumult of those who do iniquity, who have sharpened their tongue like a sword. They aimed bitter speech as their arrow, to shoot from *concealment* at the blameless; suddenly they shoot at him, and do not fear. They hold fast to themselves an evil purpose; they talk of laying snares *secretly*; they say, 'Who can see them?' They devise injustices, saying, '*We are ready with a well-conceived plot ... .*'" (PSALMS 64:1–6)

This conspiracy is currently in full swing and will not be destroyed until the return of Messiah Jesus (DANIEL 7:19–22). Since God's supernatural concealment is one of the only things that can protect the righteous in the days ahead, I believe that David's prayer should also be our prayer.

The Hegelian Dialectic

This philosophy is expressed in the Latin phrase *Ordo Ab Chao*, which translated means "Order out of Chaos." It operates according to the concept that *conflict brings change* toward a new order, and *controlled conflict brings controlled change*. Since the beginning, this philosophy has been the Order's war cry and has been effectively passed down throughout the generations.

This method of operation was popularized during the 1800s by a German philosopher named George Wilhelm Friedrich Hegel and was loosed in mania fashion in the German Universities during the early 1900s. It is better known today as the "Hegelian Dialectic," and is viewed by many as the philosophy behind the French, American, and Marxist Revolutions, as well as both world wars.[47]

Webster's Dictionary defines this dialectic as:

> "The Hegelian process of change whereby a 'thesis' is transformed into an 'antithesis,' and preserved and fulfilled by it, the combination of the two being resolved in 'synthesis.'
>
> "The Marxian process of change through the conflict of opposing forces, whereby a given contradiction is marked as a primary and secondary aspect, the secondary succumbing to the primary, which is then transformed into the aspect of a new contradiction."[48]

Simply put, Hegelian philosophy is a change that is deliberately planned. First, there is "thesis," which brings "antithesis," which produces "synthesis" or the desired outcome.

Take World War I, for example—the "thesis" was Germany and her allies' attempt to conquer Europe. The "antithesis" was the allied powers who opposed and defeated them. The "synthesis" was the first open attempt to form a world government through the League of Nations.

Since the League of Nations failed, World War II was obviously the next Hegelian model. Again, the "thesis" was Germany's move to conquer Europe, North Africa, and Russia. Again, the "antithesis" was the allied powers who opposed and ultimately defeated them. The "synthesis" was the successful creation of the United Nations, which appears to be the apparatus of the soon coming new world government.

It is important to note that at the beginning of World War II, Illuminist James P. Warburg put forth the Order's real goal of globalism when he testified before the 1941 Senate Foreign Relations Subcommittee. Warburg was very clear about the Order's willingness to do whatever it took to accomplish world government when he declared that:

> "We shall have world government, whether or not we like it. The only question is whether world government will be achieved by consent or by conquest."[49]

Warburg's statement goes a long way to explaining why men do the evil that they do. It also explains why the international banking elite have financed both sides of every major war since 1776.

King David described these warmongers in his prayer for protection:

> "Rescue me, O Lord, from evil men; preserve me from violent men, who devise evil things in their hearts; they continually stir up wars." (PSALMS 140:1–2)

When considering the Hegelian model of the Cold War, it is

easy to see that Communism could not have been the head of the conspiracy, because it was merely the "thesis" of the Cold War. The "antithesis" was the West's forty years of opposition to it. The "synthesis" was the collapse of Russia and its merger into the new global system that was built by the West to fight Communism.

Even Y2K was a Hegelian model. Y2K was the "thesis" which brought the "antithesis" in the form of a US$1 trillion global effort to solve the 2000 date cross-over problem. This effort made sure that all the various systems around the world would interface properly. The "synthesis" was the creation of a completely interactive global communications network and financial system, with the Internet (World Wide Web) leading the way.

While the globalists do not create every "thesis," they exploit circumstantial situations that might provide the basis for one. For example, the 2000 U.S. election controversy over the Florida ballot recount could never have been planned, but it provided a perfect "thesis" for revamping the election system. The "antithesis" will undoubtedly be the standardization for voter identification, registration, and casting of votes. In some counties and states, this standardization may even include "smart card" technology with a bio-identification system. This will add to the ongoing "synthesis" of the mark-of-the-beast system that is being developed on numerous technological fronts. It will be interesting to watch the "antithesis" that develops out of Florida's ballot debacle.

With this revelation, it is easy to see that the entire progression of world events, since May 1, 1776, has been a series of Hegelian models that have moved us step by step toward the completion of Mystery Babylon and its NWO system.

Mystery Babylon Goes Public

Although secrecy was the Order's way of conducting its operations for over two centuries, it eventually had to go public. That appointed time was the 1990–1991 Iraq War, which provided a unique place from which the Order could publicly announce to the whole world on CNN their plans to establish a NWO.

This announcement took place on January 29, 1991, during the state of the union address, when President George Bush (CFR, TLC) said:

> "We know why we are there. We are Americans: part of something larger than ourselves ... What is at stake is more than one small country; it is a big idea: *a New World Order*, where diverse nations are drawn together in *a common cause to achieve the universal aspirations of mankind* ... The leadership of the *United Nations* is now confirming its founder's vision ... The world can therefore seize this opportunity to fulfill the *long held promise of a New World Order.*"[50]

At the June 1991 Bilderberg RTG meeting, which took place after the Iraq War and Bush's public announcement of the NWO, fellow Illuminist, David Rockefeller made a tell-all statement. After thanking the press for their conspiratorial efforts to keep their NWO plans secret for nearly forty years, he confirmed that now was the time for the Order to go public with their agenda for establishing a world government. Not only does this statement confirm the conspiracy, but it also implicates the press as co-conspirators, which explains why the truth has been suppressed in the global media:

"We are grateful to *The Washington Post, The New York Times, Time Magazine* and other great publications whose directors have attended our meeting and respected their promises of discretion for almost forty years. It would have been impossible for us to develop our plan for the world if we had been subject to the bright lights of publicity during those years. *But, the world is now more prepared to march toward a world government. The supranational sovereignty of an intellectual elite and world bankers is surely preferable to the national autodetermination practiced in past centuries.*"[51]

For decades, the United Nations lay dormant and powerless in international affairs. However, the Hegelian model of the Iraq War was designed to empower the United Nations as the Order's new political, financial and military authority.

The "thesis" was Iraq's invasion of Kuwait, which produced the "antithesis" of a worldwide political, financial, and military coalition to defeat Iraq. This produced the "synthesis," which was the public announcement and empowering of the U.N. as the seat for the NWO.

When President Bush said that the coalition's purpose was to achieve "the universal aspiration of mankind" and "fulfill the long held promise of a New World Order," he was referring to the NWO plans that originated in ancient Babylon on the plains of Shinar during the time of Nimrod. The fact that this announcement came out of a Hegelian war that gathered the whole world to Iraq and Kuwait in a common cause was no coincidence, because today the ancient plains of Shinar are in the modern day countries of Iraq and Kuwait.

This means we have come full circle, and the end of the age is upon us. Mystery Babylon has been publicly proclaimed as the New World Order, and the U.N. is its throne.

Getting Control of the Money

All of this brings us back to the subject of this book, which is the Order's control and manipulation of money and wealth for the purposes of establishing Mystery Babylon. Since it takes a tremendous amount of economic resources to finance the overthrow of society, the reader must understand the Order's clandestine plans to capture and control all the world's financial systems and forge them into one.

As a fellow insider who understood their plans and modus operandi, Professor Quigley clearly states that this was the Order's long-term goal:

> "In addition to these pragmatic goals, the powers of financial capitalism had another far-reaching aim, nothing less than to *create a world system of financial control in private hands able to dominate the political system of each country and the economy of the world as a whole.* This system was to be controlled in a feudalist fashion by the central banks of the world acting in concert, by secret agreements arrived at in frequent private meetings and conferences. The apex of the system was to be the Bank for International Settlements in Basle, Switzerland, a private bank owned and controlled by the world's central banks

which were themselves private corporations. Each central bank ... *sought to dominate its government by its ability to control Treasury loans, to manipulate foreign exchanges, to influence cooperative politicians by subsequent economic rewards in the business world.*"[52]

As I have already pointed out in chapter three, the heart of monetary and political control is housed within the world's central banks. Therefore, it was imperative for the Order to get control of all central banks. To do this in the U.S. was a more difficult task than in other countries, because the U.S. constitution stated that only "Congress shall have the power to coin money, regulate the value thereof, and of foreign Coin, and fix the standard of weights and measures."[53]

This meant that the U.S. central bank had to appear non-threatening to the government's authority to print and coin money. In other words, it had to appear as though it were an official government institution, while control was passed to the private bankers.[54]

In the beginning, they also had to make the central bank appear as though it were independent of Wall Street, without being independent. This was the overall plan behind the secret meeting on Jekyl Island, Georgia, November 22, 1910, that laid the foundation for America's central bank of the Federal Reserve.

The secret meeting on Jekyl Island included Nelson W. Aldrich, Republican "whip" in the Senate and Chairman of the National Monetary Commission; Henry P. Davison of J.P. Morgan & Company; Frank A. Vanderlip, President of the Rockefeller-owned National City Bank; A. Pratt Andrew, Assistant Secretary of the Treasury; Benjamin Strong of the Morgan's Bankers Trust

Company, and of course Paul Warburg, who represented the Rothschild Banking dynasty.[55]

During an interview with the *Saturday Evening Post*, Rockefeller's agent, Frank Vanderlip, later admitted:

> "Despite my views about the value to society of greater publicity for the affairs of corporations, there was an occasion, near the close of 1910, when *I was as secretive—indeed as furtive—as any conspirator* ... I do not feel it is any exaggeration to speak of our *secret expedition to Jekyl Island* as the occasion of the actual conception of what eventually became the Federal Reserve System."[56]

The original plan that came from Jekyl Island was introduced in the Senate as the Aldrich Bill. It was defeated primarily because Senator Aldrich, father-in-law to John D. Rockefeller, was too closely associated with Wall Street titans. However, the Order's relentless efforts finally produced the Federal Reserve Act, which passed the House of Representatives on December 22, 1913 by a vote of 298 to 60 and the Senate by a vote of 43 to 25.[57]

It was at that time that the U. S. Congress lost its constitutional control of America's monetary system, which began a new era of control and manipulation of the financial markets. In 1916, just three years after the Federal Reserve Act was passed, President Woodrow Wilson admitted that:

> "... the growth of the nation ... and all our activities are in the hands of a few men ... We have come to be one of the worst ruled; one of the most completely controlled and dominated governments in the civilized

world ... no longer a government by conviction and the free vote of the majority, but a government by opinion and duress of small groups of dominant men."[58]

America's Role in the NWO

Since that time, the Order has confidently established the U.S. as the financial and political muscle behind its agenda for a NWO. This message was made loud and clear when the Great Seal of the U.S. was placed on America's one-dollar bill in 1935. The backside of the seal contains the Latin phrase *Annuit Coeptis Novus Ordo Seclorum*, which translated means, "Announcing the Beginning of the New Order of Secularism", i.e. New World Order.

With this system fully operational, the Order set out to manipulate the price of investments through the expansion and contraction of debt in the world's financial markets.

Figure 4: *The Great Seal*

Chapter 7

MANIPULATING FINANCIAL MARKETS WITH DEBTS

"But those who want to get rich fall into
temptation and a snare and many foolish and
harmful desires which plunge men into
ruin and destruction."
1 TIMOTHY 6:9

Although *Debt Pyramid Investing* (DPI), described in chapter four, has been around a long time, the financial elite quickly discovered that DPI only expanded the *use* of the same investment dollars and not the *supply* of investment dollars. This limited their ability to manipulate investment values, so they began to develop new ways of expanding the supply of investment dollars within the investment system.

Margined Investing

These dishonest traders realized that just as the increase of debt is used to manipulate prices in the economic system, so too the increase of debt could be used to manipulate prices in the investment system. To do this, they simply took a page from the FRB play-book for the economy and applied it to investments.

This produced a form of *fractional reserve investing* known as "margined investing."

Margined investing is when the investor borrows money to buy stock. Margin is the minimum down-payment needed for the purchase. Simply put, the investor borrows fractional reserve type ledger book money to buy more stocks than he could afford otherwise. Manipulated margined investing was the major force behind the 1929 stock market crash, but more on that later.

For example, if an investor purchased 1,000 shares of XYZ stock at $10 per share ($10,000 total) on 50% margin, he could make that purchase by advancing the broker $5,000 and borrowing the other $5,000. If the stock goes up $1 (10%), he can sell the stock for $11,000, which is a gain of $1,000 (20%) on his $5,000 margin, less interest for the time the money was borrowed. Without the margin, he would only realize a $500 (10%) gain.

However, if the stock price goes down $1 (10%), and he liquidates it for $9,000, he loses $1,000 (20%) on his $5,000 margin plus interest. Without the margin, he would lose only $500 (10%).

The same principles of inflation that apply to the economy also apply to investments. In other words, as loans to buy stocks increase, the purchasing power of the investor's dollar goes down, thereby driving prices higher. But unlike in the economic system, higher investment prices are very much welcomed. In the same way that the economy heats up because of too much money (debt) in the system, investments can also overheat because of too much money (debt) being injected through margined investing.

When this happens, the Federal Reserve, empowered by the

Securities Exchange Act of 1934, can raise margin requirements. Current margins are 50%, like in the example above. If the Fed raised them to 60%, this would have an enormous slowing effect on the stock market, and prices would plummet. On the other hand, if the Fed were to lower margins to 40%, this would speed the market up and stock prices would soar.

Another way the Fed can directly affect margined investing is to raise or lower interest rates, which raises or lowers the cost of money as a whole. In late 1999 and early 2000, Fed Chairman, Alan Greenspan, raised interest rates mainly to slow down what he called the "irrational exuberance" of the markets. The result was a 60% drop in the Nasdaq and a 20% drop in the Dow.

As you can see, this ability to control both margins and interest rates allows the financial elite to manipulate the price of investments by controlling the amount of investment dollars entering the market.

Futures and Options

Since margined investing is limited to 50%, other devices had to be created, which would expand the elite's manipulating power in both the scope of investments and amount of leverage. This birthed the futures and options contracts, which are different in application, but the same in principle. While originally developed for price discovery and risk aversion, they have both evolved into tools for manipulating investment values.

Futures is a contract that allows an investor to buy or sell a commodity (gold, orange juice, coffee, etc.) or a financial instrument (government bond, foreign currency, stock index, etc.)

on varying margins at a predetermined price. It allows the buyer to control much more investment than he has actual money for.[59]

The influx of margined *futures* buying creates an artificial demand for that commodity or financial instrument, which drives the price artificially high. On the other side, the influx of margined *futures* selling creates an artificial supply of that commodity or financial instrument, which drives the price to an artificial low.

The operative word on both sides of a *futures contract* is "artificial." This allows the financial establishment to use their vast financial resources in the futures market to manipulate investment values, up or down, according to a predetermined purpose.

Options differ from a *futures contract* in that the *option* buyer only purchases the "right" to buy or sell the "underlying" security (stock, stock index, commodity, bond, etc.) at a fixed price before a specified date. For this "right," the *option* buyer pays a fee called a premium (like a down-payment), which is forfeited if the buyer does not exercise the option before the expiration date.[60]

Options were originally used to hedge the financial risks that farmers faced from big swings in the price of their crops. In the beginning this was a good thing, but man's love of money caused him to pervert that purpose by using their leveraging ability for get-rich-quick speculation in those markets. Many options traders made fortunes, while at the same time many lost fortunes. However, in the hands of the financial elite, it becomes a tool that enables them to manipulate markets with debt created by dishonest scales.

The best example of this type of manipulation took place on October 27–28, 1997. On Monday the 27th, the U.S. stock markets experienced a record-setting crash. However, on Tuesday the 28th, those same markets set new records for one-day gains as they recovered over 50% of their losses. It was obvious that the average investor was not the major force behind the recovery. So what happened to make that recovery possible?

The Clinton administration's "Plunge Protection Team," led by the Federal Reserve, leveraged an estimated $200 billion of Treasury and Fed funds and injected it into the markets.[61] They bought S&P 500 and other stock index futures contracts and provided funds to purchase select Dow Jones and Nasdaq stocks.

They also gave IBM $3.5 billion dollars in federal loan guarantees, so that IBM could borrow money to buy back their own stock. This produced an artificial recovery in the price of IBM stock that had crashed the day before with the rest of the markets. Because IBM is such a large component of the Dow, it provided a significant contribution to Tuesday's recovery. This was a desperate move to save the financial system that only added to Wall Street's collapsing debt bubble.

Forward Contracts

A *forward contract* is a completed contract that actually purchases or sells a specific amount of a commodity or financial instrument at a price specified now, with delivery and settlement at a specified future date.[62] Although it differs slightly from *futures* and *options* contracts, both *futures* and *options* are often used to either hedge the investor from potential risk or to multiply the effects of the forward contract.

The most prolific forward selling took place in the gold market during the Asia, Russia, South America financial crisis of

1997–1999. Billions of dollars of gold were forward sold on margin in order to keep the global paper markets afloat and depress the price of gold.[†]

Black-Scholes Formula for Options Trading

As man's love of money through unjust gain grew, the original formula for options trading became too limited in its scope of investments and ability to leverage. So, in 1973, the spirit of the world moved on Fischer Black (deceased), Myron Scholes and Robert Merton, and led them to develop the 1973 "Black-Scholes Model for Options Trading" (Myron Scholes and Robert Merton are important names to remember for later):

$$C = SN(d) - Le^{-rt}N(d - \sigma\sqrt{t})$$

This complex pricing model revolutionized how options could be used. It expanded the scope of investments to include a multitude of financial instruments, and dramatically increased the user's leveraging ability.[63] In other words, more fractional reserve type debt could be created out of nothing to buy or sell investment assets, which further enhanced the elite's ability to manipulate the markets.

Derivatives

The Black-Scholes Model was the ultimate set of dishonest scales, because it was flexible enough to do almost anything with. When applied to the advances in computer processing and telecommunications, this formula virtually created a multi-trillion dollar investment market out of thin air.

---

† See *Forward Selling of Gold* on page 221.

Like standard options, *derivatives* are financial contracts whose value is *derived* from the underlying or "notional value" of the borrowed investment. The high degree of leverage associated with these financial instruments (50%–90%) makes them highly volatile and subject to huge losses in the blink of an eye. As president of an investment firm in 1987, I had the unfortunate experience of witnessing their volatility. Referred to then as "programmed trading" and "portfolio insurance," these debt-based *derivatives* underwent a collapse, which exacerbated the stock market crash of October 19, 1987.[64]

After the 1987 crash, Wall Street and the rest of the investment world began using these explosive investments even more. This produced another debt bubble ($6.4 billion) that exploded in 1993 and broke the financial backs of corporate conglomerates like Kidder Peabody, Barings Bank, and the government of Orange County, California.[65]

Fluctuating market prices continued to move against the basket of borrowed securities that formed the underlying value of the derivatives contracts. This not only made the derivatives contracts big losers, but they also became very difficult to liquidate. This forced the derivatives contractors to execute a second derivatives contract to offset the losses in the first one. But instead of a wash, the new contract increased the size of the derivatives market.

These new derivatives were usually something "exotic" such as "leveraged interest rate swaps," "structured notes," and "kitchen-sink mortgages." When the second level of derivatives contracts had trouble, then the contractor could only execute a third, even more exotic, level of derivative to offset the losses in the second, and so on, down the line to multiple generations of derivatives.

At this point, the derivatives market was increasing at an alarming rate. They even created a "weather derivative" that allowed investors to bet on how the weather would affect businesses. It was like a financial "Pac Man" that was gobbling up every securities investment in its path. As a result, there was an exponential growth in securities borrowing.

By April 1994, the "notional value" of the *derivatives* market had grown to $13 trillion. But what is important to understand is that the worldwide investment market (stocks, bonds, mutual funds, currencies, money markets, etc.) only totaled about $48 trillion at that time. This meant that over 27% of the global investment market had been leveraged in the derivatives market and was at risk of collapse.[66]

Global Financial Markets at Risk

Up to this point, only higher-risk securities were used to conjure up derivatives, but as the supply of the higher risk securities had been borrowed up, derivative dealers were forced to borrow securities from mutual funds, money markets, bank deposits, and other safer investments.

Derivatives also showed up in numerous quasi-governmental agencies. Agencies such as the Federal National Mortgage Association (Fannie Mae), Federal Home Loan Mortgage Corporation (Freddie Mac), and the Student Loan Marketing Association (Sallie Mae) quickly became major users of these exotic derivatives.

If these derivatives get into trouble, the U.S. government is expected to bail out investors at the taxpayer's expense.[67] This means that even the safest investments, such as money markets, low-risk securities, and taxpayer-backed government investments are being gobbled up by derivatives dealers.

The potential problem was so bad that in May 1994, the General Accounting Office (GAO) of the United States reported:

> "The rapid rise of complex financial transactions known as derivatives and the huge size of the market for these products pose potential risks for the U.S. financial system. ... The sudden failure or abrupt withdrawal from trading of any of these large (derivatives) dealers could cause liquidity problems in the markets and *pose a risk to others, including federally insured banks and the financial system as a whole.* Federal intervention could involve industry loans or a financial bail-out paid for by taxpayers."[68]

By August 1994, the derivatives market had burgeoned to $35 trillion and was growing almost exponentially. This meant that *derivatives* dealers had borrowed roughly 75% of available securities to play this high-risk, high leveraged *derivatives* crap game.[69]

In many instances, the value of derivatives actually exceeded the "notional value" of the underlying securities. For example, Eurodollar derivatives trading had grown to approximately $6.5 trillion, while actual Eurodollars only totaled a modest $500 billion. In this case of the tail wagging the dog, the derivatives market was trading at 13 times the existing amount of Eurodollars.[70]

Mexico joined this high stakes crap game in an effort to keep its own currency (the peso) afloat. Then, on December 20, 1994,

President Zedillo of Mexico was the first major derivatives player to fail, and the world watched a sovereign nation go bankrupt overnight. The instant devaluation of the peso was followed by the immediate collapse of its paper markets (stocks, bonds, mutual funds), which shook the entire world's financial system.

Derivatives Shake the World Economy

This began a series of financial shakings like the world had never seen before. Mexico's crisis released a pattern of currency devaluations that spread throughout Thailand, Malaysia, Singapore, Indonesia, South Korea, the Philippines, India, Pakistan, Russia, South America, South Africa and Australia. Unfortunately, this is all part of the great end time financial shaking that will ultimately bring the nations of the world to their knees.

Chapter 8

THE END TIME FINANCIAL SHAKING

"And His voice shook the earth then, but now He has
promised, saying, 'Yet once more I will shake not only
the earth, but also the heaven.' And this expression,
'Yet once more,' denotes the removing of those things
which can be shaken, as of created things, in order that
those things which cannot be shaken may remain."

HEBREWS 12:26–27

The Scriptures say that before this age is over, God is going
to shake every "created thing" that can be shaken, so only that
which cannot be shaken will remain. Since God Himself is the
only thing that is uncreated, everything not of God will fail. This
is not the wrath of God, but a time when God tests everyone and
everything in preparation for His coming.

Part of this great shaking is currently underway in the world's
financial system, where the purifying fire of God's Word is testing
every investment and financial institution. In other words, every
financial investment that is built upon God's biblical standard of
honest scales will remain, but every unjust investment will not.

It is easy to see how the recent financial shakings have actually
served to uncover the true nature of each investment. I believe
that God is using the current financial shakings to show us which
investments are built upon the principles of His Word and which

investments are not. He is trying to show us that debt-based paper investments are unstable because they are not part of His Kingdom. Rather, they are part of the world's kingdom built on dishonest scales.

With this in mind, let us examine the performance of each investment as they have experienced the end time financial shaking up until now. To better distinguish investment groupings, I have divided them into "Loanership Assets" and "Ownership Assets."

Loanership Assets
Futures, Options, and Derivatives

As I have already pointed out, this investment segment is the most volatile and damaging, because it allows speculators to create and multiply investment debt out of thin air. This debt is used to leverage every other investment segment (currencies, bonds, stocks, commodities, etc.) up or down according to a predetermined purpose.

The result is a debt bubble that always collapses eventually, and forces the markets into a sell-off. During a market sell-off, these hedge funds actually multiply paper losses and the speed at which they devalue. As a result, they negatively affect the price of every investment traded in the marketplace.

Cash and Currencies

The most recent financial shaking has predominantly been played out in the global currency markets. Remember that all paper currency is FRB debt that has been loaned into existence as money. Today's banks and brokerage houses can create money virtually at will and then channel it into both the economy and the financial markets through loans and leveraged investments.

The more money is printed, the less each currency unit is worth. To keep the currencies from devaluing and consumer prices from rising too soon, currency speculators use derivatives to buy the weaker currencies, which artificially props them up. This creates a currency debt bubble that speculators always sell off, thereby flooding the market with the unwanted currency.

The sell-off collapses the purchasing power of the unwanted currency and inflation immediately sets in. Interest rates skyrocket, which stops the borrowing process and creates a cash flow shortage. The government ceases its support of the currency and is forced to monetize its deficits. All of this accentuates the devaluation already underway and starts another round of currency liquidation.

Everyone holding the currencies that were devalued or investments denominated in those currencies would have experienced proportionate losses in value. In varying degrees, this is what has happened in all the crisis countries (Mexico, South America, Russia, India, South Africa, Latin America, and all of Southeast Asia) and is what will eventually happen in every country of the world to one degree or another.

Money Markets and CDs

Traditionally, these investments have been a safe haven for cash holdings. However, when a currency devalues due to an inflationary cycle or during a derivatives sell-off, these cash investments lose their purchasing power in direct proportion to the devaluation. Investors may eventually get their money back, but its buying power would be virtually destroyed.

In America, we have not experienced a currency devaluation, so this crisis has not yet manifested. However, fund managers have been using derivatives in an effort to enhance money market returns. This has increased investment risk and caused several U.S. money markets to go bust.

The best example of a money market bust took place on September 28, 1994, when the Denver-based Community Asset Management (CAM), an $82.2 million money market fund, fell victim to derivatives. CAM was the first money market to "break the buck," when its net asset value fell below $1 to 94 cents per share. CAM's 94 institutional shareholders reimbursed investors, sold off the derivatives, and shut the money market down.[71]

Fortunately, the financial institutions that funded CAM had the reserves to reimburse investors—but what would have happened if they did not? Today, the practice of investing money market funds in derivatives is the norm. This means that CAM's default is just a shadow of things that will eventually come to the entire money market industry.

Credit Market Investments

Credit market investments primarily consist of bonds, treasury securities and mortgages. As the currency devalues and interest rates rise, bond prices and other credit instruments collapse. This produces an immediate liquidity problem that renders financial institutions (especially banks and brokerage houses) vulnerable to insolvency. Insolvent institutions cannot redeem depositors' money, and this leads to an immediate run on the banking system, forcing it to close.

This scenario happened to hundreds of banks throughout the crisis countries. They all had to close their doors until they could be merged, or bail-out money was found to cover depositors' losses. In some cases, like Thailand and Indonesia, the country's entire financial system shut down for a time because the central banks went bust.[72]

Although America has been spared a derivatives-driven currency devaluation, U.S. institutions are not immune to blowouts in derivatives-laced credit portfolios. For example, Harris Trust & Savings lost $51.3 million in a type of derivative known as "Floating Rate Collateralized Mortgage Obligations." The Wall Street Journal reported that those derivatives made up 34% of the total accounts managed by Harris on behalf of pension funds and other institutional investors. This meant that pension fund money, normally invested in safer investments, was being gambled away in the high-risk derivatives market.[73]

This was being done illegally and without the pension funds' knowledge. According to a spokesperson for the bank:

> "There is an implicit agreement between Harris and its clients that the accounts would be invested in short-term securities such as Treasury Bills and Commercial Paper. *The derivatives should have never been in these accounts in the first place.*"[74]

Fortunately, Harris had the reserves to cover the losses, but what would have happened if they did not? Derivatives are part of the normal investment strategy currently employed by bank investment departments, which makes the threat of future shakings in the U.S. credit markets that much greater.

Insurance Products

Many believe that cash value insurance products (whole life, universal life, and annuities) have some sort of mystical safeguard that protects them from financial collapse. Unfortunately, insurance simply borrows money from its customers in the form of premium payments and then loans them out again into the same debt pyramid that has been crashing all over the world. This makes them just as vulnerable to collapse as any other financial institution. In fact, failed insurance companies in both Mexico and Asia were among those needing IMF bail-out money.

In America, interest rates spiked in the early 1990s and seriously shook the credit markets. As a result, 1991 saw the collapse of six major U.S. insurance companies that were all big players in the investment system. The most notable was Mutual Benefit Life (MBL), a 146 year-old insurer that even survived the "Great Depression."[75]

MBL sold its pension fund clients high-yield debt called Guaranteed Investment Contracts and Collateralized Mortgage Obligations, two favorite investments of Section 401(k) retirement plans. MBL turned around and invested (reloaned) this money into bonds, mortgage securities and real estate. As interest rates rose, these investments devalued, and MBL began to unwind into insolvency.[76]

When pension fund managers, who were afraid of getting sued by retirees, began to move money out of MBL, it caused a "run on the bank" so to speak, and regulators were forced to shut MBL down. The collapse of MBL had a negative financial impact on over 400,000 people and hundreds of associated companies.[77]

In 1993, the $10.2 billion Executive Life Insurance Company experienced the collapse of its $6.7 billion bond portfolio, and the company was forced into insolvency. Investors (annuity and other cash value holders) who depended on their monthly retirement check from Executive Life, were left holding empty paper promises with no way of redeeming them.[78]

This type of failed debt pyramid scheme has contributed significantly to the multi-trillion dollar shortfall in U.S. pension funds. Pension funds own about one-quarter of the stock and bond market, which means that retirees are particularly vulnerable when the market goes wrong.[79] Just don't tell any of them who were affected by the crashes that insurance companies cannot fail.

Ownership Assets

Precious Metals

History has proven that precious metals are the only unchallenged ark of financial safety during any type of financial crisis. For example, when the debt bubble collapsed during Wall Street's crash of 1929, cash was very scarce. This meant that, if you had cash, you could buy just about anything for pennies on the dollar.

However, in 1929, cash was gold and silver. In other words, wealth was preserved in the precious metals, which not only maintained, but also increased, its purchasing power during the financial shaking (more on this later).

Today, on the other hand, we have a fiat monetary system that is no longer backed by precious metals. As such, currencies fluctuate up and down according to the amount of money (debt) that is put into or taken out of the system. When a currency is strong like the

U.S. dollar has been, it buys more goods and services and prices remain low. Since world precious metals prices are calculated in the stronger U.S. dollar, the international price of metals has remained low.

However, when a currency devalues, it results in immediate inflation, and the paper costs of goods and services go up along with the price of precious metals. For example, when Mexico's peso devalued 40% in one day, the price of silver in Mexico rose from 16.5 pesos per ounce to 23 pesos per ounce, while silver remained at US$4.75 per ounce on the international markets.

If left alone, precious metals values do not fluctuate significantly. It is actually the debt-based, unjust, fiat currencies that fluctuate up and down against them. But since precious metals are priced in paper currencies and not the other way around, it appears as though it is the precious metals that are fluctuating in price. This is a major part of the NWO's financial delusion.

Whether it is a currency devaluation or a financial collapse of a single company or whole system, the only monetary asset that is not destroyed is the precious metals complex. Why? Because precious metals are the only monetary asset that is not someone else's debt. Therefore, they always maintain their purchasing power in the midst of a financial crisis.

This truth vividly came to light during the collapse of Executive Life Insurance, as a host of annuity holders descended on the corporate headquarters in California to retrieve their money, only to find the doors locked and the money gone. CNN was there and interviewed one retiree, who had the lion's share of his retirement funds invested in an Executive Life annuity. I will never forget what he said:

"I used to laugh at the guys who have gold buried in their back yard—now I wish I had some."[80]

From Genesis to Revelation, precious metals are the only God-ordained monetary assets that maintain their purchasing power until the day of the Lord's wrath (GENESIS 2:11–12; EZEKIEL 7:19; REVELATION 18:11–12). Unfortunately, most do not accept this truth until it is too late.

Stocks

Stocks (paper equities) are the only biblically-based paper investments out there. That is because they represent real ownership in a company, complete with voting rights. Unfortunately, publicly traded "over the counter" (OTC) stocks can be bought and sold on margin or leveraged with derivatives debt. This allows them to be manipulated as a method of unjust gain, which perverts their value and puts them into the same category as loanership assets.

As a result, stocks are highly susceptible to leveraged *Momentum Investing*, which creates a market madness that is as unstable as nitroglycerin. Simply put, when investors begin to leverage stocks up, other investors jump on board with more margined buying, which adds to the upside momentum in that market.

The resulting rise in stock prices is not based on value, earnings or any other technical reasons, but simply the momentum behind the borrowed money (debt) that is flooding the market. Unfortunately, when the margined debt bubble bursts, the downside is even more volatile.

This makes OTC stocks highly susceptible to currency devaluations and rising interest rates. A currency devaluation causes stocks to decline in direct proportion to the devaluation, and higher interest rates force margined traders to sell off. When this happens, investors get trapped in a stock market freefall, which is the heart of what happened throughout the crisis-hit countries.

In the U.S., the best example of how leverage (debt) can affect the stock market took place in the Nasdaq (National Association of Securities Dealers Automated Quotation). Armed with the "new economy" hype surrounding high-tech and *dotcom* Internet stocks, the Nasdaq was on the receiving end of multiple trillions of dollars of leveraged buying from institutional speculators and Internet "day traders." Additional money came into the market from investors who took second mortgages on their homes, while others borrowed from their credit cards at 16% to chase the higher stock returns in hopes of getting rich quick. This leveraged momentum-buying caused the Nasdaq to post a record 85.6% gain during 1999, which topped out at 5048.62 points on March 10, 2000.[81]

In an open effort to curb the market's "irrational exuberance," Fed Chairman Alan Greenspan began raising interest rates at the end of 1999, and extended it through late summer of 2000. This caused the Nasdaq to crash 58% to 2118.63 points by March 2, 2001. Individual stocks like *iVillage.com* dropped 88% from a high of $113.75 per share to $13.63; *DrKoop.com* dropped 91.7% from $36.90 to $3.06 per share; and *eToys.com* collapsed from $85.25 to 8 cents per share, posting a breathtaking loss of 99.9%. When *eToys.com* finally announced it was filing for bankruptcy, it kindly informed the investment community that its stock was "worthless."[82] Duh!

Many investors, including Christians, borrowed every dollar they could get their hands on, and invested it on margin into these stocks. Like the Church of Laodicea, for a while they were rich and wealthy and had need of nothing, but when the debt bubble collapsed many lost everything and were forced into bankruptcy.[†]

Real Estate

Just like stocks, real estate is an ownership investment whose value depends largely on the availability of credit. The more money is loaned for real estate, the more property values artificially inflate. As inflation sets in and interest rates rise, it produces higher payments. This reduces the number of qualified buyers, and lenders are forced to cut back on the number of loans. With fewer loans, property sales dry up. This floods the market with unsold real estate and property prices crash.

For example, the economic boom of the 1920s was predicated solely on the expansion of debt and credit. Much of that debt was loaned for real estate, which artificially inflated property values. When the debt bubble popped, interest rates rose, real estate prices crashed and borrowers defaulted on their mortgages. This collapsed the Bank of the United States, which was over-exposed in real estate loans, and was a major catalyst behind the "Great Depression" of the 1930s.[83]

The same basic scenario has taken place in every country that has recently experienced a currency devaluation. In Mexico, high-flying real estate values collapsed 50%, and most people defaulted on their loans. In Asia, real estate values dropped anywhere from 40% in Singapore and Hong Kong, to 60% in Thailand and Indonesia.

---

† See *Church of Laodicea* on page 224.

People who owned their property free and clear, that is, as a sanctuary rather than an investment, were relatively unfazed by the devaluations. However, those who had investment properties lost most of their equity. In February 1998, one Singapore real estate millionairess told me that if she had understood the biblical truths concerning Commercial Babylon before the crisis, she would have saved millions of dollars in lost equity.

Those who had real estate mortgages quickly learned that they did not actually own their property, but were slaves to their lenders. When property prices dropped below loan values, lenders demanded a loan equity buy-down. If they did not have the cash, they found themselves in default, with the lenders threatening to foreclose.[†]

In May 2000, I met with two respected Hong Kong businessmen. One was a former stockbroker, and the other, a real estate baron who represented millions of dollars in Hong Kong properties. They explained how, even though the Hong Kong dollar was not devalued, lenders were not giving real estate loans. The shortage of available mortgage money caused prices to fall 40%. As a result, they both felt strongly that Hong Kong real estate might never recover unless new real estate investment financing could be developed.

In the U.S., a growing number of bankruptcies will force lenders to become more conservative in their lending, which will undoubtedly shake the U.S. real estate market. Lower interest rates throughout 2001 may cause a short-term stay in prices, but for the most part, I believe that the bonanza in real estate appreciation is most likely over in the U.S.

_____

† See *Real Estate and Financial Crisis* on page 226.

To force debtors into additional financial bondage, Congress passed legislation on March 1, 2001 that makes it more difficult for debtors to default on their debt. The legislation is a prelude to future legislation that will hold debtors accountable for their debt, even when it is impossible for them to pay it back. This will produce a modern day "debtor's prison" designed to enslave today's debt-ridden society.

It's All Part of the Plan

During times of financial shaking, a distinct financial pattern has emerged. The financial elite exploit man's love of material possessions by providing him with easy money in the form of FRB debt and credit with which to acquire them. This allows artificial wealth to be built through inflation, which gives everyone the image of greater prosperity.

Then the same lenders conspire to dry up the money supply (debt) and deliberately collapse the debt bubble. This forces the borrowers into default and allows the international lenders to confiscate the assets acquired with the borrowed money.

It is important to understand that this process is nothing new, and it did not originate with Hegel or even Weishaupt. It was birthed by Satan on the plains of Shinar and is part of Mystery Babylon's financial dialectic.

Chapter 9

MYSTERY BABYLON'S FINANCIAL DIALECTIC

"The rich rules over the poor, and the borrower
becomes the lender's slave."
PROVERBS 22:7

The use of unjust scales by the wicked rich to put people in bondage to debt has been the foundation of Satan's plan from the beginning. Once the debt pyramid supersedes the collateral to the point that the debt can never be paid back, the lenders collapse the system and confiscate the assets.

The first man-made economy that used this dialectic was, of course, ancient Babylon. *The Encyclopaedia Britannica* records this process as follows:

> "Economically, Mesopotamia suffered under the blight that besets cereal farmers everywhere: *the burden of debt that ruins the farmer*, ... the tax claims of the administration and the practice of farming out the actual land, ... The kings of the dynasties up to the end of the Old Babylonian period

combated the continuous crisis with repeated *releases of all noncommercial debt, with redistribution of ameliorated land*, with regulations concerning rates of interest, etc., all apparently without much success."[84]

High prices were also a recurring problem in Babylon.[85] This indicates that the debauching of the currency, through the use of dishonest scales, was probably the source of both the debt and the inflation. This dialectic of accumulating too much debt, followed by an inflationary collapse and confiscation (redistribution) of the land, is the economic Mystery of Babylon that Satan has used from the beginning.

Unjust Transfer of Wealth

In this dialectic, wealth is not lost during the economic collapse; it is merely transferred from one individual to another through the monetary and investment assets they are holding at the time. The prophet Amos points out how this unjust transfer of wealth led to economic slavery for many in Israel:

> "Hear this, you who trample the needy, to do away with the humble of the land, saying, 'When will the new moon be over, so that we may buy grain, and the Sabbath, that we may open the wheat market, *to make the bushel smaller and the shekel bigger, and to cheat with dishonest scales, so as to buy the helpless for money and the needy for a pair of sandals ... ?'"*
> (AMOS 8:4–6)

When Israel debauched the currency and created debt through the use of dishonest scales, not only did it produce an inflationary collapse (AMOS 8:7–10), but those who defaulted on their debt actually became the property of their lenders.

In China, Marco Polo reported that Genghis Khan forced everyone in his dominion to use debauched paper money. Khan obviously confiscated the gold and issued paper notes as money, which transferred the wealth of the people to himself. He ensured compliance by decreeing, "Nor does any person, at the peril of his own life, refuse to accept it [paper notes] in payment."[86] This will be the same ploy of the antichrist when his mark-of-the-beast system is invoked, and no one is able to buy or sell without his electronic money (REVELATION 13:16–18).

The Crash of 1929

The stock market crash of October 28, 1929 was a classic case of Babylon's financial dialectic. In 1966, a younger and wiser Alan Greenspan described it as follows:

> "The excess credit which the Fed pumped into the economy spilled over into the stock market— triggering a fantastic speculative boom. Belatedly, Federal Reserve officials attempted to sop up the excess reserves and finally succeeded in breaking the boom. But it was too late: by 1929 the speculative imbalances had become so overwhelming that the attempt precipitated a sharp retrenching and a consequent demoralization of business confidence.

> As a result, the American economy collapsed. ... The world economies plunged into the Great Depression of the 1930s."[87]

To be more explicit, during the sixteen months prior to the crash, the Fed increased the money supply by 62%.[88] Investors borrowed money to buy stocks, which pushed stock prices artificially high. During the rise in prices, the financial insiders (Rockefellers, Warburgs, Mellons, Rothschilds, etc.) coaxed small investors into the stock market with the prospects of doubling or even tripling their money in a short period of time. As more and more small investors clamored to buy stocks at the higher prices, the insiders, who owned the low-priced stocks, sold off to them.

Then, the insider-controlled Fed shut the money supply off and the market crashed. This caused a massive transfer of wealth to move from small investors into the coffers of the financial elite, who were manipulating the system. The average investor could not cover his margins and had to forfeit his stocks.

This did not even begin to cover the investors' debts, so many were forced to liquidate cars, real estate and other personal assets. Unfortunately, in many cases, that was not enough either. The thought of becoming slaves to their lenders drove many to commit suicide by jumping out of windows or shooting themselves.

The central bank's increase of money supply to inflate market prices, followed by a decrease in money supply to crash prices is what Thomas Jefferson warned us of when he said:

> "If the American people ever allow private banks to control the issue of their currency, first by inflation

and then by deflation, the banks and the corporations that will grow up around them, will deprive the people of all property until their children wake up homeless on the continent their fathers occupied."[89]

The Fed kept the money supply tight, which bankrupted the U.S. government and pushed the whole world into the depression of the 1930s. This led to the next and greatest transfer of wealth, when President Roosevelt confiscated privately-owned gold under Executive Order 6102.† During this time, the insiders, who had all the money from the 1929 crash, forged new financial empires by buying up real estate, manufacturing plants, and just about everything else.

Black Monday 1987

The collapse of the Bretton Woods system of fixed gold prices and exchange rates in 1971, followed by the debt crisis of the early 1980s, led to a new generation of corporate mergers and acquisitions (M&A). In turn, this precipitated a new generation of debt-based financial instruments used to fund them.[90] These highly leveraged investments led to an early form of derivatives called "portfolio insurance," which used the "Black-Scholes Model for Options Trading" to hedge these new debt instruments.

Unfortunately, these derivatives were also based on debt, and their ability to leverage investments up or down exploited man's love of money to make quick profits in other markets. This created a mini-version of Babylon's financial dialectic, and ultimately collapsed the stock market on "Black Monday", October 19, 1987.

---

† See *Executive Order 6102* on page 228.

As president of an investment firm during that crash, I personally experienced this dialectic. I witnessed the programmed sell-off of these early forms of derivatives, which crashed the stock market 22.6% in one day. This collapse shook financial markets around the world and wiped me out personally, as I explained earlier in chapter three.

1994–1995 Mexico Crisis

One would normally think that if derivatives were causing this much chaos in the markets, investors would stop using them. However, just the opposite is true. Remember that wealth is not lost during a financial crisis; it is merely transferred. So the huge losses suffered by the average investor translated into huge gains for the insiders who were manipulating the markets with derivatives.

This gave birth to a new generation of institutional speculators, who actually raised investment money (both debt and equity) to play the derivatives markets. Governments also began to use derivatives as a hedge to protect their currency from devaluation, which led to the first currency default by Mexico.

When money began pouring into Mexico's markets from global investors, it inflated the supply of currency (pesos), which normally causes higher prices. However, institutional speculators, along with Mexico's central bank, used derivatives to buy the Mexican peso on margin, which strengthened it. This allowed Mexico's economy to grow at a quickened pace without much price inflation in the economy.

Unfortunately, the derivatives debt bubble exceeded Mexico's ability to participate, and they were forced to stop buying the peso. On December 20, 1994, President Zedillo announced that Mexico's central bank was no longer going to support the peso, but let it float freely on the currency market. This meant that all the investment money from around the world that had been injected into Mexico's economy through stocks, bonds, and mutual funds, was going to sling-shot back to its true value.

Immediately, the stock market plunged 30%, as billions of dollars left Mexico on the first day after the announcement. By the end of the week, the markets (currency, stocks, and bonds) were down 50%, and inflation rose to over 75%. Interest rates instantly shot up to 100%, which collapsed the real estate market and left real estate loans in default.

This allowed the international banking cartels to come in and buy up Mexico's businesses and real property for dimes on the dollar.[91] In other words, Babylon's financial dialectic transferred Mexico's wealth to the very conspirators who control the system.

1997–1998 Asian Crisis

This transfer of wealth only spurred the financial elite on to using derivatives on a wider scale. By 1995, the daily volume of derivatives-based foreign currency transactions had reached $1.3 trillion dollars. This type of leveraged currency trading was especially prevalent throughout the countries of Southeast Asia. Governments, banks, and institutional speculators like George Soros of Quantum Fund, were doing the same propping up of

Asia's financial system that had been done in Mexico before it collapsed.

Then, on July 2, 1997, Soros and other institutional derivatives players sold off their leveraged holdings of Thailand's currency (the baht). This resulted in a 38% drop in the baht, which produced an inflation rate of 65%. Interest rates skyrocketed, which collapsed the real estate market, and the Thai stock exchange plunged 70%.[92] By August, the Thai government was bankrupt, and they were forced to come to the International Monetary Fund (IMF) with hat in hand, seeking a bail-out.

However, from the standpoint of international trade, Thailand's products would cost less in countries with stronger currencies, such as the U.S. and most of Europe. This gave Thailand the lowest prices when the West came shopping in Asia.

In order for other Asian countries (Malaysia, Indonesia, the Philippines, and South Korea) to compete with Thailand in international trade, they were all but forced to devalue their inflated currencies also. This is known as a "competitive currency devaluation," and it caused the same devastating contagion that happened in Thailand to quickly spread throughout Asia.

All of this produced a run on Asia's financial institutions, causing over 150 Asian banks, securities firms and insurance companies to go bankrupt. The insolvency was so bad that many of the bankrupt companies could not even be merged with other stronger companies in the same industry, but were defaulted upon and completely shut down. The failure of Asia's financial systems destroyed the life savings of millions of people, while at the same time throwing millions more out of work overnight. This was all due to a modern day dishonest scale called "derivatives".

1997 Nobel Prize for Economics

At this point, it is important to reiterate that all derivatives are an off-shoot of the *Black-Scholes Model For Options Trading*. The only thing that made Asia's financial crisis worse was the fact that, on October 15, 1997 (during the height of Asia's financial debacle), the global elite awarded Black-Scholes and its creators, *Myron Scholes* and *Robert Merton*, the 1997 Nobel Prize in Economics.

By awarding this unjust financial instrument, the Nobel Prize, while simultaneously using it to plunder Asia, the global elite were mocking the nations that they had seduced. They were also mocking God, who commands all men not to use dishonest scales when trading.[†]

Somebody Please Say Something!

Over the years, there has been only a remnant of political leaders who have had the courage to expose and challenge the conspiracy of the power elite. Among them was President Andrew Jackson who openly waged war against the conspirators by saying:

> "You are a den of vipers. I intend to rout you out, and by the Eternal God I will rout you. If the people only understood the rank injustice of our money and banking system, there would be a revolution before

---

† See *God Judges Nobel Prize for Economics* on page 232.

morning!"[93]

This kind of rhetoric never works. In fact, it was probably this open challenge that earned him the assassination attempt on his life in 1835.

In more recent times, Prime Minister Mahathir Mohamad of Malaysia emerged as the only political leader in the world who had the courage to stand up to the currency raiders, the IMF and the NWO as a whole. Mahathir recognized that derivatives were something evil, and he spoke out boldly against them and their users.

The *USA TODAY* reported Mahathir's righteous indignation as follows:

> "Mahathir blames the West. He made headlines around the world last month by demonizing free markets in general and billionaire currency player George Soros specifically. *The prime minister called currency trading 'unnecessary, unproductive and immoral.'*"[94]

In defense of Malaysia's currency (the ringgit) and its financial markets, Mahathir slapped trading restrictions on the Kuala Lumpur Stock Exchange (KLSE). These restrictions forced all paper trades to be conducted openly, and monitored by the KLSE.

Mahathir also set up a currency board that fixed Malaysia's currency at 3.8 ringgit to the US$1. I have spoken with two high-ranking Malaysian officials, who attended conferences that I conducted in Malaysia and Singapore, and we all agreed that Mahathir's actions saved Malaysia's financial system from complete collapse.

Unfortunately, Mahathir's financial safeguards have been systematically dismantled by Malaysia's own need for international investment capital. The need for capital forced him and others to call for a global funding system. When international capital was slow in coming, he began to seek regional capitalization, which led him and other leaders in the region to establish the Asian Monetary Fund. However, I believe that he now realizes that regionalization is just a stepping stone toward globalization.

During my September/October 2000 trip to Asia, the inside word was that PM Mahathir was greatly discouraged because he realized that he could not beat the globalist's debt trap. PM Mahathir has been a "voice of one crying in the wilderness" of the global political arena, and I admire him for it. Unfortunately, he, like every other world leader, is in a no-win situation. Therefore, I encourage Christians everywhere to pray for their leaders.†

Globalization Through Regionalization

Financial crisis always brings about political change. Each financial dialectic, therefore, works to move the political systems toward a NWO. Globalization is not an overnight process, but a series of step-by-step Hegelian models that are forcing countries to merge their economic and political systems into regional blocks.

Zbigniew Brezezinski, a spokesman for the Trilateral Commission (TLC), briefly outlined its plans for regionalization in a speech given at Mikhail Gorbachev's "State of the World Forum" meeting in October 1996:

> "We cannot leap into world government in one quick

---

† See *Pray for Rulers and Those in Authority* on page 265.

step ... [This objective] requires a process of gradually expanding the range of democratic cooperation ... a widening, step by step, stone by stone of existing relatively narrow zones of stability. ... The precondition for eventual globalization—genuine globalization—is *progressive regionalization,* because thereby we move toward large, more stable, more cooperative units."[95]

Remember, conflict brings change and controlled conflict brings controlled change. This simply means that, until the Day of the Lord comes, there will be a lot of Hegelian-type manipulation in the financial and political systems of the world. This manipulation will move to divide the world up into regional blocks that are considered to be more cohesive and easier to manage than the 181 nations that argue over the non-binding UN resolutions of today.

Understanding the NWO's plan for globalization through regionalization is paramount for overcoming the financial and political crises yet to come. Therefore, let us be wise as serpents but gentle as doves as we seek God's wisdom and understanding about the coming regionalization of the global world system.

Chapter 10

REGIONALIZATION OF THE GLOBAL WORLD SYSTEM

"The fourth beast will be a fourth kingdom on the earth, which will be different from all the other kingdoms, and it will devour the whole earth and tread it down and crush it. As for the ten horns, out of this kingdom ten kings will arise; and another will arise after them, and he will be different from the previous ones and will subdue three kings."
DANIEL 7:23–24

Bible prophecy in Daniel Chapter 2 has taught us that there would be four world kingdoms from Nebuchadnezzar's Babylon to the coming of the antichrist. History concurs with prophecy and has proven those kingdoms to be Babylon, Medo-Persia, Greece and Rome. The fourth kingdom of ancient Rome is seen by Daniel as a divided kingdom that would revive at the end of the age to become the final world kingdom of the antichrist.

In the above Scripture, Daniel also describes this last kingdom as a ten-horned beast that will be different from all other kingdoms. He says that this kingdom will come together under the authority of the ten horns, who are ten kings, and they devour the whole earth and tread it down and crush it. At that point, another king (the antichrist), who is distinct from the ten kings, will arise and become the beast of the last days. Even though the antichrist must subdue three of these kings, there will ultimately be ten world leaders who give their power and authority over to him (Revelation 17:12–13).

Club of Rome Plans the Revived Roman Empire

In April 1968, an Italian industrialist named Aurelio Peccei formed the RTG known as the Club of Rome (CR). In an effort to maintain the unity of globalistic thought, most of its members were drawn from the Council on Foreign Relations (CFR) and the Bilderbergs.[96]

In September 1973, the CR published a confidential report entitled *The Regionalized and Adaptive Model of the Global World System.* Compiled by CR members Mihajlo Mesarovic and Eduard Pestel, this study proposes to divide the world up into ten social, economic, and political regions. The original report even refers to these ten regions as "ten kingdoms," which is very intriguing

Figure 5: *Remake of 1973 Club of Rome map*

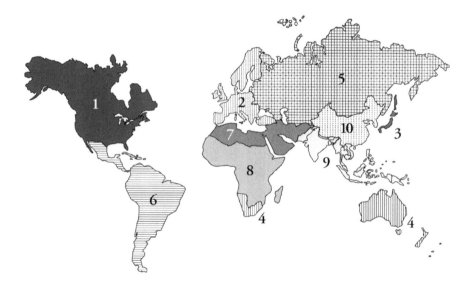

when you consider that they would eventually need "ten kings" to govern them (see Figure 5).

This plan was later published in a book *Mankind at the Turning Point*, which serves as a NWO directive for establishing ten regional blocs that encompass the whole world.[97]

Constitution for the Federation of Earth

The plan to divide the world system into ten more manageable regions is also promoted in the *Constitution for the Federation of Earth*, written and published by the World Constitution and Parliament Association (WCPA) of Lakewood, Colorado. Although founded in 1959, the WCPA did not ratify and begin circulating its world constitution until May 1991, just after the Gulf War when the NWO went public.

The WCPA's *Constitution for the Federation of Earth* calls for the world to be divided into what they define as "ten magna-regions," which are very similar to the CR's "ten kingdoms."[98] This leads me to believe that this plan will probably be the fulfillment of Daniel's ten-horned beast of the last days.

Ten Horns Update 2001

As I said earlier, globalization is not an overnight process, but a series of step-by-step Hegelian models that force countries to merge their economic and political systems into these ten regional blocs, which will ultimately come together in a global world system. However, even though the outcome is pretty well determined in advance, the process is still subject to rogue operators and God's sovereign intervention.

That is why the boundaries of the 1973 CR map were not set in stone, and some obvious changes have taken place since the original study was published. The most notable change occurred when the North America Free Trade Agreement (NAFTA) took Mexico out of kingdom #6 and put it into kingdom #1 along with the U.S. and Canada (see Figure 6).

Another change was made when kingdom #3 expanded from Japan (only) into what investment brokers now call the "Pacific Rim Countries." In other words, South Korea, Thailand, Malaysia, Singapore, Indonesia, the Philippines, Vietnam, and Cambodia have been moved from kingdom #9 into kingdom #3. This region is still in the process of working through a Hegelian economic crisis that may further change the regionalization of East Asia.

When South Africa voted Nelson Mandela in as President, communist theology came in with him. As a result, South Africa is on the verge of declining into becoming a Third World country that will probably be merged into Third World Central Africa of kingdom #8. If this scenario holds true, then Australia and New Zealand become kingdom #4 by themselves.

The breakaway Muslim states of Russia have separated from kingdom #5 and will most likely become part of the Moslem dominated kingdom #7. This would appear to make up the end time confederation that attacks Israel in EZEKIEL chapters 38 and 39. The important thing to notice as we proceed from here is how a series of Hegelian-style financial crises have served to force these regions together economically with political union in the offing.

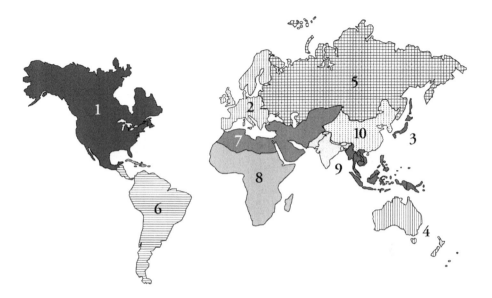

Figure 6: *Franz—2001 updated map*

Horn #1: NAFTA

The North America Free Trade Agreement (NAFTA) is far more than just a free trade agreement. It is a plan to create a supranational regional block consisting of the U.S., Canada and Mexico. This merger will produce horn #1 of Daniel's ten-horned beast, and the dialectic process is well underway:

Merging NAFTA economically

NAFTA's free trade arrangements was the economic first phase of merging North America. This was promoted in the financial markets as something that would be good for the economies of North America and the world. The financial elite funneled leveraged investment dollars from all over the world into Mexico's paper markets, which drove them artificially high. The Mexican government was also cooking the books with false economic reports, and since it all looked good on paper, NAFTA was passed.

The next step of this financial merger was taken on April 24, 1994, when the central banks of the NAFTA countries created an $8.8 billion joint currency account. This currency account was available to all three NAFTA members if and when any of their currencies came under pressure.

Then followed President Zedillo's public announcement on December 24, 1994 not to defend the peso, but to let it float freely against all foreign currencies. This resulted in a devaluation of the peso by 40% in one day, which created a domino effect in all the other paper markets, and the "Mexico Crisis" was birthed.[99]

Overnight, Mexico was bankrupt and on the brink of defaulting on $17 billion in loans, made from Wall Street banks and bond houses. If allowed to default, Wall Street and the world's financial system would have collapsed. This forced the U.S. to dip into NAFTA's joint currency account, along with some G7 funds for the bail-out. During the February, 1995 G7 meeting, U.S. Treasury Secretary Robert Rubin justified the use of G7 funds, saying, "We only had a few hours to make a decision."[100]

President Zedillo is a trained economist who knew that his actions would collapse his country's financial debt bubble. So what was the upshot? It unleashed a Hegelian financial crisis that was designed to further merge NAFTA's financial systems one step closer to becoming a regional economic bloc.

Merging NAFTA politically

The merging of NAFTA's financial systems means that a merger of NAFTA's governments (Canada, America and Mexico) is not far behind. Confirmation of this comes from the U.S. Internal Revenue Service (IRS), which is part of the President's executive branch of the U.S. government. After NAFTA became law in 1995, the IRS issued an order to U.S. corporations on how they must legally make their Federal Employee Tax Deposits. The order states:

"PROVISIONS OF THE NORTH AMERICAN FREE TRADE AGREEMENT (NAFTA) LEGISLATION REQUIRES DEPOSITS TO BE BY ELECTRONIC FUND TRANSFER (EFT)."[101]

If NAFTA is only about free trade, then why is it dictating to the executive branch of the U.S. government how American companies are to make their employee tax deposits? It is because NAFTA's purpose is to create a supranational regional government, which will become kingdom #1 of Daniel's ten-horned beast.

A New North America

The globalist's plan to merge the governments of North America was outlined in a *Los Angeles Times* special report entitled *A New North America*. The report focused on how the current "global reconfiguration" currently taking place will change the national boundaries of most sovereign nations, including the U.S.[102]

The tone of the report was set by U.S. State Department Chief Geographer William Wood, who said:

"What we are dealing with is the recreation of countries."[103]

George Demko, another geographer and director of the Rockefeller Center at Dartmouth College, echoed this plan:

> "As we're challenging the traditional idea of state sovereignty, globalizing economies and communications, and breaking up the last empires, the geography of the world is unhooking old connections and hooking up new ones."[104]

Julian Minghi, U.S. representative to the International Geographers Union (IGU) on the World Political Map, also agrees with this plan:

> "The notion of boundaries as we've known them, in terms of absolute sovereignty and legalities, will in time dwindle."[105]

The report went on to describe how numerous third-level ministates will unite to form second-level regional blocs that will come together under the authority of the U.N.:

> "*A stratified system of governance* and power is likely to replace traditional states ... *At the **top** will be the stronger United Nations* or an equivalent body responsible for peace, environment and other global issues ...
>
> "He [Minghi] places *regional groupings like the European Community* on the *second* tier, while the tiny ethnically and linguistically based mini-states of the future will be on the *lowest level*.
>
> "The latest [second level of governance] is the new *continental pact forming the North American Free Trade Agreement ...* "[106]

As you can see, the globalists consider both NAFTA and the EU to be *second-level regional governments* that are subservient to the global government of United Nations.

Ethnic mini-states

The global reformation of the ethnic and linguistic mini-states into the lowest (third) level of government has been going on for over ten years. It is clear to anyone that the political and ethnic battles which have led to border changes in the fifteen Commonwealth of Independent States that broke away from the former Soviet Union, the Baltics, Yugoslavia (Bosnia, Serbia and Herzegovina), and East Timor in Indonesia, are all part of this plan.

Even the Israeli-PLO conflict is about reconfiguring third-level borders along ethnic lines within kingdom #7. However, Jehovah God has set the borders of Israel and not even the U.N. is going to change that for long (GENESIS 15:18–19).

Jesus forewarned of the spread of worldwide ethnic conflict when He said that "nation will rise against nation " during the last days (MATTHEW 24:3, 7). The Greek word for "nation" is *ethnos* from which we get the English word "ethnic." Jesus was saying that ethnic wars would increase in frequency and intensity like the birth pangs of a woman in labor just prior to His return (MATTHEW 24:3, 7–8). In effect, Jesus was describing the Hegelian-style ethnic conflicts that would be used for creating disorder among the nations, in an effort to manipulate them into accepting the antichrist's NWO.

The globalists also plan to internally reconfigure NAFTA by dividing it up into numerous ethnic and linguistic third-level mini-states (see Figure 7).

Figure 7: *Remake of LA Times "New North America" map*

The Los Angeles Times reports:

> *"Even the U.S. may not be immune to the forces reshaping the globe ...* Instead of Canada, the U.S. and Mexico, the North American Free Trade Agreement could eventually contain a dozen smaller pieces—or more. *Even after losing two independent autonomous zones, Pacifica and Angelica, the United States may be vulnerable to further splits."*[107]

In other words, through NAFTA, the NWO is planning to carve North America up like a Halloween pumpkin and bring it under U.N. control.[108] What does dividing up North America have to do with free trade? The answer is "nothing." Even the geographers recognize that NAFTA is about creating a supra-national, second-level regional government that internally consists of ethnically-divided third-level groupings.

Unfortunately, to accomplish this, there are a lot of Hegelian-style crises (financial, political and ethnic) yet to come in North America, especially in the United States. For out of chaos comes order—the New World Order.

Horn #2: The EU

The greatest move toward regionalization is taking place in Europe, with the formation of the European Union (EU). The EU has effectively established the office of President, who will serve as one of Daniel's ten kings. It is also merging its currencies into the new Eurodollar that will be completed in 2002.

In the past, prophecy teachers have mistakenly concluded that the ten horns of the revived Roman Empire would be limited to the geographic boundaries of ancient Rome. As a result, they have mistaken the EU for the whole of the fourth beast. As a former political and monetary economist, I can tell you that it is impossible to *"devour the whole earth and tread it down and crush it"* from ten nations of Europe. It is systemically impossible.

A world government with that kind of power would have to incorporate elements from every region and nation on earth. Those who understand this reality will tell you that the Club of Rome's scheme of establishing ten regions that merge into a world government is a real possibility, whereas the scheme of "Europe only" becoming ten rulers of a world government is not.

This truth makes it clear that the EU alone is not the ten horns of the beast, but simply one of the ten horns. In other words, two Hegelian World Wars and decades of planning are coming together as kingdom #2 of the NWO.

Horn #3: ASEAN

In the past, it seemed like East Asia was a hodgepodge of economic and political dysfunction. Only Japan, which is a member of the Trilateral Commission, was able to successfully design its economic and political systems to integrate with the global plan for a NWO. As a result, the original CR plan for kingdom #3 only included Japan.

The Association of Southeast Asian Nations (ASEAN) is an economic bloc of ten nations[109] that had in the beginning made only superficial attempts at establishing trade agreements and political coalitions. Additional alliances such as the Asia-Pacific Economic Community (APEC) and Southeast Asian Economic Caucus (SAEC) were also unable to overcome the political hurdles necessary to bring economic and political unity.

However, after the 1987 U.S. stock market crash shook the economies of the world, East Asia began moving toward greater economic cohesiveness. Since 1991, ASEAN has launched the ASEAN Free Trade Area (AFTA), the ASEAN Regional Forum (ARF), and the Asia-Europe Meeting (ASEM). This produced an influx of international investment capital and some remarkable economic growth in the region, which is why Southeast Asia was moved out of kingdom #9 to join Japan in kingdom #3.

Unfortunately, independent politicos and rogue central banks still refused to submit to the globalist's plan for economic and political uniformity of the region. Therefore, the Hegelian financial crisis of 1997–98 was unleashed to bring Southeast Asia into line.

Soon after this happened, a group of Christian investment bankers from Singapore who had seen my video about Mexico's collapse, asked me to come and minister about Asia's financial crisis from a biblical perspective. Part of my February 7, 1998, lecture was about the NWO's plan to regionalize East Asia into kingdom #3 of Daniel's ten-horned beast. I shared this same message in Indonesia and Malaysia, and even told them that a regional currency proposal was undoubtedly in the works.

Sure enough, on Wednesday, February 18 (the last day of my speaking tour), an article entitled *Coin of the Regional Realm: Welcome the 'Asian'* appeared in *The Asian Wall Street Journal* as a confirmation that this prophetic scenario is accurate. It was written by Mark Mobius, head of emerging markets at Templeton Asset Management, who is also a member of the NWO financial elite.

In the article, Mobius makes the case for the regionalization of Asia beginning with a regional currency called the "Asian":

> "*Asia needs a regional currency and the creation of an 'Asian' would result in a boom in investment, trade and tourism.* The Asian currency unit should be initiated by Indonesia, the Philippines, Singapore, Malaysia, Thailand and Brunei. These countries share political and geographical proximity and could form

the core group of countries sharing the same currency conveniently. ...

"The time has never been better to consider such an idea. *At times of crisis critical evaluations must be made of where we have been, where we are, and where we are going.* Asia is experiencing a confidence crisis caused by the collapse of currencies in the region. ... The new Asian, in sum, will mean more convenience and less risk for trading and investment—all lending to a more prosperous Asia as the region embarks on its next big growth wave."[110]

Mobius is unmistakably pointing out that the Illuminati's strategy of "order out of chaos" is clearly at work in Asia. He is openly explaining how Asia's financial crisis was a Hegelian model of regionalization. The "thesis" was the collapse of the individual currencies. The "antithesis" is the promotion of a regional currency, and the "synthesis" will be the regionalization of Asia into kingdom #3 of Daniel's ten-horned beast.

Devouring the Whole World

During that same trip to Asia in February 1998, I met with Herman Mantiri, the Indonesian Ambassador to Singapore. Ambassador Mantiri, a Christian, asked me what I thought about the currency board that President Suharto was trying to implement as a means of stabilizing Indonesia's currency (the rupiah).

I shared with him how Daniel's ten-horned beast would devour the whole earth and tread it down and crush it economically and politically. I told him that if Suharto refused to submit to the IMF austerity measures and became part of Kingdom #3, the globalists would overthrow his government.

I do not think that Ambassador Mantiri or anyone else with whom I shared this prophetic truth believed that a military strongman like Suharto could ever be overthrown. As it turned out, violent protests forced Suharto to resign just three months later in May 1998.

Time and space prevent me from covering the other seven regions. However, now that we know what to look for, we will be able to track their progress as they all come together to form the ten horns of the beast.

Globalization Will Come

I believe that we are supposed to expose and righteously resist the rising tide of globalism (EPHESIANS 5:11). However, we must also realize that the ten horns (regional blocs) with their ten kings are going to come, and no one can stop it. Even three of the original ten kings will resist the antichrist, but they will eventually be subdued, just as President Suharto was.

In the end, the final ten kings will give their power and authority to the beast, and he will rule the NWO. The apostle John saw this end time scenario in his prophetic vision of the last days:

> "And the ten horns which you saw are ten kings, who have not yet received a kingdom, but they receive authority as kings with the beast for one hour. These have one purpose and they give their power and authority to the beast (antichrist)." (REVELATION 17:12–13)

The continued march toward a NWO will undoubtedly result in one Hegelian crisis after another. Each crisis (financial, political, social, ethnic or military) will serve to further define and draw us closer to the ten regional kingdoms that will eventually unite as a global world system.

I believe that the final thrust into a global system will come via a domino-style crash of the world's debt bubble. This will produce a worldwide financial collapse that will force the debt-ridden nations of the world into the waiting arms of a NWO.

Chapter 11

WORLDWIDE FINANCIAL COLLAPSE

*"'Woe to him who increases what is not his—for
how long—and makes himself rich with loans?'
Will not your creditors rise up suddenly, and
those who collect from you awaken? Indeed,
you will become plunder for them."*
HABAKKUK 2:6–7

Although regionalization is currently on the globalists' front
burner, their ultimate goal has always been globalization.
Remember, globalization is a demonic blend of economics,
politics and religion that the Bible calls "Mystery Babylon."

To bring this new global system on-line, the NWO elite plan to
systematically bankrupt the current mishmash of dysfunctional
systems, while at the same time establish a new global
infrastructure under the surface. This plan was expressed during
the Great Depression, when Henry Morgenthau, former Treasury
Secretary for Franklin D. Roosevelt and member of the CFR, said:

> "We can hardly expect the nation-state to make itself
> superfluous, at least not overnight. Rather, what
> we must aim for is recognition in the minds of all
> responsible statesmen that they are nothing more than

caretakers of a bankrupt international machine which
will have to be transformed slowly into a new one."[111]

The first phase of Morgenthau's new machine was our current
UN system that rose out of the ashes of World War II. However,
this system was also scheduled for collapse from its very
beginnings.

John Maynard Keynes

Fellow Illuminist and NWO apostle John Maynard Keynes (1883–
1946) is the author of our current post-World War II economic
system. Concerning his economic design, Keynes said:

> "There is no subtler way, no surer means of overturning
> the existing basis of society than to debauch the
> currency. The process engages all the hidden forces
> of economic law on the side of destruction, and does
> it in a manner which not one man in a million is able
> to diagnose."[112]

In other words, Keynes designed this system to fully employ the
debauchery of Fractional Reserve Banking (FRB) as the primary
scheme for funding economic growth. He understood that it was
nothing more than a debt machine that would produce a debt
bubble so huge it would ultimately destroy the system itself.

Keynes did this with such satanic cunning that less than one man
in a million people could diagnose it. However, he failed to realize
that God's Word had diagnosed it from before the foundation of
the world, and that diagnosis is being revealed in this book.

The Consumer Debt Bubble

FRB debt has produced varying degrees of spending booms and debt busts since the 1920s. However, there is an ominous foreboding about the spending binge and resulting debt bubble of the 1990s.

One of the most noticeable aspects of the 1990s debt bubble is the enormity of its size. This is largely due to the "cradle-to-grave" debt syndrome that has developed in America.[†] In addition, a larger-than-average portion of it has been built on the weak foundation of household borrowing. By the end of 1999, consumer debt (including mortgage debt) soared to an all-time high, with household debt alone rising to 71% of GDP.[113] From the historical pattern of Babylon's financial dialectic, it is reasonable to assume that this record debt bubble will also produce a record number of bankruptcies when it pops.

During an April/May 2000 ministry trip to Southeast Asia, the government of Indonesia defaulted on a multi-billion dollar loan to the IMF. At that time, the Lord began to speak to me about a landslide of personal and corporate bankruptcies that was coming upon the world. The West (including the U.S.) will not escape it, nor will Christians who have used debt as a scheme to get rich quick.[††]

Statistics show that U.S. filings for personal bankruptcy in 2000 hit $1.26 million, which was just slightly lower than the $1.28 million filed in 1999. However, the real concern is that the rate of personal bankruptcies is increasing at an alarming rate. Estimates are that bankruptcies will increase by 15% in 2001, easily surpassing the record 1.4 million bankruptcies set in 1998.[114]

---

† See *Debt and America's Children* on page 234.
†† See *Landslide of Bankruptcies* on page 235.

The Corporate Debt Bubble

The consumer spending binge of the 90s was accompanied by a corporate spending binge of equal proportions. U.S. corporate debt (bonds, junk bonds, bank loans, etc.) increased $1.73 trillion (43.6%) from $3.97 trillion in 1995 to $5.70 trillion in 1999.[115]

Unfortunately, only about $300 billion (15%) actually went into capital expenditures (plants and equipment). This means that approximately $1.5 trillion (85%) was spent on speculative deals like mergers and acquisitions (M&A), stock repurchases, and leveraged financial transactions (margined stocks, futures, options, and derivatives), which added significantly to the U.S. debt bubble.[116]

Much of that debt was spent on acquiring *dotcom* ventures that started going broke in mid-2000. According to Moody's Investors Service, which sets the global index for credit-rating, most of the *dotcom* companies have run out of money and cannot get any more from the banks, bonds, or the stock markets to finish building their venture. This calls to mind what Jesus said about counting the cost (LUKE 14:28–30).

As of October 2000, corporate bond defaults were up 68.6%.[117] Companies that have filed Chapter 11 bankruptcies include Iridium LLC, Planet Hollywood, eToys.com, Harnischfeger Industries, Laidlaw Inc., Pathmark Stores, Montgomery Ward, and AmeriServe Food Distributors. Just to give you an idea how bad the debt bubble was, AmeriServe's $1.5 billion debt bubble was nine times its annual cash flow.[118] That is suicidal and will kill any company in any economy.

On October 25, 2000, Moody's reported that troubled loans of $20 million or more had risen over 100% since 1998. Moody's also reported that the overall corporate credit quality had been declining for ten straight quarters.[119] As more and more *dotcoms* fail, America will see a virtual landslide of corporate bankruptcies and bond defaults that will domino through the system.

The Bank Debt Bubble

Many have been told that the banking crises of the past have taught today's banks how to properly make loans and manage their risk—i.e., their derivatives portfolio. However, according to the Comptroller of the Currency, David Gibbins, every indication is that they are headed for more of the same kind of trouble.[120]

With the Glass-Steagall Act[121] virtually gone, banks have been actively merging commercial banking, investment banking and insurance together. These financial institutions represent the three major pools of capital that the financial elite have always wanted to bring under the control of one big NWO roof.

With all this money needing to earn a return on investment, the banking industry virtually loaned or invested it into anything that moved. This is where the *dotcoms* got a large portion of the money that ran the stock market up so high. Unfortunately, the *dotcom* bust will soon cause problems throughout the banking industry. *Look out for an increase in bank and brokerage house mergers during 2001–2002 as a way of hiding debt problems in the financial services sector.*

The Investment Debt Bubble

Margined investing in the U.S. exploded 653% from $35 billion in 1990 to $228.5 billion in 1999. In 1998 alone, it rose $141 billion (62%), and by mid-February 2000, it had grown another $15 billion to an unprecedented $243.5 billion.[122]

Many mainstream Americans even mortgaged their homes up to 125% of their value, and invested it into the stock markets on margin. They were seduced into believing that real estate, stocks, and the new economy would continue to grow forever, but found out that what goes up must come down.

Some even began to "day trade" on margin individually over the internet. They invested in high-flying *dotcoms* that have mostly gone bust. The hype about becoming rich overnight failed them miserably, and the consequences have been devastating.

When the bubble started to burst on the "day traders," some of them did not just commit suicide but also killed their families and their "day trader" colleagues at the trading office before taking their own lives. I know it is horrible to even talk about, but it is a sign of the last days.†

Japan's Debt Bubble

Currently, Japan is on the financial ropes and is about to go down for the count. On March 9, 2001, Kiichi Miyazawa, Japan's Minister of Finance, warned that, "Japan's public finances are very near collapse."[123]

For the past ten years, the Japanese government has fed hundreds

† See *Day Trader Killings* on page 237.

of billions of dollars of taxpayers' money into the economy to keep it going. Unfortunately, this has created the worst debt problem in the industrialized world and it is all coming home to roost.[124]

Japanese interest rates have been 0.5% or less for years in hopes that people would borrow and spend. This has not worked, because regardless of how low interest rates fall, if the credit card is maxed out people simply cannot borrow anymore.

Japan has been suffering under this scenario for a long time, and people are financially worn out. This has led critics of the newest government bail-out plan to argue for Japan to just let the system collapse and start over again. They contend that it would be painful at first, but a new and better economic system would emerge. In other words, out of Japan's economic chaos will emerge a new economic order. Sound familiar?

An unbelievably blatant Hegelian statement was made by Yoshiaki Murakami, formerly with Japan's Ministry of International Trade and Industry, who said:

> "A crisis would be good! Good, good, good, good, good. ... If such a crisis does strike, it could provide an excellent opportunity to rebuild the economy."[125]

This NWO rhetoric means that another Hegelian-style financial crisis is about to bankrupt the second largest economy in the world. This will force Japan into doing everything it can to stay afloat. Unfortunately, that probably includes selling its $250 billion U.S. bond portfolio, something they have threatened to do before.

In 1997, during Asia's financial crisis, Japan's Prime Minister more or less threatened to start selling off U.S. bonds if the U.S. did not "maintain foreign-exchange stability."[126] This veiled threat threw the U.S. stock market into a frenzy, and triggered the second-largest point decline in Dow Jones history up to that point.

When Japan actually starts to liquidate U.S. bonds, it will depress bond prices and devalue the dollar. The only thing that could stop the bond market from collapsing is for the Fed to step in and buy back those bonds under the table. At that point, the Fed would be directly monetizing U.S. debt, which would also devalue the dollar. Either way, both the bond market and the dollar will be shaken as more pressure is put on the U.S. debt bubble.

The U.S. Debt Bubble

When you add consumer, investor, and corporate debt together with the $5.6 trillion of U.S. government debt, America has a total domestic debt of approximately $25 trillion, *not counting derivatives.*[127] Unfortunately, the M-2 money supply is only $4.8 trillion, which means the U.S. is technically bankrupt (see money supply table on page 129).

The even more serious flip side to the debt problem is that $20.2 trillion of the debtors have been asked to pay back loans (debt) with money that does not exist. Let us do some math:

Total U.S. Debt	$25.0 trillion
– Total M-2 Money Supply	*– $ 4.8 trillion*
Unredeemable Balance	$20.2 trillion

Money Supply Table

Money Supply is the total stock of money in the economy, consisting primarily of (1) currency in circulation, and (2) deposits in savings and checking accounts. Since banking deregulation in the 1980s, the various forms of money are now grouped into two broad divisions: M-1, M-2, and M-3, representing money and near money; and L, representing short-term government and corporate debt. The accompanying table shows a detailed breakdown of all four categories.[132]

M-1 $1.104 Trillion

Currency in circulation
Commercial bank demand deposits
NOW and ATS (automatic transfer from savings)
Credit union share drafts
Mutual savings bank demand deposits
Non-bank travelers checks

M-2 $4.759 Trillion

M-1 plus
Overnight repurchase agreements
Overnight Eurodollars
Savings accounts
Time deposits under $100,000
Money market mutual fund shares

M-3 $6.664 Trillion

M-2 plus
Time deposits over $100,000
Term repurchase agreements

L No Figures Available

M-3 plus other liquid assets such as:
Treasury bills and Savings bonds
Commercial paper and Bankers' acceptances
Eurodollar holdings of U.S. residents (non-bank)

There are only two things that can be done in this situation. One is to monetize the debt (print money), which will create more debt followed by massive inflation and loss of purchasing power.

The other is a system-wide default. This means that consumers will be unable to pay back their bank and other loans. However, a default also means that the credit markets will be unable to pay back the money they have borrowed from investors who bought Treasury securities, bonds, mortgage securities, bank deposits, and other loanership investments. Therefore, all of these paper investments are at risk of being defaulted upon (see investment default chart on page 131).

This is why a biblical year of jubilee (cancellation of debt), as some Christian groups have suggested, is not a feasible solution. Since all money and investments are built on debt, the cancellation of that debt means that every individual and institution holding paper money and investments would be instantly wiped out. We may have a jubilee year, but like Japan, it is coming in the form of a bankruptcy. U.S. banks have known this is coming and have been preparing to protect themselves for years.[†]

The Trigger of Global Collapse

Derivatives make up the largest and most volatile portion of this debt. As early as 1993, the Bundesbank warned that the derivatives market could potentially "trigger chain reactions and endanger the financial system as a whole."[128] Since then, the collapse of various derivative debt bubbles has triggered the bankruptcy of whole regions of the world.

---

† See *U.S. Banks Preparing for Collapse* on page 240.

Investment Default Chart

Borrower	Loanershop Investments that will be defaulted on
Federal Government	Treasury Bills Treasury Notes Treasury Bonds Treasury Bond Mutual Funds Treasury Money Market Funds
State Governments	General Obligation Bonds Revenue Bonds State Bond Mutual Funds
County Governments	General Obligation Bonds Revenue Bonds County Bond Mutual Funds
Municipal Governments	Municipal Bonds Municipal Bond Mutual Funds
Banks	Passbook Savings Certificates of Deposits (CDs) Bank Money Markets Funds
Corporations	Corporate Bonds • Investment Grade Bonds • Junk Bonds Corporate Bond Mutual Funds
Consumers	Bank & Other Consumer Loans Consumer Credit Cards Primary Mortgages
Federal National Mortgage Association (FNMA) Government National Mortgage Association (GNMA)	Fannie Maes (Moody's downgraded these debt securities in March 2001) Ginnie Maes

In March 2000, worldwide derivatives debt was estimated to be $150–200 trillion (it is growing so fast no one can get an exact figure on it).[129] It is also estimated that U.S. banks alone are holding approximately $36 trillion in derivatives, and that $28 trillion (78%) of them are in interest rate swaps.[130] The collapse of these same types of swaps[131] exacerbated all the recent global financial crises (1994–1999), and the U.S. is not immune.

Simply put, the derivatives market is the atomic bomb of the world's debt bubble that will most likely trigger the collapse of the entire world's financial system. When that happens, the globalists plan to roll ownership of the entire world over to themselves in one gigantic debt-for-equity swap.

Chapter 12

DEBT-FOR-EQUITY SWAPS

"Woe to those who scheme iniquity, who work out
evil on their beds! When morning comes, they do
it, for it is in the power of their hands. They covet
fields and then seize them, and houses, and
take them away. They rob a man and his
house, and man and his inheritance."
MICAH 2:1–2

A debt-for-equity swap is simply another term for the confiscation
and redistribution of the assets held by those who have defaulted
on their debt. This is Babylon's financial dialectic, and it will
soon be forced on every individual and country in the world who
cannot repay their debt.

Debt-for-equity swaps have been going on since the early
1990s,[132] and they play a major role in the current austerity
measures that the IMF and the World Bank have imposed on the
crisis countries. Unfortunately, the swaps also appear to be the
standard method of transferring control of the world's financial
system over to the United Nation's System.

Africa's Debt-for-Equity Swaps

The most blatant debt-for-equity swap of the 1990s took place in Africa, when everyone finally recognized that the nations of the sub-Sahara would never be able to pay back their debts. In 1995, *The New York Times* published a special report that described the debt-for-equity process as follows:

> "For more than a decade the economies of Africa have been caught in a relentless downward spiral. As a result, countries ... are finding themselves more than ever under the thumb of outside powers. ...
>
> "Now the external powers are the International Monetary Fund and the World Bank. These institutions ... have become the overlords of Africa in the 1990s. ... The IMF and the World Bank are the purveyors of a new orthodoxy. *They come in to bail out a country that is bankrupt.* They do so by drawing up a 'structural adjustment program' [SAP]. ...
>
> "Because the package is tied to millions of dollars in aid from Western donor countries, it is an offer that can't be refused. And so the IMF and the bank end up calling the shots on a broad range of issues, ... even political matters ...
>
> "Through its 'structural adjustment programs' *the IMF and the [World] bank now effectively oversee and supervise the economies of some 30 countries in sub-Saharan Africa.*"[134]

Almost everyone acknowledges that Africa has become a bankrupt slave of the United Nation's system. It must be understood that the

UN, the World Bank, and the IMF are simply the global political and banking fronts that cater to the dictates of the international bankers who pay the bills. In other words, the international bankers have used debt to take financial and political control over much of sub-Saharan Africa.

Mexico's Debt-For-Equity Swaps

Mexico's financial crisis produced several debt-for-equity schemes. First, Mexico was forced to pledge its oil as collateral for the $52 billion loan bail-out, and deposit all revenues from its global oil sales into an account in the New York Federal Reserve Bank. Today, Mexico's debt has been refinanced several times, and its oil reserves are still collateral for the debt.

Another form of debt-for-equity transfer occurs after a financial crisis, when international banks and global business conglomerates buy up bankrupt businesses and real estate for pennies on the dollar. For example, in September 1997, *The Wall Street Journal* reported that Mexico's fifth largest financial company was purchased by the international financial group of Santander Investment SA.[135] Technically, every asset (business, real estate, cars, boats, chattel, etc.) held as collateral for debt becomes the property of the financial elite who bought them out.

The report goes on to describe how completely Mexico's wealth was transferred to the multinationalists:

> "In a huge transfer of ownership from Mexican to foreign hands, foreign multinationalists have spent more than $7 billion in the past two years buying up stakes in everything, from a maker of tequila bottles to Mexico's most famous brewer."[136]

It is clear to see that these various debt-for-equity schemes have reached deep into Mexico, transferring both its wealth and sovereignty to the globalists.

Asia's Debt-For-Equity Swaps

In Thailand, banks borrowed money from the international banking community, converted it to baht (Thailand's currency) and loaned it wildly throughout the economy.[137] Much of that money was loaned for real estate, which artificially inflated property prices.

When the baht collapsed in a de facto devaluation on July 2, 1997, borrowers began defaulting on their real estate loans. This left the Thai banks holding billions of dollars of illiquid over-priced real estate as collateral, which caused them to default on their loans to the international bankers.

When the IMF bail-out came, so did the international bankers who literally raided the country. As early as November 1997, *USA TODAY* reported:

> "'*We already see some foreign banks making acquisitions in Thailand and that is likely to emerge as a trend in the other Asian countries,*' says Ron Mandle, banking analyst at Sanford Bernstein.
>
> "Adds James Cramer, president of hedge fund Cramer Berkowitz: 'The only companies that are going to prosper in that environment are U.S. financial companies.'
>
> "Citicorp has already broken the ice, becoming the first foreign bank announcing plans to take a majority stake in a Thai bank."[138]

In this case, not only did ownership of the Thai bank pass to Citicorp (David Rockefeller), but so did the real estate that the Thai banks held as collateral. In other words, the global elite have successfully implemented another financial dialectic of Mystery Babylon, and they now own Thailand.

Confirmation that this was being done throughout Asia came late one night during Asia's financial crisis. I was at home in Colorado watching the day's news about Asia's financial problems when an investment banker friend called me from Indonesia. He told me of how the investment bank he worked for had been hired by the IMF to assess distressed commercial ventures and properties for acquisition by the globalists.

My friend, a Christian, was amazed to see himself actually become a part of end time Bible prophecy. Jokingly, I told him that the next time he read the Bible where it talks about how the beast system takes over the world, he could tell his children that he was literally a part of the take-over.

Since then, my friend has left that bank and started his own company, where he works to create investment opportunities built around real wealth and honest scales. He and his associates are end time Josephs, who are working to come out of financial Babylon and biblically prosper *in* the world (Egypt) without being *of* the world.[†]

America's Debt-For-Equity Swaps

America as a nation has seen numerous types of debt-for-equity schemes throughout its history. For example, at the end of the Civil War, the U.S. owed $2.8 billion to the House of Erlinger

---

† See *End Time Josephs* on page 243.

in London and the House of Rothschild in Paris, both of which literally financed both sides of the war. When the Union could not pay the debt immediately, the natural resources (gold, silver, timber, etc.) of the states were put up as collateral.[139] Although this debt was later internalized, the principle of collateralizing national debt with the equity of its natural resources was established in the U.S.

We have already seen how, during the 1929 crash and the Great Depression of the 1930s, massive amounts of wealth were transferred when lenders confiscated the assets (equity) of those who could not pay their debt. However, the biggest debt-for-equity swap during that time came in 1933, when Franklin D. Roosevelt confiscated gold by "executive order." In the name of "national security," U.S. citizens were forced to surrender tangible gold (equity) in exchange for empty paper promises (debt) called Federal Reserve Notes.[†]

In the 1960s, during the initiation of "The Great Society" and the beginning of the Vietnam War, America began to externalize its debt again by selling U.S. bonds in the international credit markets. When U.S. borrowing became excessive, France and others challenged America's ability to redeem its debt with gold. When the U.S. government insisted that it could redeem its debt with gold, foreign creditors surprised America by requesting that their loans (U.S. bonds) be redeemed with gold rather than U.S. dollars (FRNs).[140]

This began a run on U.S. gold reserves, which Richard Nixon stopped by closing the gold window on August 15, 1971. However, without sufficient collateral to back its debt, America's credit rating was at risk, and a sell-off of U.S. bonds became a

---

† See *Executive Order 6102* on page 228.

real threat. To save the U.S. Treasury market, Nixon had to find another way to collateralize external U.S. debt. He did so by pledging America's natural resources in the Western states, similar to what was done during the Civil War.

To show foreign creditors that those resources would not be developed but preserved as collateral for its debt, Nixon set up the Environmental Protection Agency (EPA). Working together with the Department of the Interior's Bureau of Land Management (BLM), the EPA began setting aside lands[141] and their natural resources as collateral for America's external debt.[142]

Environmental Protection and U.S. Debt

Under the guise of "environmental protection," government and non-government agencies (Sierra Club, Friends of the Earth, UNESCO and others) began pressuring Congress to pass oppressive environmental legislation that slowed or stopped drilling, mining and logging in the Western United States. One such piece of legislation is the Federal Land Policy and Management Act, which allows the BLM to arbitrarily restrict access to the natural resources of certain lands. For example, "Areas of Critical Environmental Concern" (ACECs) limits access to historical, cultural, scenic areas, and wildlife resources. By 1992, the BLM had set aside the natural resources of 4.5 million acres throughout ten Western states as ACECs.[143]

During the same time, the BLM also set up "National Conservation Areas" (NCAs) that have "certain resource values identified in Public Law Statutes."[144] These statutes set arbitrary values on "historic, scenic, archeological, environmental, biological, cultural, educational, recreational, economic, geological, ecological, scientific, or paleontological values; aquatic and wildlife resources; and other wilderness resources." Under these classifications, the BLM can lock up virtually any wilderness areas it wants. By 1992, the BLM was able to capture nearly 14 million acres of resource-rich lands through NCAs, and the EPA served as the government's enforcement agency.[145]

Every trick in the book has been used by these agencies to disenfranchise ranchers, farmers and others from harvesting the natural resources on their own land. In his book, *War on the West: Government Tyranny on America's Great Frontier*, author and lawyer William Perry Pendley sums it up this way:

> "Quite simply, the environmental extremists' vision of the American West does not include the rancher. ...
>
> "Like most issues embraced by environmental extremists, the fight is neither about money nor the buzzwords of environmental policy—safety, survivability, and sustainability. *The fight is over who will control millions of acres of Western land. ...*
>
> "If the ranching families of the West can be driven off their federal grazing allotments, if their private holdings can be rendered uneconomic and they are forced to sell those lands, if water rights become unsustainable and the lands worthless, then vast expanses will be snapped up by the federal government. ... *Economics and the environment—like the northern spotted owl—are only window dressing for the real goal: to drive people off the land.*"[146]

Clinton-Gore Land Grab

From 1992 to 2000, the Clinton-Gore White House acquired 4.515 million acres of additional resource-rich lands by way of executive order.[147] Much of this was done without state or congressional approval. When confronted by Congress, the Clinton Administration threatened more unconstitutional land confiscations through executive order if Congress did not capitulate.

In a special report on the landmark case of *Hage* versus *The United States*, *The Ashville Tribune* describes one such confrontation:

> "During a Congressional hearing regarding Federal land acquisitions that have been done without State or Congressional consultation, Republican John Shadeqq asked Secretary of the Interior Bruce Babbitt to provide Congress with a list of other lands that were being considered for further federal acquisition. Babbit sternly responded, 'No.' After a stunned silence, the secretary added, 'I don't mean to be disrespectful.' However, *Babitt told the Committee that if they did not cooperate, he would ask the President [Clinton] to 'use his [executive] power' to get more lands with or without their approval.*"[148]

This type of land grab is draconian in nature and reflects the same methods used when communist governments nationalize the assets of a nation once they take control. Since communist methods are unacceptable in the free world, land confiscation is disguised under the banner of "environmental protection," and placed in what the government now calls "biospheres."

In the case of U.S. oil reserves, this action effectively prohibits America from harvesting much of its own oil. This has caused the U.S. to become dependent on foreign oil and has forced it to buy oil from both friendly and unfriendly sources. As American dollars flow overseas to purchase oil, it causes an unnecessary increase in the U.S. trade deficit. To add to America's embarrassment, foreigners then lend those U.S. dollars back to Uncle Sam by purchasing U.S. Treasury securities, for which we pay them 5%–6% interest.

This takes us right back to the beginning, where America's creditors require that its resources be set aside in protected biospheres as collateral for the debt. It is common knowledge that Japan has been trying to swap American debt they hold in U.S. bonds for Alaskan oil reserves for years. When the U.S. dollar begins to devalue, watch for Japan and others to begin a new push towards a debt-for-equity (bonds-for-oil) swap.

Biodiversity and Earth Worship

At the same time Nixon established the EPA, he also signed on to the United Nations Environmental Programme (UNEP),[149] which oversees the environmental debt-for-equity land grab on a global scale. UNEP's legal guide is the "Global Biodiversity Assessment" (GBA), which outlines its plan to organize society into "bioregions." Section 10.4.2.2.3 of the GBA Treaty commits to protecting global "biodiversity" by setting aside vast amounts of land that permits "no human use" or "extremely limited use."[150]

UNEP's five-step confiscation plan goes as follows:

1 Redraw land maps to differentiate biological characteristics rather than political jurisdiction.

2 Regroup human populations into self-sustaining settlements that minimize impact on biodiversity.

3 Educate humans in the "gaia ethic," which holds that gaia is the creator of all life and all life is part of the creator.

4 Create a new system of governance based on local decision-making within the framework of international agreements.

5 Reduce the use of natural resources by (a) reducing population; (b) reducing consumption; and (c) shifting to "appropriate" technology.[151]

Redrawing land maps, reducing and regrouping the human population into self-sustaining settlements, and creating a new system of governance are all major NWO catalysts for overturning the existing basis of society. However, in order for this plan to be fully successful, a common beliefism (religion) must be established as a rallying point.

It is important to note how the "gaia ethic" of step 3 gives this movement a moral and religious base for confiscating these lands. It is the new global religion that replaces the biblical worship of "Father God" with the pagan worship of "mother earth." Mother earth worship represents a large part of the "woman on the beast"† in the book of REVELATION 17:1–7, and is even being preached in some of today's apostate Christian denominations.

---

† See *The Woman on the Beast* on page 253.

In other words, the NWO plans to substitute the worship of Jehovah God with its own standards of pagan earth worship, with the intention of completely overthrowing (subduing) Judeo-Christian society. King David prays against this form of pagan overthrow:

> "Thine adversaries have roared in the midst of Thy meeting place [church]; they have set up their own standards for signs .... They have burned Thy sanctuary to the ground; they have defiled the dwelling place of Thy name. They have said in their heart, '*Let us completely subdue them.*'" (PSALMS 74:4, 7–8)

Global Debt-For-Equity Swap

As the global debt bubble reaches new highs, the NWO will continue to use the banner of "environmental protection" in their attempt to cordon off the world's natural resources. Although these energetic earth worshipers think they are preserving "gaia" the mother goddess of earth, they are actually gathering the collateral that will be confiscated by the NWO elite when the global debt bubble collapses.

This collapse will loose chaos among the nations of the world unlike anything it has ever seen before. I believe this is when the ten kings take power and actually establish a new one-world political and financial order.

In exchange for canceling the debt of the nations, ownership of the earth will be transferred into an escrow account of the World Central Bank and used to capitalize the New World Financial System.

Chapter 13

THE NEW WORLD FINANCIAL SYSTEM

"And he causes all, the small and the great, and the
rich and the poor, and the free men and the slaves, to
be given a mark on their right hand, or on their forehead, and he provides that no one should be able to
buy or to sell, except the one who has the mark … ."

REVELATION 13:16–17

The cries for a one-world government have been going out for
centuries, but never before have they reached the fever pitch we
are hearing today. Ever since the 1990–91 Iraq War, when the
globalists openly announced their plans to build a NWO, the
large majority of the United Nations has embraced the creation
of a one-world government.

Writing for the U.N.'s *Human Development Report*, economic
Nobel Laureate Jan Tinbergen states:

"Mankind's problems can no longer be solved
by national governments. What is needed is a
World Government. This can best be achieved by
strengthening the United Nations system. …

"Some of the most important new [UN] institutions
would be financial—a World Treasury and a World
Central Bank. The World Treasury would serve as

a world ministry of finance. Its main task would be to collect the resources needed by the other world ministries through one or more systems of global automatic taxation. … In addition, there should be a World Central Bank based on a reformed IMF to deal, among other things, with monetary, banking and stock exchange policies."[152]

In essence, Tinbergen is talking about establishing a UN controlled world system, which integrates a New World Government together with a New World Financial System.

New World Treasury

The first stage of the UN's financial plan is to create a World Treasury, which will gather tax revenues to fund its program for world governance. Since governments are the only ones that can legally impose tax, global taxation, by definition, means global government.

The term "global automatic taxation" refers to a type of sales tax that will be automatically received at the point of sale and immediately disbursed to the World Treasury. From there, it is paid out proportionately to the regional and local governments down-line. This method of taxation allows for the creation of an all-powerful world central government that commands complete financial control over the nations.

Wealthier countries will pay higher taxes than poorer countries as a way of redistributing everyone's wealth. The *Human Development Report* (*HDR*) confirms this, stating that:

"We [the UN] collectively believe that our world cannot survive one-fourth rich and three-fourths poor, half democratic and half authoritarian, with oases of human development surrounded by deserts of human deprivation. We pledge to take all necessary actions, nationally and globally, to reverse the present trend of widening disparities within and between nations. ..."[153]

The report goes on to say:

"Just as each nation has a system of income redistribution [taxation], so there should be a corresponding 'world financial policy' to be implemented by the World Bank and World Central Bank. Redistribution is the core political issue of the [21st] century. ..."[154]

The redistribution of wealth through global taxation is largely what world socialism is all about. It levels out the masses financially and allows the NWO elite to control the social and economic behavior of the nations.

New World Central Bank

The UN also plans to establish a World Central Bank.[155] Just as today's national governments need central banks to function financially, the World Government will also need a World Central Bank to interact with the global economy. The *HDR* describes this interaction as follows:

"A World Central Bank is essential for the 21st century—for sound macroeconomic management, for global financial stability and for assisting the economic expansion of the poorer nations."[156]

In other words, the New World Central Bank will work hand-in-glove with the World Treasury to create an international financial control center. Its real goal will be to coordinate global economic growth with global taxation in an effort to redistribute (transfer) the wealth of the world into the hands of the wicked financial elite. This is a satanic counterfeit of God's plan to redistribute (transfer) the wealth of the wicked into the hands of His people at the end of the age (PROVERBS 13:22).

Building Global Consensus

As I have pointed out, the controlled collapse of the various international financial systems will ultimately force the nations into accepting a New World Central Bank. Interestingly enough, the UN seems to suggest this very thing in its *HDR*, which states:

> "It will take some time and probably some *international financial crisis* before a full-scale world central bank can be created."[157]

This astounding statement was published in the *HDR* on March 16, 1994. Nine months later, on December 20, 1994, an "international financial crisis" broke out in Mexico, just like what the report suggested would be necessary to bring about a world central bank.

The collapse of Mexico's financial system provided just the excuse the NWO criers needed as they renewed their call for a New World Financial System. Some financial leaders even warned that there would be future financial crises. These warnings were directives to the IMF and the World Bank to revamp themselves into some sort of global financial institution that could deal with this new type of international financial crisis.

The Los Angeles Times reported one such warning by NWO elitist Robert Rubin as follows:

> "Treasury Secretary Robert E. Rubin warned ... that *events like the Mexican peso crisis could become common* in a world of rapid and overwhelming movement of capital.
>
> "Rubin called for revamping global financial institutions to provide faster responses to emergencies. ... 'We need international financial institutions as modern as the problems they face,' Rubin said. He urged changes in the International Monetary Fund (IMF) and the World Bank to help deal with fast-moving currency and trade crises."[158]

Several years later, during the 1997–98 Asian financial crisis, NWO leaders stepped up the rhetoric about why the world needed a new global financial system. International financier George Soros, a major force behind the collapse of Asia, blamed it on the "inherent instability of the world's financial system," which lacked the common global institutions necessary to manage global markets.[159] Then he called for the IMF to reform and provide the framework for a new global financial system:

> "A regulatory framework which must at least smooth the effects of capital flowing from the periphery to the center is needed. And the IMF, with all its deficiencies,

must reform in order to meet exactingly this challenge and infuse some measure of equilibrium in a basically unstable environment."[160]

During this same period, Japan's top financial diplomat, Eisuke Sakakibara, suggested that world leaders form a "New Global Monetary Fund."[161] NWO apostle Henry Kissinger called for a "New World Financial System,"[162] and the IMF proposed a "Global Financial Supervisory Agency."[163]

Clearly, each international financial crisis provides the "thesis" for building global consensus towards the "antithesis" of a New World Financial System. In the end, this will produce the "synthesis" of actually creating a World Central Bank that becomes the financial clearing-house for "Mystery Babylon" (REVELATION 13:16–18).

Earth Financial Credit Corporation

Political and financial pundits of the NWO outside of the conspiracy, are also promoting various "one world" campaigns. They are being led by the "spirit of the world" which is united in its call for both a New World Government and a New World Central Bank.

One such group is the World Constitution and Parliament Association (WCPA), which calls their version of a World Central Bank the "Earth Financial Credit Corporation" (EFCC). They aggressively promote it as "The Key to a New World Economic Order,"[164] and some of the main features and benefits include:

- Provides unlimited financial credit for all worthy projects in all countries where people are available to work.

- No prior savings or capital formation required. *Credit is created as an accounting procedure* based on potential productive capacity.
- Releases developing countries from the bondage of debts. No interest; only low administrative and accounting fees.
- No more foreign exchange fluctuations, manipulations or conversions. All financing is in terms of a single global monetary system, calculated in Earth Dollars.[165]

In other words, the EFCC proposes to create as much ledger book money (debt) as needed, freely loaning out this money at will without anyone incurring debt. Some think that freely giving money away like this sounds like a great idea, but it is not.

First of all, the massive release of all the new "Earth Dollars" would create rampant inflation as they circulate through the global economic system.[166]

Second, no one would own anything. As I have already pointed out, debt is backed by some sort of collateral (real estate, vehicles, chattel, etc.), and the lender is the ultimate owner. If there is no debt incurred, then everything built or purchased with borrowed money would be the property of the bank. And believe it or not, that is exactly where we are heading.

This new world financial order is not new at all. It is simply old world Babylon's financial dialectic wrapped up in a little different package. Only this time, when the debt bubble pops, the wealth of the world is going to be confiscated and transferred onto the balance sheet of a New World Central Bank.

Global Resource Bank

Another global bank proposal, which offers the clearest picture of what the New World Central Bank will probably look like, is being promoted by the Global Resource Bank (GRB). The GRB's primary focus is on "Capitalizing the Wealth of Nature" into a spendable one-world electronic "telecomputer" currency.

The introduction of the GRB proposal states that:

> "There is no greater store of wealth than in nature, nor better medium of exchange than telecom-munication.
> "The Global Resource Bank issues global dollars that value the production of nature. The Bank's currency quantifies the economy of the ecosystem. The money measures the capacity of nature to produce the commodities that sustain life on earth."[167]

The bank proposes to place a value on the earth's ecosystem at 6,000 trillion GRB dollars ($6 quadrillion) and use it to capitalize the bank itself. This newly created electronic money (e-money) would provide the necessary working capital to pay off the debt of the Old World System and fund NWO operations.[168]

Pricing Nature's Economic Value

This type of valuation "integrates people and nature at the market" by computing the economic worth that each one contributes to the whole.[169] Placing a price on the ecosystem is also part of the UN agenda, which is clearly stated in its *HDR*:

> *"The lifestyles of the rich nations will clearly have to change.* The North has roughly one-fifth of the

world's population and four-fifths of its income, and it consumes 70% of the world's energy, 75% of its metals and 85% of its wood. *If the ecosphere were **fully priced**, not free, such consumption patterns could not continue.*"[170]

Various universities and environmental groups are actually conducting studies that calculate nature's economic value to mankind. One such study appeared in *USA TODAY*:

"Cornell University ecologist David Pimentel has computed nature's economic value to humanity to be about $2.9 trillion annually.

"That figure reflects the economic benefits, goods and services that humans reap as a direct or indirect result of the environment. For example, Pimentel calculated that bees pollinate about $40 billion worth of crops globally each year, while predator insects perform about $17 billion in extermination services killing pests. ...

"Pimentel estimated the environmental benefits in the United States to be worth about $320 billion ... ."[171]

These two examples reveal the basic plan of how the "spirit of the world" plans to level everyone out by "fully pricing" the ecosphere. The goal is to bring about a NWO utopia where nobody owns anything and everyone is forced to buy resources from the NWO monopoly. Unfortunately, it also means that all the world's wealth will have to come under the control of a global financial redistribution center like the GRB.

Pricing Man's Economic Value

In exchange for paying off man's debt, all private property would be transferred over to the world bank.[172] The cancellation of all debt would serve as a counterfeit year of jubilee. Unfortunately, instead of the land reverting back to the original owner (God), the earth and everything in it will become the property of Satan's New World Central Bank.

Under the GRB proposal, man is then given an allowance of "10,000 dollars per year for ten consecutive years."[173] This totals 100,000 dollars, which just so happens to be what each "Depositor" is insured for under the FDIC. The GRB actually calculates the total value of humanity at $600 trillion by multiplying the world's population of six billion people times $100,000 per person. Then, it lists humanity's value of $600 trillion on the bank's balance sheet as "working capital."

In this scenario, the sin of debt causes man to default on his dominion over the earth, and he becomes the property of Mystery Babylon. This is the ultimate fulfillment of King Solomon's warning that the borrower becomes a slave to the lender. It also fulfills an old saying among opponents to FRB debt, which says:

> "*Gold* is the money of kings; *silver* is the money of gentlemen; *barter* is the money of peasants; but *debt* *is the money of slaves.*"

Man's default will allow him to be bought and sold as a commodity by the international merchant elite in a similar fashion to what happened during the famine in Egypt (GENESIS 47:19–23; REVELATION 18:11, 13). This completes the global debt-for-equity swap, and the financial side of Mystery Babylon will become a prophetic reality.

The Rise of Mystery Babylon

Although the GRB proposes that each person in the world owns one share of the whole, prophet Daniel and apostle John both prophesied that the ten NWO kings will eventually take ownership of everything and give it over to the beast (antichrist).

John specifically warns that:

> "These [ten kings] have one purpose and they give their [financial] power and [political] authority to the beast." (REVELATION 17:13)

Once the antichrist ascends the throne as world ruler, Satan will empower him to finish the end time city (system) of Mystery Babylon. This is all part of the "mystery of lawlessness" that comes into its fullness when the "man of lawlessness" (antichrist) is revealed (2 THESSALONIANS 2:1–11).

During this time, Daniel warns that the power to prosper through wicked means will climax and continue until Satan's "indignation" against God and His people is complete:

> "Then the king [antichrist] will do as he pleases, and he will exalt and magnify himself above every god, and will speak monstrous things against the God of gods; and *he will prosper until the indignation is finished, for that which is decreed will be done.*" (DANIEL 11:36)

For a season, everything that the antichrist does produces prosperity, which he shares with his NWO supporters.† As the new CEO of the World Central Bank (which owns the earth), the antichrist will have the power to parcel out a piece of land to each

† See *Why the Wicked Prosper* on page 255.

of his supporters in payment for their allegiance.

This will fulfill the prophecy of Daniel that says:

> "… he [antichrist] will give great honor to those who
> acknowledge him, and he will cause them to rule
> over the many, and *will parcel out land for a price*."
> (DANIEL 11:39)

During this same time, he will impose a closed financial system that supports a one-world electronic currency (e-money). This system will monitor and tax every financial transaction, from multi-trillion dollar stock trades to garage sale purchases. All transactions will be conducted via an expanded Internet system, which provides a financial transaction station in every business and home computer.

E-money will be transferred from one account to another via an electronic biochip, which is implanted in the right hand or the forehead of all NWO patrons.† This brings us right back to the "mark of the beast" mentioned in REVELATION 13:16–18, which is at the heart of Mystery Babylon's New World Financial System.

What Can the Righteous Do?

Before you allow a spirit of hopelessness to overwhelm you, it is important to note that the NWO conspiracy and the rise of Mystery Babylon did not catch God by surprise. In fact, as we have discovered in this book, God actually recorded their plans for us in His Word, so that we would not get caught by surprise either.

---

† See *Mark of the Beast* on page 256.

God has made it abundantly clear that this plan will run its course. However, He also makes it clear that since this unrighteous world system is built on the root sin of the love of money, it will ultimately fall under His judgment.

Therefore, when Mystery Babylon's New World Financial System finally collapses, God's people need to be separated from it. This is why God admonishes us to come out of her now before Babylon falls (REVELATION 18:4).

Chapter 14

COME OUT BEFORE BABYLON FALLS

"And I heard another voice from heaven, saying,
'Come out of her [Babylon] my people, that you may not
participate in her sins and that you may not receive of her
plagues; for her sins have piled up as high as heaven, and
God has remembered her iniquities.'"
REVELATION 18:4–5

Throughout the Scriptures, God draws the contrast between good
and evil and calls His people out of that which is evil. In His
mercy, God even shows us the judgment of the wicked in the
hope of revealing to His bride just how futile it is to walk (whore
around) in the ways of the world. I believe that God's purpose
in all this is to persuade His people to come out and be separate
from Babylon before it falls.

The Fall of Mystery Babylon

The apostle John reveals how God actually uses Mystery Babylon
as a gathering point for everyone and everything that is wicked
and unclean in His eyes. Once the gathering is complete, the
Lord will release His wrath, and "Babylon the great" will fall to
destruction:

"After these things I saw another angel coming down from heaven ... And he cried out with a mighty voice, saying, 'Fallen, fallen is Babylon the great! And she has become a dwelling place of demons and a prison of every unclean spirit, and a prison of every unclean and hateful bird.'" (REVELATION 18:1–2)

Mystery Babylon is where the mystery of lawlessness culminates in preparation for its destruction. I know this is hard to grasp, but, in His sovereignty and foreknowledge of the beginning to the end, God actually uses Satan's plans as a weapon against him.†

This judgment is complete and will destroy Mystery Babylon across the political, financial and religious board. However, the prophet Ezekiel specifically identifies God's judgment of the dishonest gain acquired through Fractional Reserve Banking (FRB):

"In you they have taken bribes to shed blood; you have taken *interest and profits*, and you have injured your neighbors *for gain by oppression* [*interest*] ... Behold, I smite My hand at your *dishonest gain* [*FRB*]." (EZEKIEL 22:12–13)

This judgment will ultimately destroy all of Satan's economic plans and bring an end to all worldly prosperity as we know it.

The End of Worldly Prosperity

If God's people fail to understand that His judgment of Mystery Babylon will bring an end to all worldly prosperity, the lust for financial gain can seduce them into seeking after the unjust

---

† See *God's Sovereignty Over Babylon* on page 264.

prosperity of the wicked.

The psalmist Asaph almost falls into this trap until he sees their end:

> "But as for me, my feet came close to stumbling; my steps almost slipped. For I was envious of the arrogant, as I saw the prosperity of the wicked. For there are no pains in their death; and their body is fat. They are not in trouble as other men; nor are they plagued like mankind. … Behold, these are the wicked; and always at ease, they have increased in wealth. … When I pondered to understand this, it was troublesome in my sight until I came into the sanctuary of God; then I perceived their end. … How they are destroyed in a moment! They are utterly swept away by sudden terrors!" (PSALMS 73:2–5, 16, 19)

Here, God reveals the destruction of the wicked rich to Asaph to persuade him not to go their way, but instead, to turn and follow the Lord's way. Asaph realizes that even though God allows the wicked to prosper for a time, He will eventually strike down all of their unjust gains in order to fulfill His Word.[†]

Babylon's Wealth Destroyed in a Moment

Note that when Asaph says the wicked rich are destroyed in a moment by sudden terrors, he is referring to God's final judgment at the end of the age. The apostle John actually gives us the general time-frame of this moment when he describes Babylon's destruction:

---

† See *Why the Wicked Prosper* on page 255.

"For this reason *in one day* her [Mystery Babylon's] plagues will come, pestilence and mourning and famine, and she will be burned up with fire; for the Lord God who judges her is strong. (REVELATION 18:8)

In this day of judgment, John specifically identifies how long it will take to destroy the unjust wealth of Mystery Babylon's New World Financial System:

"The merchants of these things, who became rich from her, will stand at a distance because of the fear of her torment, weeping and mourning, saying, 'Woe, woe ... *for in one hour such great wealth has been laid waste!*" (REVELATION 18:15–18)

Not only does this destruction come all at once, but it also comes while the world is carrying on business as usual. Jesus best describes this sudden financial obliteration of the end time economic system by correlating God's final judgment to that of Sodom and Gomorrah:

"It was the same as happened in the days of Lot: they were eating, they were drinking, they were buying, they were selling, they were planting, they were building; but on the day that Lot went out from Sodom it rained fire and brimstone from heaven and destroyed them all. It will be just the same on the day that the Son of Man is revealed." (LUKE 17:28–30)

Understanding the Times

Again, let me say there is a distinction between the shaking of God and the wrath of God. The shaking of God that we are experiencing today will lead to the eventual collapse of our current world political, financial and religious order. From the midst of that collapse will arise the ten kings (horns) of the beast, who will continue to build the ten social, political and economic regions of the NWO beast system.

The NWO will continue to shake until the man antichrist comes and brings the missing pieces of Mystery Babylon together.[174] He will govern the world for seven years and rule with impunity for forty-two months (three-and-a-half years) (REVELATION 13:5–7; DANIEL 7:23–25). If God's people are here for any portion of that time— and I believe we will be—it is imperative that we understand the times and how to properly respond.

Throughout the Scriptures, God constantly reminds us to understand the times we are living in and prepare accordingly. I believe the Lord wants us to be like the sons of Issachar "who understood the times, with knowledge of what [God's people] should do" (1 CHRONICLES 12:32). That's because, according to God's plans for the times, He will show us to what extent we can be involved in the world system.

For example, there are actually times when God directs His people to go into the world system and even prospers them while they are there. This would be like the time he allowed Abraham to go down to Egypt (world system) to escape a famine (GENESIS 12:10). Later, He sent Joseph, followed by all Israel, to go down to Egypt to avoid another famine (GENESIS 39–45). He also sent Judah into 70 years of captivity to Babylon (world system), and used the system to sustain them while they were there (JEREMIAH 29:4–7). Finally, He sent Joseph and Mary to Egypt to escape Herod's attempt to murder the Christ Child (MATTHEW 2:13–14).

There are also times when God tells us *not* to go to the world system for refuge. This would be like when Isaac thought he was supposed to go down to Egypt during yet another famine, but God told him to stay and sow in the Promised Land (GENESIS 26:1–17). If Isaac had gone to Egypt without God's permission, it would have been a financial disaster.

Then there is eventually the time when God specifically calls His people to *come out* of the world system. An example of this is when He called the children of Israel out of Egypt after 430 years of slavery (EXODUS 3:7–10). Another time was when He called Judah out of Babylonian captivity to return to the land of Israel and rebuild the temple (2 CHRONICLES 36:22–23; EZRA 1:1–4). Yet another was when He called Joseph and Mary to come out of Egypt and bring Jesus back to Israel after Herod's death (MATTHEW 2:15).

Missing God's Financial Timing

If we miss God's timing concerning our relationship to the world's financial system, it can cost us everything. The prophet Isaiah warns that going down to Egypt—the world—without God's permission will lead to shameful financial losses in the lives of His people:

"Woe to the rebellious children [God's people] ...
who execute a plan, but not mine, and make an
alliance, but not of My Spirit, in order to add sin to
sin; who proceed down to Egypt [the world system],
without consulting Me, to take refuge in the safety of
Pharaoh [government programs], and seek shelter in
the shadow of Egypt! Therefore the safety of Pharaoh
will be your shame, and the shelter in the shadow
of Egypt, your humiliation. ... *Everyone will be
ashamed because of a people who cannot profit them,
who are not for help or for profit, but for shame and
also for reproach.*" (ISAIAH 30:1–3, 5)

Today, many of God's people have turned to the world's
financial system for safety and profit without God's permission.
They continue in the world's ways, even when they see that the
system is not working anymore.

Because Egypt/Babylon is all they know, many of God's people
continue to use the dishonest scales of FRB debt to prosper in the
world's financial markets, only to rack up mountains of debt they
cannot pay back. This has forced many of them into bankruptcy,
and their shame has become a reproach to the ways and purposes
of God.

Even those who have prospered in the ways of Egypt/Babylon
in the past are being cut off. In His mercy, God is trying to tell
them that the days of doing it by the world's ways are over for
the church. Based on the evidence in this book and the financial
shaking described in chapter eight, I believe God is telling us that
it is time to come out of the unclean world's financial system.

Come Out of the World's System

God's ultimate call has always been for His people to come out of Satan's unrighteous world system. To "come out" of the world system does not mean to stop functioning within the system. It means, do not trust or look to it as your source because, when you do, it becomes your god.

That is why so many people will actually worship the beast, because otherwise they would not be able to get the "mark of the beast" to buy and sell in the world economy (REVELATION 13:15–18). Isn't it amazing how everything comes back to the root sin of the love of money?

Coming out of the world system is a delicate balance, especially in light of the fact that Jesus said that we are to be *in* the world, but not *of* the world (JOHN 17:13–19). According to this reality, when God commands us to come out of the world, He is actually telling us to come out from being *of* the world.

Being *of* the world means that a person is trusting in the world system and its unrighteous ways for their provision. To come out from being *of* the world simply means to stop following the world's ways and start walking in God's ways.

God's Model for Coming Out

God has been trying to separate the clean from the unclean and the holy from the unholy since the beginning (EZEKIEL 44:26). The apostle Paul urges God's people to come out and be separate of the unclean thing (political, financial and religious world system) (2 CORINTHIANS 6:14–18). Paul was actually quoting from the prophet Isaiah, who best describes how God intends to bring us out:

"Depart, depart, go out from there, touch nothing unclean; go out of the midst of her [Egypt/Babylon], purify yourselves, you who carry the vessels of the Lord. But you will not go out in haste, nor will you go as fugitives; for the Lord will go before you, and the God of Israel will be your rear guard." (ISAIAH 52:11–12)

Notice how Isaiah says God will lead us out in an orderly fashion. When he says that "you will not go out in haste, nor will you go out as fugitives," he means we would not come out all at once and be destitute with nowhere to go. God will lead us out according to His master plan, and bring us into our promised land. We may have to go through some wilderness wandering, but God will be there to comfort, guide and protect us.

When Isaiah says that God will be our "rear guard" as we come out, he is referring to what happened when Israel came out of Egypt. He is specifically speaking about when Jehovah went behind Israel in the pillar of the cloud and separated them from Egypt, so they could cross the Red Sea and come out of Egypt (the unclean thing) unmolested (EXODUS 14:19–21). This would seem to establish that Israel's exodus out of Egypt is the best model for us to use when coming out of the world system of the last days.

Show Me the Way Out

When God plagued Egypt, Israel remained in the land during all the ten plagues, throughout which God protected His people from each plague. Some protection was extended supernaturally according to God's divine favor, while some came as a result of

Israel's obedience to God's commands. The plagues of Egypt are all but identical to the plagues prophesied in the book of Revelation and, just as God protected Israel, I believe He will protect us from the plagues of the last days, both supernaturally and through our obedience.

Israel's settlement in Goshen represents how God's people can be *in* the world without being *of* the world. However, it is important to note that God's separation was not primarily between the land of Goshen and the land of Egypt; it was between the people of God and the people of Egypt. When God protected His people, the fact that they lived in Goshen meant that the land was also protected (EXODUS 8:22–23).

This truth is evident from the times that Israel was protected from certain plagues while conducting business outside of the land of Goshen. For example, when the fifth plague of pestilence among the livestock struck, God made a distinction between Israel's livestock and Egypt's livestock. This distinction supernaturally protected Israel's livestock even while they were grazing in the fields of Egypt (EXODUS 9:4–6). In other words, God's protection was primarily extended to His people as opposed to the land they were occupying.

Some have misinterpreted this metaphor as an all-inclusive principle that God will always protect our investments, regardless of where we have them. However, the plague of hail shows us that obedience to the commandments of God is also necessary for His financial protection.

Obey and Prosper

Instead of allowing the Israelites' cattle to remain in the fields of Egypt during the seventh plague of hail, God commanded Israel to come out of Egypt and bring their cattle home to Goshen. It is interesting to note that even the Egyptians who obeyed Jehovah's commandment to bring their livestock indoors, were also protected from the hail (EXODUS 9:19–26).

The moral of the story is that whoever obeyed God's instructions—whether Israelite or Egyptian—protected themselves and their livestock, while the disobedient perished in the field along with their livestock.

In addition, while the livestock/investment that remained in Egypt (the world system) perished, the livestock/investment that was taken out and brought to Goshen (God's ways) increased in value (EXODUS 10:24). This effectively produced a major transfer of wealth from the hands of the Egyptians (wicked) into the hands of Israel (God's righteous).

As we apply this principle of coming out of the world system of unrighteous investments (Egypt/Babylon), not only does God promise to protect us, but we will also be partakers of the end-time transfer of wealth.

Chapter 15

THE END TIME TRANSFER OF WEALTH

"A good man leaves an inheritance to his
children's children, and the wealth of the
sinner is stored up for the righteous."
PROVERBS 13:22

God promises there is eventually going to be a transfer of
wealth from the world's wicked to His righteous. Although the
full measure of this wealth transfer does not come until Jesus
physically returns and establishes His Kingdom on the earth, I
believe that a part of it does take place prior to Messiah's coming
in order to finance the completion of the great commission. This
is commonly referred to as the end time transfer of wealth.

Wealth Only Transfers to the Righteous

It is paramount that we understand from the above verse that
wealth is only going to be transferred to the righteous. Job best
explains how the wicked are cursed with judgment, but their
wealth is transferred to the just who are walking innocently
before God:

"This is the portion of a wicked man from God, and the inheritance which tyrants receive from the Almighty. Though his sons are many, they are destined for the sword; and his descendants will not be satisfied with bread. His survivors will be buried because of the plague, and their widows will not be able to weep. Though he piles up silver like dust, and prepares garments as plentiful as the clay; *he may prepare it, but the just will wear it, and the innocent will divide the silver.*" (JOB 27:13–17)

Some teach that the end time transfer of wealth comes to everyone who is born again, whether they are living righteously or not. This is a misguided and self-serving teaching that is part of an array of unscriptural teachings concerning this subject.[†]

Simply put, God is not going to transfer the wealth of the wicked to those who are unwilling to obey His Word. The end time transfer of wealth is going to come to the same righteous group that God has always prospered. Therefore, we must conduct ourselves and our business affairs according to the ways and purposes of God.

The Wealth of the Wicked

Many find it difficult to believe that the wealth of the vast international bankers, who use the dishonest scales of Fractional Reserve Banking (FRB) to rob the nations, could possibly be

---

† See *How Wealth Does Not Transfer* on page 266.

transferred to God's people. However, King Solomon prophesied that this is exactly what will happen:

> "He that by usury [interest] and unjust gain [dishonest scales of FRB] increaseth his substance, he shall gather it for him that will pity the poor." (PROVERBS 28:8, KJV)

How is it that the unjust gain of the wicked is both destroyed by God *and* transferred to the righteous at the same time? The answer is simple. There are three categories of unjust gain.

The first category of unjust gain is the debt-based monetary and investment assets (currencies and credit markets) created by the dishonest scales of FRB debt. Just as they have always done in the past, these assets will fail several times over, even before Messiah's return.

The second category of unjust gain includes the artificial price increase (inflation) that results from the debauching of currencies to make the value of paper assets appear to be worth more than they really are.

The first two categories of unjust gain have already been severely shaken during the various financial crises, but they will ultimately be completely destroyed "in one hour" when Mystery Babylon is overthrown in the Day of the Lord (REVELATION 18:15–18).

The third category of unjust gain consists of tangible assets that the wicked unjustly obtained through their debauchery. This will be the full measure of what is transferred back to the righteous, when Jesus returns to judge the world's financial system.

Wealth Transfers During
the Great Financial Shaking

As I said earlier, most of this wealth transfer will take place at the Lord's coming, but some of it is taking place during the great worldwide financial shaking that has already begun. The prophet Haggai gives us a clear prophetic word that a sizeable portion of the wealth of the nations is destined to be transferred to God's people during this shaking:

> "For thus says the Lord of hosts, 'Once more in a little while, I am going to shake the heavens and the earth, the sea also and the dry land. *And I will shake all the nations; and they will come with the wealth of the nations; and I will fill this house with glory,*' says the Lord of hosts." (HAGGAI 2:6–7)

I believe "this house" has a two-fold meaning. One is obviously God's ancient Jewish people who would return to the land of Israel, and the other is God's people, the church. God promises to prosper the church as they pray for the peace and prosperity of Jerusalem and Israel as a whole (PSALMS 122:6–9; ISAIAH 40:1–2).

It follows that if we desire to be successful in financing the great end time harvest, we must discover how God plans to transfer this wealth during the financial shakings that we are continuing to experience.

Mechanics of Wealth Transfer

Other than simply prospering those who are operating righteously in the marketplace, the end time transfer of wealth will take place in numerous ways. The following is a short list describing the mechanics of how I believe God plans to transfer a portion of the world's wealth to the church during this time of financial calamity.

Get Out of Debt

All of the end time transfer of wealth begins by getting out of debt. Becoming debt-free transfers back the tangible wealth that is held captive as collateral for the loans we have made. It is important to note that the first piece of collateral that is set free when debt is redeemed is the debtor himself, because he is no longer slave to the lender.

Digging your way out of debt is never easy. It takes commitment, discipline, a plan and some time. Unfortunately, very few of God's people are willing to commit the time it takes to get out of debt. Most are impatient and want out of debt instantly. Failure to wait on the Lord was what got them into debt in the first place, and if they fail to repent from this attitude they will only open themselves up to even greater deception.[†]

What About Bankruptcy?

I am often asked for my opinion on bankruptcy. I think King David answers this question best by pointing out how "the wicked borrows and does not pay back ..." (PSALMS 37:21). Filing for bankruptcy is the world's way of doing things, which actually plays into the hands of the NWO.

In my opinion, there are very few reasons for a believer to be in debt.[††] Therefore, there are very few reasons for a believer to ever file bankruptcy. Do not look for the easy way out, because there

---

[†] See *False Hope from False Prophets* on page 268.

[††] See *When God Allows Debt* on page 283

isn't one. There is always a price to pay for rebellion against God's Word. Just repent and start coming out God's way. If He wants to deliver you instantly, He will. But if He doesn't, following biblical principles is still the only way to righteously get out of debt.

Evangelism Transfers Wealth

I believe one of the major ways that God has always transferred the wealth of the wicked into the house of the Lord (church) is to win the wicked to Christ. This is another reason why we pray for kings and rulers of this world system. As they turn to Jesus and come into His Kingdom, their wealth is transferred into the kingdom with them.[†]

But some say that such money is dirty and should not be used in the church. In some cases this would be true, especially as it pertains to bribes, murder and any *ongoing* unjust gain. If the new believer can make reparations for his dishonest gain he should always attempt to do so in a humble manner.

However, we must remember that money is not the problem. It is the *love of money* that is the root of all evil. So, for the most part, it is perfectly legitimate to use wealth that has been acquired up to the point of salvation, for kingdom purposes. That's because money has no moral characteristic of its own. It simply takes on the characteristics of the one who controls it. So, when a sinner becomes righteous through his salvation in Christ and begins to walk in God's financial laws, his wealth takes on his new character and is transferred into the kingdom with him. Just as he now belongs to Jesus, so does his wealth.

---

† See *Missions and Financial Crisis* on page 269.

Investments Transfer Wealth

One of the major ways that wealth will be transferred in the last days will be through the different types of investments. As we have seen, that's because wealth is not really lost during an economic crisis; it is merely transferred from one individual to another through the monetary and/or investment assets they are holding at the time.

King Solomon says that diversification is one of God's primary rules for protecting our wealth from unseen financial crises:

> "Divide your portion to seven, or even eight, for you do not know what misfortune may occur upon the earth." (ECCLESIASTES 11:2)

I remember how, as a former financial planner, I used this principle to recommend that people invest in mutual funds because of their diversification. This is the standard sales pitch of most investment advisors. Unfortunately, you cannot apply the biblical principle of diversification to unbiblical paper investments and expect it to protect you.

When the shaking comes, every investment that is not built on sound biblical principles will crash, no matter how diversified they are. Therefore, our diversification must be grounded in investments that are built around real wealth that cannot be artificially pumped up through the use of dishonest scales.

As I have already pointed out, neither debt-based paper investments nor artificially inflated profits survive any type of serious financial shaking. In fact, their ultimate destiny is total destruction. Only the values of righteous tangible assets will survive the financial shakings in the days ahead. Therefore, holding righteous investments, at righteous prices, under righteous terms is the only way we can hope to participate in the end time transfer of wealth.

Public versus Private Stock

As I mentioned earlier, stocks are the only legitimate paper investments that represent real ownership. Unfortunately, the price of publicly traded OTC stock can be leveraged up or down through margined buying and selling. This puts them in the same category of unjust investments, and any artificial price appreciation will be destroyed during any future financial crisis.

However, private stock better reflects the true value of a company because it cannot be traded on margin. As a result, private stock better maintains its value during a financial crisis, and should be considered as a practical way of building and retaining investment value in the future.

Even worldly companies are discovering this truth. During my October 2000 trip to Asia, Renong Berhad, Malaysia's largest publicly-traded conglomerate, announced that it was planning to go back under private stock ownership.[175] Renong's stock had dropped to 2 ringgit per share after the crisis even though its book value was closer to 5 ringgit per share.

This meant that the value of Renong's publicly traded stock was being artificially suppressed, which limited the company's ability to raise investment capital. By delisting the company from the Kuala Lumpur Stock Exchange (KLSE) and taking it back under private ownership, Renong would increase shareholder value 60% and drastically improve its chances for refinancing.

Private stock ownership virtually eliminates the artificial price inflation that takes place in today's OTC markets, because stock prices are limited to the real value of the company. It also keeps the company focused on building real wealth as opposed to the artificial gains resulting from the leveraged purchase of its stock.

Although it is not as liquid as public stock, it better lends itself to building real, long-term wealth according to the biblical standards of investment finance that Jesus established in the parable of the talents (MATTHEW 25:14–28).[176] As a result, numerous public companies have begun delisting their stock and going private. These include Pacific Carrier of Singapore and Seagate Technologies of the U.S. just to name a couple.

I believe this is a prophetic sign for God's people to come out of worldly paper investments that can be manipulated with debt. If Christian investors will commit themselves to investing consecrated capital into consecrated Christian businesses under these basic guidelines, their enterprises will transfer real wealth into God's house in the last days.

Real Estate

As I pointed out in chapter eight, the strength of today's real estate market depends largely on the availability of real estate loans. However, when the loans are cut off, the debt bubble pops and homeowners lose much of the artificial equity that they thought was real wealth.

In the U.S., the "American Dream" of owning a home has produced a real estate feeding frenzy that is gobbling up properties at an unprecedented rate. Mortgage lending chains have sprung up in every corner and strip mall across America. They have flooded the real estate market with new, low-interest loans that have artificially inflated property values to unrealistic and record-setting highs.

Unfortunately, this has also produced a real estate debt bubble that is unprecedented in all the world. As the debt bubble maxes out, a real estate bust is waiting in the wings.

To those who say a real estate collapse cannot happen in America, I would remind them that every real estate debt bubble in the world has collapsed sooner or later—and so will America's.

In fact, part of God's judgment for participating in different types of unrighteous gain is the destruction of the real estate market:

> "'I will also smite the winter house together with the
> summer house; the houses of ivory will also perish
> and the great houses will come to an end,' declares
> the Lord." (Amos 3:15)

Real estate's artificial price appreciation that has been created through the unrighteous use of debt, simply cannot be maintained for much longer. With this in mind, a review of your real estate holdings is probably in order. A properly timed liquidation of real estate could be a prudent financial move. You may have to rent for a while, but that is better than losing thousands, perhaps millions, of dollars of equity in a real estate market crash.

Many people mortgage their homes because they do not like renting. However, unless you own your real estate free and clear you are, in fact, still a renter. You either rent the real estate itself, or you rent the money at interest to buy the real estate. But either way, you are renting.

In America, investment real estate is probably near its peak, which is a good time to liquidate and take your profits. If you are worried about capital gains, look at it this way. You can either pay capital gains on your inflated equity or lose your equity when the bubble pops, like most people in the crisis countries already have.

Precious Metals Transfer Wealth During the Great Shaking

In HAGGAI 2:6–7, when God spoke about the end time transfer of wealth that would take place during the global financial shaking, he goes on to give us a good idea of how this transfer will take place. As we revisit the Scripture, notice that in verses 8–9, the Lord clearly identifies a major vehicle of wealth-transfer:

> "For thus says the Lord of hosts, 'Once more in a little while, I am going to shake the heavens and the earth, the sea also and the dry land. And I will shake all the nations; and they will come with the wealth of the nations; and I will fill this house with glory,' says the Lord of hosts. *'The silver is Mine and the gold is Mine,'* declares the Lord of hosts. 'The latter glory of this house will be greater than the former,' says the Lord of hosts, 'and in this place I shall give peace,' declares the Lord of hosts." (HAGGAI 2: 6-9)

Notice that God does not say that the stocks, bonds and mutual funds are His, but the silver and gold. God actually appears to indicate that at least part of the end time transfer of wealth is going to come through the honest weights of precious metals.

The best and most recent example of paper wealth transferring to precious metals took place during Asia's financial crisis. Prior to July 1997, Asia's currencies were relatively strong, which kept precious metals prices low in their national currencies. However, when their currencies devalued, the paper cost of goods and services, including precious metals, went up.

In Malaysia, for example, the ringgit devalued 48% from 41 U.S. cents per ringgit to a low of 21 U.S. cents per ringgit. At that precise point in time, the price of gold rose 57% from 870 ringgits per ounce to a high of 1,370 ringgit per ounce (see Figure 8 below).

In effect, Malaysia and all the other crisis countries experienced a transfer of wealth from the dishonest weights of debt-based paper currencies to the honest weights of precious metals. This manifested as inflation that destroyed (devalued) the purchasing power of all paper investments.

Figure 8

(A) Malaysian currency (the ringgit) against the U.S. dollar between June 1997 and November 1998

(B) Price of gold in Malaysian currency between June 1997 and November 1998

It also led to the devaluation and confiscation of real estate as people were financially wiped out overnight. Only the precious metals maintained their purchasing power, while paper money and other investments that are influenced by debt were destroyed.

Precious Metals Protect Private Property

By debauching the currency, first through inflation, then by deflation, the financial elite are able to confiscate the real wealth of a country. Prior to his appointment as chairman of the Federal Reserve, Alan Greenspan pointed out how the honest money of precious metals was designed to stop this unrighteous transfer of wealth.

In his 1966 writings on *Gold and Economic Freedom*, Mr. Greenspan says:

> "The abandonment of the gold standard made it possible for the welfare statists to use the banking system as a means of unlimited expansion of credit. *In the absence of the gold standard, there is no way to protect savings from confiscation through inflation.* There is no safe store of value ...
>
> "The financial policy of the welfare state requires that there be no way for the owners of wealth to protect themselves. ... This is the shabby secret of the welfare statists' tirades against gold. Deficit spending is simply a scheme for the 'hidden' confiscation of wealth. *Gold stands in the way of this insidious process. It stands as protection of property rights.*"[177]

Unfortunately, Mr. Greenspan has been seduced by the "dark side," and now heads the world's largest unjust money monopoly—namely, America's central bank of the Federal Reserve. Even though you will not hear him even hint at establishing a gold-backed currency, he still understands the importance of owning gold. This truth is reflected in the fact that the Fed has approximately 40% of its assets invested in 262 million troy ounces of gold. Why? Because Mr. Greenspan understands the "Golden Rule," which is: "He who owns the gold—Rules."

God's Unchanging Word

For over 5,000 years, precious metals have maintained their purchasing power through wars, revolutions, the fall of empires, inflation and economic crisis. No other form of money offers the proven long-term stability of precious metals. Why? Because it is honest money, which has a lasting store of value that continues to purchase the same amount of goods and services it always has.

For example, in ancient Rome, a good suit of clothes cost roughly one ounce of gold. In 1920, the same good suit of clothes could be obtained for a twenty dollar gold piece, which contained roughly one ounce of gold. Today, (early 2001) that same suit of clothes can be bought for roughly $250 (FRNs), which is the approximate value of one ounce of gold. In other words, precious metals protect private property (the suit) from being confiscated through inflation.

Therefore, as we begin to come out of this world's financial system and its debt-based paper investments, we should begin moving a significant portion of our long-term savings into precious metals, because they are the only tangible monetary assets that are not someone else's debt. So when the system crashes, you are not dependent on someone else to get your money back.

The best rule of thumb for average investors is not to do what the insiders tell them to do, but to do what the insiders actually do themselves. In other words, having somewhere up to 40% of your long-term money in a diversified portfolio of precious metals, just like the Fed, is probably a good position to be in.[†]

The End of Unrighteous Mammon

In the end, all unrighteous mammon (debt-based money and investments) will be destroyed under the curse of dishonest scales. This will fulfill the words of the prophet Micah who said:

> "Is there yet a man in the wicked house, along with treasurers of wickedness, *and a short measure that is cursed? Can I justify wicked scales and a bag of deceptive weights?* For the rich men of the city are full of violence, her residents speak lies and their tongue is deceitful in their mouth. So also I will make you sick, striking you down, desolating you because of your sin." (MICAH 6:10–13)

At the same time, real (Godly) wealth is going to be transferred to those who are walking in God's standards of righteousness, where He promises to teach us His ways of prosperity.

---

† See *Precious Metals in the Last Days* on page 271.

Chapter 16

GOD'S WAYS OF PROSPERITY

"I am the Lord your God, who teaches you to profit.
Who leads you in the way you should go. If only
you had paid attention to my commandments! Then
your well-being would have been like a river, and
your righteousness like the waves of the sea. …
Go forth from Babylon!"

ISAIAH 48:17–18, 20

When we pay attention to God's commandments, it releases
well-being in our lives, and God promises to teach us His ways
of prosperity. However, God has always made it clear that His
blessing is not automatic, but conditional on our hearing and
obeying His commandments. Simply put, God has never blessed
man's disobedience in any dispensation, nor will He do so in the
last days. Just as the world's financial system is failing because of
its disobedience to God's ways, biblical prosperity will only come
through our obedience. Therefore, if we want to be partakers of
God's end time transfer of wealth, we must learn and implement
God's commandments concerning money and wealth.

Ten Commandments Of Biblical Prosperity

The following is a list of what I call the *Ten Commandments
of Biblical Prosperity*. In essence, I believe that they are ten

foundational keys to releasing true biblical prosperity into the body of Christ in the last days.

#1: Obey All of God's Commandments

> "Now it shall be, *if you will diligently obey the Lord your God, being careful to do all His commandments* which I command you today, the Lord your God will set you high above all the nations of the earth. And all these *blessings* shall come upon you and overtake you, *if you will obey the Lord your God. … the Lord will make you abound in prosperity …* But it shall come about, *if you will not obey the Lord your God, to observe to do all His commandments* and His statutes with which I charge you today, that all these curses shall come upon you and overtake you." (DEUTERONOMY 28:1–2, 11, 15)

When King Solomon said, "It's the blessing of the Lord that makes rich and He adds no sorrow" (PROVERBS 10:22), it was with the understanding that the blessing came as a result of obedience. From the beginning, God's eternal spiritual law of blessings for obedience and cursings for disobedience has been on the books—i.e., *the law of the Spirit of life in Christ Jesus and the law of sin and death* (GENESIS 2:16–17; ROMANS 8:2).

Moses makes it clear that one of the main benefits of obeying God's word is prosperity:

> "So keep the words of this covenant† to do them, *that you may prosper in all that you do*." (DEUTERONOMY 29:9).

---

† God's covenant is His commandments (DEUTERONOMY 4:13).

When Israel entered the "Promised Land" under Joshua, God reiterated the same commandment linking prosperity with obedience:

> "This book of the law shall not depart from your mouth, but you shall meditate on it day and night, so that you may *be careful to do according to all that is written in it; for then you will make your way prosperous, and then you will have success.*" (JOSHUA 1:8)

King David, whose tabernacle God restores in the New Covenant (ACTS 15:15–18), gives this same instruction to his son Solomon, saying:

> "Obey the laws of God and follow all his ways; keep each of his commandments written in the law of Moses so that you will prosper in everything you do, wherever you turn." (1 KINGS 2:3, *LB*)

On the flip side, the prophet Zechariah clearly warns us that when we disobey God's commandments, we do not prosper:

> "Then the Spirit of God came on Zechariah the son of Jehoiada the priest; and he stood above the people and said to them, 'Thus God has said, *"Why do you transgress the commandments of the Lord and do not prosper?* Because you have forsaken the Lord, He has also forsaken you.'" (2 CHRONICLES 24:20)

If those transgressions—i.e., sins (1 JOHN 3:4)—stay hidden and are not dealt with, Solomon also says that we will not prosper:

> "He who conceals his transgressions will not prosper, but he who confesses and forsakes them will find compassion." (PROVERBS 28:13)

Simply put, both prosperity and the end time transfer of wealth are going to come the same way that godly prosperity has always come, through our obedience to God's Word. This is one reason why the Holy Spirit is currently emphasizing that we should return and learn the ancient paths of God's laws (Torah) that we might find *rest for our souls* (Jeremiah 6:16).

#2: Seek the Prosperity of Your Soul

"Beloved, I pray that in all respects you may prosper and be in good health, just as your soul prospers." (3 John 1:2)

The apostle John prays that we prosper physically and financially in direct proportion to how much our soul prospers. Prosperity of soul comes through the study and application of God's Word in our lives. That is why Solomon says, "He who keeps the commandment keeps his soul" (Proverbs 19:16).

King David further confirms that prosperity of soul comes through God's law when he says:

"The law of the Lord is perfect, restoring the soul; the testimony of the Lord is sure, making wise the simple. The precepts of the Lord are right, rejoicing the heart; the commandment of the Lord is pure, enlightening the eyes. The fear of the Lord is clean, enduring forever; the judgments of the Lord are true; they are righteous altogether ... Moreover, by them Thy servant is warned; *in keeping them there is great reward."* (Psalms 19:7–9, 11)

It is clear that God will prosper us physically and financially to the same degree that our soul prospers in His Word. If we don't understand His laws, commandments, statutes, precepts, judgments and testimonies concerning biblical prosperity, we can never come into the fullness of that prosperity in spirit, soul or body.

As we learn to walk according to God's ways, He promises to prosper our souls with the wisdom, purity, endurance, truth, and righteous knowledge of Him. It is also interesting to note that Solomon said, "He who gets wisdom loves his own soul" (PROVERBS 19:8).

#3: Acquire Wisdom and Knowledge

> "Because you had this in mind, and did not ask for riches, wealth, or honor … nor have you even asked for long life, but you have asked for yourself wisdom and knowledge … wisdom and knowledge have been granted to you. And I will give you riches and wealth and honor … ." (2 CHRONICLES 1:11–12)

When Solomon asked God for wisdom and knowledge, he knew that he was committing himself to obey His commandments. As a student of the Torah, Solomon understood that wisdom and knowledge came as a result of obedience to God's Word, just as Moses said:

> "See, I have taught you statutes and judgments just as the Lord commanded me … *So keep and do them, for that is your wisdom and your understanding*

in the sight of the peoples who will hear all these statutes and say, *'Surely this great nation is a wise and understanding people.'"* (DEUTERONOMY 4:5–6)

Solomon acquired this understanding from his father, King David, who taught him that God's Law (Torah) made him wiser than all his enemies and gave him more insight than all his teachers (PSALMS 119:97–100). David also said that the blameless walk in the Law of the Lord and are *blessed* by God (PSALMS 119:1–3), further confirming that obedience brings God's blessing that makes one rich.

Solomon never taught obedience to God's commandments for salvation, but for *length of days, peace and favor in the sight of God and man* (PROVERBS 3:1–4). That is because the birthright of salvation has always been by grace through faith in God's blood atonement (LEVITICUS 6:6–7; EPHESIANS 1:7; 2:8–9), but the blessings have always come through obedience to God's laws (GENESIS 26:4–5).

Solomon goes on to prophetically personify God's Word as "wisdom" that brings witty inventions, riches, glory, enduring wealth, and righteousness (PROVERBS 8:12–21). In verse 14, He says that wisdom actually cries out saying, "power is mine." This is undoubtedly the same "power to make wealth" that God gives us in order "that He may establish His covenant" (DEUTERONOMY 8:18).

#4: Bless Israel and Pray for the Peace of Jerusalem

"Now the Lord said to Abram, … 'I will bless those who bless you, and the one who curses you I will curse.'" (GENESIS 12:1, 3)

In the Abrahamic covenant, Jehovah extends the law of the Spirit of life in Christ Jesus and the law of sin and death to our relationship with Israel. He promises to release His blessing (that makes rich) on all those who follow His commandment to bless Israel, and to curse all those who curse Israel. [*It is interesting to note that this law of blessing is actually established before the law of tithes is established in* GENESIS 14:18–20.]

Along the same lines, He commands us to pray for the *peace and prosperity of Jerusalem*, and to seek after Israel's good "for the sake of the house of the Lord" (PSALMS 122:6–9).

The house of God includes both natural Israel and the gentile church that has been grafted into the commonwealth of Israel (ROMANS 11:17–21; EPHESIANS 2:11–13). This inexorably links the New Testament church into the Abrahamic covenant, as the apostle Paul clearly points out:

> "And if you belong to Christ, then you are Abraham's offspring [spiritual seed†], heirs according to promise." (GALATIANS 3:29)

Therefore, God's promise to the spiritual seed of Abraham (both Jew and gentile in Christ) is that He will bless them as they bless the natural seed of Abraham (physical Israel). For this reason, the church needs to invest in Israel in order to build them up, both physically and spiritually. Whoever does this "to the least of these My brethren [Jews]" will be blessed, and whoever does not do this will be cursed (MATTHEW 25:40–46). This phenomenon can be seen throughout the history of blessings or cursings of every nation under heaven, down to this very day.

---

† GALATIANS 3:16.

#5: Honor the Lord with Your Wealth

"Honor the Lord from your wealth, and from the first
of all your produce; so your barns will be filled with
plenty, and your vats will overflow with new wine."
(PROVERBS 3:9–10)

The first of all our produce refers to the tithe, which belongs to
the Lord (LEVITICUS 27:30–34). The tithe is important because it
is considered the first lump of our finances, which is always holy
(sanctified) to the Lord (NUMBERS 15:18–2; NEHEMIAH 10: 37;
ROMANS 11:16). If we fail to give back to God the first fruits of
our tithes, then it and our whole lump becomes cursed (MALACHI
3:8–9).

The Hebrew word for "cursed" is the prime root word *awrar*,
which means, "to execrate."[178] Execrate refers to *something that
is abhorrent, because it has become unsanctified/unholy and
separate from God and His way of doing things*. In other words,
if we fail to tithe, our whole financial lump becomes unholy and
is placed outside God's protection where it is subject to attacks
of the enemy.

Because tithes and offerings are holy unto the Lord, our motives
for giving must also be pure. If we give with *impure motives* or
while we are *willfully practicing sin*, our gifts actually become
"unrighteous offerings" that God despises (ISAIAH 1:10–15;
MALACHI 1–2).[179]

Unfortunately, many believers in the church today actually give
offerings out of their love of money. By this I mean their primary
motive for giving is to make a thirty, sixty, or a hundred-fold
return on their money. Theirs is an *unrighteous offering* and is
the major reason why today's prosperity message is not working.

I believe that when we give tithes and offerings with a proper motive, God uses it as a tool to help us overcome the love of money. Therefore, keeping ourselves and our wealth holy begins by the honoring of the Lord with our tithes and offerings that are given with the right motives.

#6: Be Generous to the Poor

> "He who is generous will be blessed, for he gives some of his food to the poor." (PROVERBS 22:9)

Ministering to the poor is one of the Lord's most sacred works. In fact, Jesus was anointed and sent into this world to minister specifically to the poor (LUKE 4:18). Having done so Himself, he then tells us to go and minister in like manner and with even greater works (JOHN 14:12).

When speaking about our calling to be generous, the apostle Paul applies the principle of sowing and reaping in a very profound manner when he says:

> "For you know the grace of our Lord Jesus Christ, that though He was rich, yet for your sake He became poor, that you through His poverty might become rich." (2 CORINTHIANS 8:9)

Paul is not saying that Jesus became poor so we could become rich and buy a bunch of nice things for ourselves. He is saying that God gives us His abundance so that we can use it to minister to those in need (2 CORINTHIANS 8:11–21). This is a work of God, and the more we minister to those in need, the more He provides what we need for this work.

God once gave me a prophetic word from 2 CORINTHIANS 9:6–10 that went something like this: "I will provide seed for the sower and bread for food. And as it passes through there will be enough for you." From this, the Lord showed me that when Solomon said, "He who gives to the poor will never want" (PROVERBS 28:27), he was not talking about the sower gaining riches for himself. He was talking about the sower having food to minister to the poor, and as the food passes through the sower's hands to the needy, there would always be enough for him.

Fortunately, God also says that those who are generous to the poor will receive more than just their daily rations, as Solomon points out:

> "He who is gracious to a poor man lends to the Lord, and He will repay him for his good deed." (PROVERBS 19:17)

#7: Don't Use Debt to Prosper

> "'Woe to him who increases what is not his ... and makes himself rich with loans?' Will not your creditors rise up suddenly, and those who collect from you awaken? Indeed, you will become plunder for them." (HABAKKUK 2:6–7)

As we have already discovered, every financial crisis over the past century has been the collapse of one or more debt bubbles. When this happens, those who have leveraged their investments (real estate, stocks, bonds, etc.), hoping to ride the artificial inflation bubble higher and higher, have suffered huge loses. Many have even been totally wiped out.

No matter how well debt seems to work for obtaining material possessions; *the borrower is still always a slave to the lender*. When there is a financial shaking (currency crisis, recession, unemployment, etc.), your creditors become your masters who rise up and confiscate your assets, and you become plunder for them.

On the flip side, we must also be careful who we lend to, because lending our wealth to the world system will eventually prove fatal. Neither should we co-sign a loan for anyone if we are not willing or are in a position to suffer the loss if the borrower defaults (PROVERBS 11:15; 6:1–5).

Man is called to prosper primarily by the work of his hands and the sweat of his brow (GENESIS 2:15; 3:19), not by drawing interest on loans. This is especially true in the light of today's unjust FRB lending scheme. Therefore, we should put our money to work by building tangible wealth that will withstand the shakings of the unrighteous world's financial system.

There are only a few biblically sound reasons why believers should borrow or even lend money at interest. That is because real wealth is what you own, not what you owe. (This is a subject that will be covered in more detail in a subsequent book.)

#8: Be Diligent

> "Poor is he who works with a negligent hand, but the
> hand of the diligent makes rich." (PROVERBS 10:4)

To be diligent means *to be alert, to be eager, to have determination, to be liquid or flow easily, to be prompt*—i.e., do not procrastinate.[180] The first place we are to exercise diligence is in keeping God's Word. When we do this, God not only promises that we will prosper, but also promises that we "shall stand before kings" (PROVERBS 22:29, KJV).

If you are called to leadership of any kind, you must understand that only "the hand of the diligent will rule" (PROVERBS 12:24). Solomon said, "the precious possession of a man is diligence" (PROVERBS 12:27), and that "the soul of the diligent is made fat [with the blessing of the Lord]" (PROVERBS 13:4).

As we approach the end of the age, diligence will provide us with an added measure of needed strength to endure the last days. Solomon warns that, "if you are slack in the day of distress, your strength is limited" (PROVERBS 24:10), and you will be sent to the rear because of your faint-heartedness (DEUTERONOMY 20:8). Even now, many are being sent to the rear because of their lack of diligence in keeping with the ways of God.

Be careful not to confuse diligence with "workaholism," because the two are clearly different. Workaholism consumes a person's life to the point were he has no life other than work. Sometimes diligence takes a little extra time and effort to do the job right, but workaholism makes work/career an idol that keeps us from honoring our other biblical obligations to God, family and church community.

It is also interesting to note that, in the New Testament, the word for diligence is sometimes translated "business" (ROMANS 12:11, KJV), which is definitely one place where believers need to be especially eager, determined, and vigilant in the ways of God.

#9: Establish God's Covenant in the Marketplace

> "And you shall remember the Lord your God, for it is He who gives power to get wealth, that He may establish His covenant which He swore to your fathers, as it is to this day." (DEUTERONOMY 8:18, NKJV)

Establishing God's covenant in the marketplace is paramount for financing the work of the ministry in the last days. Remembering that God's covenant is His commandments (DEUTERONOMY 4:13), forces us back to God's model of learning and implementing His laws (Torah) when conducting business and trade.

Since the marketplace is the birthplace of Lucifer's original sin (see chapter one), it is understandable why the business world is the most difficult arena to walk in obedience to God's commandments.

I call the marketplace a "ministry," because the Hebrew word for business is *melawkaw*, which translated means *"the ministry of work in the form of an industrious occupation or business involving property, work, workmanship, service, or public business such as politics or religious service."*[181]

Melawkaw comes from the root word *mal'ak*, which means *to dispatch as a deputy or a messenger of God in the form of a prophet, priest or teacher.*[182] In other words, Scripture teaches that a businessman or woman is a messenger of God, who has been dispatched as a prophet, priest or teacher to do the work of the ministry—i.e., establish God's covenant—in the marketplace.

Surprisingly enough, the first marketplace minister was God Himself. Scripture says that after the Lord finished conducting the business of creating the heavens and the earth, "He rested from all the 'work' [*melawkaw*] He had done" (GENESIS 2:2). In fact, the six-day workweek followed by the seventh day of rest is an expression of God's Kingdom pattern of *melawkaw* (business), which He established within the creation itself.

Later, when the Lord became flesh and dwelt among us, He did it as a businessman. Jesus was a carpenter from the age of thirteen when he entered manhood, until age 30 when He entered fulltime ministry. During this time, He grew in favor and stature with God and man. I believe that His seventeen years in the marketplace ministry actually served as a training ground for His three-and-a-half years of fulltime preaching ministry. That is a 5:1 ratio of training in the marketplace in preparation for fulltime pulpit ministry.

If you are a businessman who feels the overwhelming call to fulltime ministry, relax. You are either in training for pulpit ministry or you are already in fulltime marketplace ministry. Whatever the case, your primary goal should be to learn and implement God's ways of prosperity that will release the wealth you need to establish His covenant.

#10: No Dishonest Scales of Any Kind

"A false balance is an abomination to the Lord, but a just weight is His delight." (PROVERBS 11:1)

By far, the most abhorrent use of dishonest scales is the Fractional Reserve Banking (FRB) within our monetary system. However,

FRB is not the only way a person can be guilty of using dishonest scales. Cheating your trading partners in any way is also classified as the use of unjust scales.

For example, cutting corners by not providing the full measure of a business contract would be classified as using unjust scales. This would also include providing a cheaper product when the contract calls for a better one. By agreeing to sell a more expensive product to a trading partner and then giving him a cheaper one, the seller becomes a "dishonest merchant" in whose hands are false balances. He is also in violation of the eighth, ninth and tenth commandments not to steal, lie, or covet his neighbor's wealth (EXODUS 20:15–17). Walking in integrity and treating our neighbors as we would have them treat us, is God's "golden rule" for life, especially when it comes to conducting business in the marketplace (LEVITICUS 19:17–18; MATTHEW 7:12).

Unjust scales include bribery (PSALMS 26:9–10), withholding wages from your employees (DEUTERONOMY 24:14–15; JAMES 5:4), charging interest on loans to the brethren (LEVITICUS 25:35–37), and taking unfair advantage of widows and orphans (ISAIAH 1:23).

If God "delights in the prosperity of his servants," and "a just weight is His delight," it follows that God will delight in prospering His people only when they operate with the integrity of just scales.

God Only Prospers the Righteous

Just remember that God only rewards those who walk righteously before Him with prosperity. King Solomon emphasizes this when he says:

> "Adversity pursues sinners, but *the righteous will be rewarded with prosperity.*" (PROVERBS 13:21)

This timeless and unwavering truth is why God commands the New Testament church to practice godly righteousness in the same manner that Jesus did (1 JOHN 2:5–6; 3:7). As we walk this out by faith, God's righteousness manifests itself in our lives (JAMES 2:20–26). This releases the very life of God into our finances, and we prosper as a result.

The *Ten Commandments of Biblical Prosperity* are just the beginning of God's plan to release His fuller prosperity to His servants in the last days. Not only will their investments and their entrepreneurial conduct be built on honesty and integrity, but their wealth will also be consecrated to the Lord of all the earth.

At that point in the believer's life, his love of money (the world's unrighteous mammon) comes to an end and true biblical wealth begins.

Chapter 17

WHEN MONEY ENDS AND WEALTH BEGINS

"Arise and thresh, daughter of Zion, for your horn I
will make iron and your hoofs I will make bronze,
that you may pulverize many peoples, *that you may
devote [consecrate] to the Lord their unjust gain and
their wealth to the Lord of all the earth.*"
MICAH 4:13

As we approach the end of the age, how we appropriate the
money and wealth that comes under our control will play a vital
role in our overcoming the financial shakings of the last days.
Therefore, we must build on the *Ten Commandments of Biblical
Prosperity* with the law of consecration. Only when we consecrate
the money and wealth of the wicked to the Lord of all the earth
will He transfer it to us.

However, before God transfers the wealth of the wicked to us,
He first tests us to determine whether we would actually devote
it to Him or not. That test comes in the consecration of our own
wealth to Him. If we can't devote our own wealth to the Lord, how
can He trust us to devote the wealth of the wicked to Him once
it transfers to us. The unfortunate truth is that most believers are
still using the unrighteous ways of FRB debt and other financial
schemes to build their own house, business, or ministry instead
of building God's house.

Consider Your Ways

When God called Israel out of Babylonian captivity it was specifically "to build Him a house [temple] in Jerusalem" (2 CHRONICLES 36:22–23; EZRA 1:1–4). However, when Israel got back to Jerusalem, they focused on building their own homes instead. This led to one financial failure after another until God sent the prophet Haggai to explain why:

> "Then the word of the Lord came by Haggai the prophet saying, 'Is it time for you yourselves to dwell in your paneled houses while [God's] house lies desolate?' Now therefore, thus says the Lord of hosts, 'Consider your ways! *You have sown much, but harvest little*; you eat, but there is not enough to be satisfied; you drink, but there is not enough [to be filled]; you put on clothing, but no one is warm enough; and he who earns, earns wages to put into a purse with holes ... *You look for much, but behold, it comes to little; when you bring it home, I blow it away. Why?' declares the Lord of hosts, 'Because of My house which lies desolate, while each of you runs to his own house.'"* (HAGGAI 1:3–5, 9)

Unfortunately, this is where many of God's people are at today. They have sown one seed-faith offering after another in hopes that God will prosper them enough to make their next house payment. Their goal is to maintain their worldly debt-based image of prosperity rather than building God's Kingdom in a biblical fashion.

God's people must stop pursuing prosperity and start pursuing the Kingdom of God and His righteousness, because only then will the wealth of the Kingdom be released to them (MATTHEW

6:33). One of the greatest heresies in the church today is that you can become prosperous by sending a "seed-faith offering" into someone's ministry, and then simply "confess that you are prosperous."

Yes, we need to give, but we need to give with the expressed purpose of building God's house rather than treating God like an investment broker who is supposed to give us thirty, sixty or hundred-fold return on our money. *This teaching actually causes us to put more trust in our giving and faith in the soliciting ministry than in God.* As a result, a large portion of the prosperity message has degenerated into nothing more than a religious get-rich-quick scheme, where the only one getting rich is the guy you are giving your money to.

This is not faith. It is foolishness that is not biblically sound. What is more, God is not going to prosper it. This will fulfill the words of the prophet Jeremiah who said:

> "From this place also you shall go out with your hands on your head; for the Lord has rejected those in whom you trust, and *you shall not prosper with them.*" (JEREMIAH 2:37)

It is not even going to work for the soliciting ministries anymore, because God is bringing a stop to it.

Building God's House

The foundational truth for successfully building God's house centers on keeping God's Laws. King David points this out to his son, Solomon, when instructing him on how to successfully build the temple:

"Now, my son, the Lord be with you that you may be successful, and build the house of the Lord your God just as He has spoken concerning you. Only the Lord give you discretion and understanding, and give you charge over Israel, *so that you may keep the law of the Lord your God. Then you shall prosper, if you are careful to observe the statutes and the ordinances which the Lord commanded Moses concerning Israel.* Be strong and courageous, do not fear nor be dismayed. (1 CHRONICLES 22:11–13)

Building the house of God through obedience takes us back to the essence of the great commission, which is about discipling the nations, *teaching them to observe all that Jesus commanded* (MATTHEW 28:19–20). Interestingly enough, only when we return and consecrate ourselves to build our Father's house in obedience to His Word, does He actually transfer the wealth of the nations into our hands (HAGGAI 1:10–2:9).

Seeking Fortune and Destiny

When so much emphasis is put on building our own house, it produces an overload of teaching about personal prosperity and career/ministry calling. Prosperity and calling are legitimate subjects to teach on, but seeking the Lord must be our primary pursuit.

Most of the current teaching concerning prosperity and calling is actually the pursuit of the false god's, Fortune and Destiny, in disguise. Isaiah specifically prophesies of a time just prior to the millennial reign of Christ (ISAIAH 65:17–25), when many of

God's people would turn away from seeking Him, and begin to seek after these two pagan deities:

> "And Sharon shall be a pasture land for flocks, and the valley of Achor a resting place for herds, *for My people who seek Me*. But you who forsake the Lord, who forget My holy mountain, who set a table for *Fortune*, and who fill cups with mixed wine for *Destiny*, I will destine for the sword ... (ISAIAH 65:10–12A)

Not only has there been an over-emphasis on personal prosperity, but there has also been a lot of teaching in the church lately about finding and fulfilling your *Destiny*. Unfortunately, that *Destiny* usually centers on career (business or ministry) calling, with a caveat on Fortune (personal prosperity). However, our true destiny is to "become conformed to the image of Jesus" (ROMANS 8:29), and when this gets mixed up with career-calling, it becomes a cup of mixed wine that we pour for a false god named *Destiny*.

Isaiah goes on to point out how God is going to distinguish clearly between those who are seeking after Him and those who are seeking after Fortune and Destiny:

> "... I will destine you for the sword, and all of you shall bow down to the slaughter. Because I called, but you did not answer; I spoke, but you did not hear. And you did evil in My sight, and chose that in which I did not delight. Therefore, thus says the Lord God, 'Behold, *My servants shall eat*, but *you shall be hungry*. Behold, *My servants shall drink*, but *you shall be thirsty*. Behold, *My servants shall rejoice*, but *you shall be put to shame*. Behold, *My servants*

*shall shout joyfully with a glad heart, but you shall
cry out with a heavy heart, and you shall wail with a
broken spirit."* (ISAIAH 65:12–14)

This has already happened to many Christian investors who
have been seeking after *Fortune* and *Destiny* in the world's
financial markets. Many have lost everything and are crying out
with a heavy heart and wailing with a broken spirit as their wealth
has evaporated before their eyes.

This has fulfilled the words of Solomon who said:

"Do not weary yourself to gain wealth, cease from
your consideration of it. When you set your eyes on
it, it is gone. For wealth certainly makes itself wings,
like an eagle that flies toward the heavens." (PROVERBS
23:4–5)

It's Not What We Do, It's How We Do It

If our primary focus is to seek after *Fortune* and *Destiny*, we end
up believing that we will succeed regardless of whether we obey
God or not. In other words, many have come to falsely believe
that what they do—i.e., prospering in their career-calling—is
more important than how they do it.

However, King David gives us the proper perspective when
he points out that if a man delights in walking according to the
law of the Lord, "he will prosper in whatever he does" (PSALMS
1:1–3). In other words it is not what we do; it is how we do it.
This gets our focus off personal *Fortune* and *Destiny* and back
on consecrating our lives and our wealth to the building of God's
Kingdom.

Consecrated Personal Wealth

Consecrating our wealth to the Lord consists of more than just giving our tithes and offerings. It means devoting *all of our wealth* to the Lord. This does not mean that you give all your money to a church or para-church ministry to fund their programs. It means you give it all to God's Kingdom model of money and wealth management.

I believe that the Lord is bringing His people to a place of living *wholly* consecrated lives, where any wealth over and above their own needs becomes consecrated (set apart) to the work of discipling the nations. In other words, wealth that we produce over and above our living expenses, budgeted savings/inheritance (PROVERBS 13:22), recreation/vacations (ECCLESIASTES 5:18–19), and feast celebrations (LEVITICUS 23) should be devoted and made immediately available to the work of the great commission as the Lord directs.

Consecrated Business Wealth

In the business arena, profits over and above standard operating expenses, expansion costs, and tithes and offerings to fulltime church and para-church ministries, should also be made immediately available for the work of discipling the nations. As I minister among the nations, I see more and more marketplace ministers using their profits to finance their own vision for ministry.

For example, a marketplace apostle friend of mine from Singapore finances his own ministry outreach in Indonesia, where he disciples about 100 of the poorest pastors from the hill country of Sumatra. I recently spoke at a conference that he sponsored for them, and as we ministered personally to those who were literally destitute, we gave them money from our own pockets to buy food with.

My friend did not advertise what he was doing. He did not ask for donations from the church. He did not even ask his pastor for permission. He just did it in obedience to the Word of God and paid for it out of his company's profits. This is the kind of true marketplace ministry that God desires to raise up in these last days.

Can you imagine an army of these guys going out to the uttermost parts of the world armed with the tangible message of the Gospel and the finances to deliver it. The problem is that there is not a proper understanding or discipling of marketplace ministers.

Most pulpit ministries are unable to meet the real needs of Christian businessmen because most of them do not understand the difference between priestly income and business income. The pastor's income is priestly in that God commands His people to provide a reasonable living for those in fulltime pulpit ministry whereas the business/working man's income, which provides the priestly income, is earned by the sweat of his brow.

The businessman is battling it out for market share in the midst of a cursed financial system that he is trying desperately to understand. He does not need to hear about how to give more offerings to the church programs, but how to implement God's ways in his business affairs so he can earn enough money to give offerings from.†

---

† See *What Every Businessman Wishes He Could Tell His Pastor* on page 279.

Unfortunately, the message on money and wealth management coming from most pulpits is one-dimensional. That message is: "Just give to the church, and God will prosper you." As a prophetic voice to the body of Christ, just let me say in the name of the Lord, "That day is over."

Discipling Marketplace Ministers

As a former senior pastor who is now a para-church minister, I have always believed that successful Christian businessmen and women (Josephs) should be actively discipling young Christian entrepreneurs in the biblical aspects of marketplace ministry. When those marketplace disciples have proven themselves faithful to the Word of God, the Joseph's should invest a portion of their consecrated capital together with them, in a business venture of their own. (This will be covered in a future book).

To aid in this end time financing of Christian business ventures, I also believe that every marketplace minister should consecrate a portion of His business wealth toward investment into other Kingdom business ventures that are dedicated to establishing God's covenant in the marketplace. The goal is to make the next generation more successful than your own, which further establishes God's covenant in the earth.

I believe this approach is vital for the last days, because it not only advances the Gospel of the Kingdom, but also prepares supernatural provision for the giver when the world's financial system fails.

Make Friends With Your Money

In LUKE 16:1–13, when the unrighteous steward knew that his master was about to fire him, he went to all of the people who owed his master money, and forgave a portion of their debt. When the master discovered this, he actually praised the unrighteous steward for his shrewdness and noted that the worldly are smarter than God's people in the use of unrighteous mammon.

The master was not condoning the unrighteous act, but the principle of how to use the world's money to secure one's future. The principle was that the steward used the unrighteous mammon (the world's money) to make friends with those who would be obligated to reciprocate the favor once the loss of his job brought financial failure:

> "And I say to you, make friends for yourselves by means of the mammon of unrighteousness; that *when it fails*, they may receive you into the eternal dwellings." (LUKE 16:9)

In the same manner, we can apply this principle to the last days as it relates to the coming failure of the unrighteous mammon of the world's financial system. By sowing the world's finances into the work of the ministry today, we are using it to make friends with the Kingdom of God, which obligates it to open its doors of financial provision to us when all the world's money fails.

As we are faithful to obey this principle with the little we have, God will give us much, because He can trust us not to serve the mammon, but to use the mammon of the world's system to serve His kingdom.

The Work of the Flesh

At this point, we must be careful not to let our obedience become a work of the flesh. If we focus solely on the biblical mechanics of cause and effect to produce wealth, we will eventually end up trusting in the work of our hands. That is generally when we reduce the ways of God into a series of formulas, in an attempt to manipulate Jehovah Himself into prospering us. At that point, the Lord says it becomes a work of the flesh that comes under a curse:

> "Thus says the Lord, 'Cursed is the man who trusts in mankind and makes flesh his strength, and whose heart turns away from the Lord. For he will be like a bush in the desert and *will not see when prosperity comes ... .*'" (JEREMIAH 17:5–6)

For years, I trusted in a certain degree of my flesh to produce financial returns until one day it stopped. I was obeying God's Word in all I knew to do, but it was not working anymore. When I asked the Lord about why His ways were not working for me, He spoke to my heart and said, "Even though you are mechanically doing it My way, you are still *trusting in the work of your hands* to bring forth My blessing. Now you need to start *trusting in Me* to bless the work of your hands."

He showed me that until my obedience comes from a heart of trust and love for Him, everything that I do is nothing more than dead works that will not prosper. That revelation set me free from the works of the flesh, and released me into a new level of Spirit-led and empowered obedience to the laws of God. This, in turn, has produced a new level of prosperity in my life, because I now live a greater degree of His life that is in me and less of my own.

God's Foremost Law of Prosperity

This brings us to the foremost commandment concerning all God-ordained prosperity, which Moses says is to love the Lord with all our heart:

> "See, I have set before you today life and prosperity, and death and adversity; in that I command you today to *love the Lord your God*, to walk in His ways and to keep His commandments and His statutes and His judgments, that you may live and multiply, and that the Lord your God may bless you … ." (DEUTERONOMY 30:15–16)

Moses further clarifies that loving the Lord is the foremost law of prosperity when he says:

> "And it shall come about, if you listen obediently to my commandments which I am commanding you today, *to love the Lord your God* and to serve Him with all your heart and all your soul, that 'He will give the rain for your land in its season, *the early and late rain*, that you may gather in your grain and your new wine and your oil. And He will give grass in your fields for your cattle, and you shall eat and be satisfied.'" (DEUTERONOMY 11:13–15)

Jesus confirmed this truth when he said that the foremost commandment was to "love the Lord with all our heart, soul, mind and strength" (MATTHEW 22:37–38). He was quoting from the *Sh'ma*, where Abba says that when we first love Him with all our heart, soul, and strength it releases His commandments to be on our hearts.

> "Hear , O Israel! The Lord our God is one! And you shall love the Lord your God with all your heart and with all your soul and with all your might. And these words, which I am commanding you today, shall be on your heart ... ." (DEUTERONOMY 6:4–6)

This empowers us to walk in His ways and enter the Promised Land, where God transfers the wealth of the wicked into our hands just as He transferred the wealth of the Canaanites to Israel:

> "Then it shall come about when the Lord your God brings you into the land which he swore to your fathars, Abraham, Isaac and Jacob, *to give you, great and splendid cities which you did not build, and houses full of all good things which you did not fill, and hewn cisterns which you did not dig, vineyards and olive trees which you did not plant, and you shall eat and be satisfied ... ."* (DEUTERONOMY 6:10–11)

Simply put, loving the Lord whth all our heart is the ultimate key to unlocking the end time transfer of wealth. Jesus also points out that our love for God is always accompanied by obedience (JOHN 14:15). For when we truly love the Lord with all our being, obedience to His commandments is no longer a burden, but simply the natural by-product of His life being manifest in us:

> "For this is the love of God, that we keep His commandments; and His commandments are not burdensome." (1 JOHN 5:3; see also DEUTERONOMY 30:11–14)

Writing God's laws on our hearts is the essence of the New Covenant, which is what brings us to a full knowledge of God (Jeremiah 31:31–34; Hebrews 10:15–17). And when we come to know Him, we always obey His Word and walk in the same manner as Jesus walked (1 John 2:3–6).

God's Love Conquers the World

From the beginning of His relationship with man in the garden, God has set His blessing of life and prosperity before us (Genesis 2:16–17). All He has ever asked is that we love Him with all our heart just as He loves us with all His heart.

Unfortunately, the day Adam transgressed God's commandment not to eat of the tree of the knowledge of good and evil, was the day that Adam stopped loving Abba with his whole heart. His love for God was replaced with the love of money, riches and the world, and he lost God's everlasting life, which is the true wealth of God's Kingdom.

However, God so loved the world that He gave His only begotten Son to die on Calvary's cross so that we could be restored, and return to Him as our first love. This process of God first loving us so that we could return to first loving God is what John was referring to when he said, "We love Him, because He first loved us" (1 John 4:19, kjv).

Only when we return to love the Lord with our whole heart, soul, mind and strength will the love of money—man's original sin and the root of all evil—cease to reign in us. At that point, our love of money will end and our love for God—the true wealth of the Kingdom—will be fully restored as it was in the garden before the fall.

In other words, just as the love of money overcame Adam's love of God, the love of Christ that is shed abroad in our hearts will overcome our love of money. This is when we arise in the fullness of Him to overcome the world, and the world will be forced to pass away. I believe this was the essence of what the apostle John meant when he said:

> "Do not love the world, nor the things in the world. If anyone loves the world, the love of the father is not in him. For all that is in the world, the lust of the flesh and the lust of the eyes and the boastful pride of life, is not from the Father, but is from the world. *And the world is passing away, and also its lusts*; *but the one who does the will of God abides forever.*" (1 JOHN 2:15–17)

The Restoration of All Things

I also believe that this will result in the "restoration of all things" that releases Messiah Jesus to return and once again establish His Kingdom on earth as it is in heaven (Acts 3:19–21). In other words, our return to Him releases His return to us. This fulfills the words of the prophet Malachi who said:

> "'From the days of your fathers you have turned aside from My statutes, and have not kept them. *Return to Me, and I will return to you,*' says the Lord of hosts." (MALACHI 3:7)

All we have to do is say, "Yes!"

ADDITIONAL INSIGHTS

"And those who have insight will shine brightly like
the brightness of the expanse of heaven, and those
who lead the many to righteousness, like
the stars forever and ever."
DANIEL 12:3

The Monetary Control Act of 1980

This piece of legislation is a long, complicated piece of monetary law that gave the U.S. Federal Reserve Central Bank (the Fed) unlimited power to monetize the debt of the world's financial system. A short review of several sections will help us to better understand how the financial and political elite manipulate the paper markets of the world in an effort to keep them from totally collapsing—at least for now.

Section 105 (2) gives the Fed authority to monetize U.S. Federal Debt, Municipal Bonds and *Foreign Debt*. This section allows the FOMC (Federal Open Market Committee) to expand the money supply to purchase (1) U.S. Treasury Securities, (2) Revenue Bonds, (3) Warrants with a maximum six month term that were issued by any state, county, district, political subdivision, or municipality, including irrigation, reclamation and drainage districts in anticipation of tax revenues, (4) *all obligations of foreign governments or their agencies*, and (5) *obligations of foreign banks if they are guaranteed by that bank's government*.[183]

In other words, it not only gave the Fed the authority to monetize all U.S. debt, but it also authorized it to monetize the debt of foreign governments, which makes the Fed the lender of last resort to the world.

The word on the street is that the Federal Reserve (Fed) has already used Section 105 (2) to buy back U.S. bonds from Japan and other financially troubled countries of Asia. The Fed has done this under the table, which kept the credit markets from being flooded with U.S. bonds. This temporary liquidity stabilized Asia's financial system and kept America's Bond market from crashing.

However, by doing this, the Fed has flooded the world with U.S. dollars. The thing that we must understand is that the inflationary implications of this action is beyond description, and a massive devaluation of the U.S. dollar is inevitable.

Section 103 (2)(D)(3) gives the Fed authority to drop the Reserve Requirement of U.S. Banks to 0%. At present it averages approximately 10%, which simply means that a bank deposit of $100,000 can be multiplied into 10 times that amount ($1 million) of ledger book debt and credit.

By lowering the write out to 0%, they can create as much ledger book money as they want. This money can then be loaned out wherever and for whatever purpose needed, thereby increasing the risk of an inflationary collapse in the case of a dollar sell-off.

Forward Selling of Gold

The most prolific forward selling took place in the gold market during 1997–99. Forward selling of gold is something that central banks began doing to strengthen their currencies. For example, numerous European central banks forward sold a portion of their gold in exchange for their own currencies. This artificially strengthened their currencies so they could meet the stringent currency requirements necessary to join Maastricht and the new Eurodollar. However, it also drove gold prices artificially low.

Australia worked this same type of forward gold selling scheme to keep its dollar from going the way of Asia's currencies during the collapse of that region's financial systems. During a spring 1999 trip to Asia and Australia, I had an opportunity to give a lecture on this at the Australian Stock Exchange in Melbourne. I explained that purchasing the Australian dollar with forward sales of gold was only a temporary measure that would eventually push the Australian dollar to new lows, which it did in 2000.

Gold Leasing

The most elaborate type of forward selling is gold leasing. This type of contract allows investors to lease gold from central banks and then forward sell the leases on margin in the futures market. Leasing gold involves paying an extremely low lease rate (approximately 1%) to obtain a marketable paper claim to a certain amount of tangible gold that never leaves the bank. The money from the sale is invested in the high-yield credit markets that earns between 5%–7%. This scheme pushes credit markets artificially higher and gold prices artificially lower.

During the same spring 1999 trip to Asia and Australia, I was fortunate enough to gain firsthand knowledge about the most exotic forward selling of gold leases that I had ever heard of. It was in Johor Bahru, Malaysia, where I met two French-Canadian currency traders, who attended one of my meetings. After the meeting, we had dinner together where they told me about their association in a multi-billion dollar financial scheme involving the IMF, the Federal Reserve, the government of Indonesia, and an unnamed bank in Switzerland.

In this scheme, the Federal Reserve (Fed) was leasing gold from a Swiss bank and forward selling those leases on margin in the futures market. The money from the sale was given to the IMF, who used it to bail-out some Indonesian banks that had defaulted on their loans to Wall Street banks and brokerage houses.

This type of financial scheme was particularly manipulative and has a big impact on the price of gold, the U.S. dollar, and paper investments (stocks, bonds, mutual funds, etc.).

The Price of Gold. When the gold paper claims are sold, it creates an artificial increase in the supply of gold for sale in the marketplace, which drives gold prices lower. The lower price is artificial because the gold itself is never sold. Only paper claims to the gold are sold, but the market treats the sale as though real gold were being liquidated into the market, and gold prices fall.

The U.S. Dollar. On the other side of this Ponzi scheme, the gold leases were being sold for U.S. dollars, which creates an artificial demand for the buck. This artificially drives the dollar higher, which affects foreign currencies, international interest rates, and world trade as a whole.

Paper Investments. With a fresh supply of bail-out money, Wall Street began to invest it back into the global paper markets. In many cases, Wall Street used margined investing to multiply these already multiplied dollars to purchase additional paper investments. This increase in investment dollars artificially drove paper investments to record-setting highs in 1999, only to see them crash in 2000–01.

On top of all this, lower gold prices made it less profitable to mine gold, so gold-mining companies forward sold their underground gold supplies on margin for the higher futures prices of one to three years down the road. This put money in their pockets immediately, which they invested in the high yield credit markets. It made them profitable even when gold prices were down, but also added to the artificial strength of paper and the weakness of gold.

When small investors read or watch the financial news, they see paper investments going up and gold going down, so they invest accordingly. However, if they are unaware of why this phenomenon is taking place, they are setting themselves up to suffer huge losses when the market slingshots back to reality, like it did in the beginning of 2000.

Gold Stronger Than Paper

At this point, it is very important to note how central banks are always selling gold in an attempt to strengthen paper currencies and investments as a whole. However, you never see them selling paper investments to strengthen the value of gold. This simply means that true purchasing power is not in paper money, but in the real money of the precious metals complex.

Debt-based money has no value except that which the market manipulators can con you into believing it has. If they could not use futures and options and margined forward selling to keep gold prices artificially depressed, gold would probably be trading at a minimum of five times its current price of US$250.

The Church of Laodicea
(*REVELATION 3:14–22*)

In chapters two and three of the book of Revelation, Jesus speaks to the seven churches of Asia Minor. He addresses both their accomplishments, as well as their on-going rebellion. Then He commands five of the seven churches to repent or they will not share in the great rewards of the overcomers in Jesus Christ.

Prophetically speaking, Jesus is also describing the condition of the worldwide body of Christ in the last days. He commends us for our accomplishments, but He also rebukes us for our sin, and commands us to repent.

The Church of Laodicea is unique in that it has no good deeds, but is a lukewarm church that ends up being spit out of God's mouth. Their lukewarmness is the result of their great love of money and their lust for riches, which has caused them to go after every type of money-making scheme imaginable. They have seduced themselves into believing that they are rich and wealthy and have need of nothing, but God says they are really wretched, miserable, poor, blind and naked (v 17).

The false teaching behind some of today's prosperity messages has caused many of God's people to believe that prosperity is the primary sign of spirituality. If this were true, Donald Trump, Bill Gates and Warren Buffet would all be apostles. Nevertheless, this false teaching has led many Christian believers into chasing after money-making schemes of all kinds. From investing in off-shore arbitrages that *never pay off*, to leveraged day trading in the stock market, many in the body of Christ have abandoned the principles of God's Word for the sake of gaining a buck.

Debt always seems to be their fallback position when all their other schemes fail. This continues to give them the image of prosperity, but they are really only servants to their lenders.

Since the Asian financial crisis started in July 1997, I have personally met with numerous people who have lost multiple millions of dollars during the 1997–98 crisis. One multi-millionaire industrialist from Indonesia said that before the crisis he had the wealth of seven generations, but since the crisis he has the debt that ten generations cannot pay back.

In other words, before July 1997, many in Asia considered themselves to be rich and wealthy and in need of nothing. However, when the debt bubble collapsed, it revealed that much of their wealth was only an image built on debt, and overnight they found themselves wretched, and miserable, and poor, and blind, and naked.

I believe that the most recent global financial crises have been prophetic signs that we are the end time church of Laodicea. This means that God is calling us to repent and return to His ways in the area of finance and investments—"He who has an ear, let him hear what the Spirit says to the churches" (v 22).

Real Estate and Financial Crisis

The following is a letter from a Singapore real estate investor who attended the February 1998 financial crisis conference in Singapore. I remember the incident very well because this person was totally broken before the Lord. At their request, I have kept their name anonymous, using only their initials.

Dear Pastor Norm,

I am C.T. from Singapore. You may remember me coming to you on the last day of the recent "Economic Shaking" seminar in Singapore requesting prayer. I shared about how *I had heard from God in 1996 to sell my residential property and downgrade to a fully paid smaller apartment, with money to spare for church work.* However, due to certain circumstances, I did not fully obey the Lord; as a result of partial obedience, I made certain unwise choices and ended in severe financial crisis.

I was stuck with two properties, which have depreciated greatly in value, one of which was mortgaged to the bank and the other requiring progressive payments. When the bankers started to call for cash top-up and interest rates kept going up, I was faced with a liquidity problem and finally had to sell my home at a loss. Even so, there was no buyer for nine months and I was close to facing a bankruptcy suit.

You may recall my desperate cry as I came forward in repentance for prayers. In fact, I was near suicidal in the weeks preceding the seminar. *I thank God for the teaching at the seminar, which set me free.* I also thank you for your encouragement as you stood with me in prayer to plead with God for His mercy and to provide a way out. Your affirmation that *"God sees the sincerity of my heart and will deliver me"* was most assuring and comforting. It restored my hope in Him.

I praise and thank our precious God for His faithfulness. *He sent a buyer on the day after the seminar for my home property, freeing me from the mortgage. Three weeks later, He sent another buyer for the new uncompleted apartment, freeing me from the need to get into another mortgage.* Even my Christian lawyer, who is struggling to accept the teaching on "Commercial Babylon" as I shared with him, exclaimed that it was a remarkable feat to be able to sell two properties in such a short time (bad times, too), especially when I have been attempting to do so in vain for the past nine months. It has to be God. Hallelujah!

Although I lost S$300,000 through this mistake, I am very grateful to our Father for setting me completely free from debt. Owning the roof over my head used to be my greatest desire and without realizing, it became a stronghold in my life. However, through this trial, our Lord Jesus has shown me so clearly how I had been fooled by the debt system and was a slave to the bank for the past 10 years.

Now that I am free, I have been sharing the teaching on "Commercial Babylon" with others, especially those in my church. Your website and videos provide a great resource. Once again, my deep gratitude for your faithful ministry. I trust that our God will continue to prosper your work and I am praying for you and your ministry. May the God of Israel bless you and keep you strong always.

Yours-in-Christ,

C.T.

Singapore

Executive Order 6102
April 5, 1933

By virtue of the authority vested in me by Section 5 (b) of the Act of October 6, 1917, as amended by Section 2 of the Act of March 9, 1933, entitled, "An Act to provide relief in the existing national emergency in banking, and for other purposes," in which amendatory Act Congress declared that a serious emergency exists, I, Franklin D. Roosevelt, President of the United States of America, do declare that said national emergency still continues to exist and pursuant to said section do hereby prohibit the hoarding of gold coin, gold bullion, and gold certificates within the continental United States by individuals, partnerships, associations and corporations and hereby prescribe the following regulations for carrying out the purposes of this order:

Section 1. For the purposes of this regulation, the term "hoarding" means the withdrawal and withholding of gold coin, gold bullion or gold certificates from the recognized and customary channels of trade. The term "person" means any individual, partnership, association or corporation.

Section 2. All persons are hereby required to deliver on or before May 1, 1933, to a Federal Reserve Bank or a branch or agency thereof or to any member bank of the Federal Reserve System all gold coin, gold bullion and gold certificates now owned by them or coming into their ownership on or before April 28, 1933, except the following:

(a) Such amount of gold as may be required for legitimate and customary use in industry, profession or art within a reasonable time, including gold prior to refining and stocks of gold in reasonable amounts for the usual trade requirements of owners mining and refining such gold.

(b) Gold coin and gold certificates in an amount not exceeding in the aggregate $100 belonging to any one person, *and gold coins having a recognized special value to collectors of rare and unusual coins.*

(c) Gold coin and bullion earmarked or held in trust for a recognized foreign Government or foreign central bank or the Bank for International Settlements.

(d) Gold coin and bullion licensed for other proper transactions (not involving hoarding) including gold coin and bullion imported for re-export or held pending action on applications for export licenses.

Section 3. Until otherwise ordered, any person becoming the owner of any gold coin, gold bullion, or gold certificates after April 28, 1933, shall, within three days after receipt thereof, deliver the same in the manner prescribed in Section 2, unless such gold coin, gold bullion or gold certificates are held for any of the purposes specified in paragraphs 9 (a), (b) or (c) of Section 2, or unless such gold coin or gold bullion is held for purposes specified in paragraph (d) of Section 2 and the person holding it is, with respect to such gold coin or bullion, a licensee or applicant for license pending action thereon.

Section 4. Upon receipt of gold coin, gold bullion or gold certificates delivered to it in accordance with Sections 2 or 3, the Federal Reserve Bank or member bank will pay therefore, an equivalent amount of any other form of coin or currency coined or issued under the laws of the United States.

Section 5. Member banks shall deliver all gold coin, gold bullion and gold certificates owned or received by them (other than as exempted under the provisions of Section 2) to the Federal Reserve Banks of their respective districts and receive credit or payment therefore.

Section 6. The Secretary of the Treasury, out of the sum made available to the President by Section 501 of the Act of March 9, 1933, will in all proper cases pay the reasonable costs of transportation of gold coin, gold bullion or gold certificates delivered to a member bank or Federal Reserve Bank in accordance with Section 2, 3, or 5 hereof, including the cost of insurance, protection, and such other incidental costs as may be necessary, upon production of satisfactory evidence of such costs. Voucher forms for this purpose may be procured from Federal Reserve Banks.

Section 7. In cases where the delivery of gold coin, gold bullion or gold certificates by the owners thereof within the time set forth above will involve extraordinary hardship or difficulty, the Secretary of the Treasury may, in his discretion, extend the time within which such delivery must by made. Applications for such extensions must be made in writing under oath, addressed to the Secretary of the Treasury and filed with a Federal Reserve Bank. Each application must state the date to which the extension is desired, the amount and location of the gold coin, gold bullion and gold certificates in respect of which such application is made and the facts showing extension to be necessary to avoid extraordinary hardship or difficulty.

Section 8. The Secretary of the Treasury is hereby authorized and empowered to issue such further regulations as he may deem necessary to carry out the purposes of this order and to issue licenses thereunder, through such officers or agencies as he may designate, including licenses permitting the Federal Reserve Banks and member banks of the Federal Reserve System, in return for an equivalent amount of other coin, currency or credit, to deliver, earmark or hold in trust gold coin and bullion to or for persons showing the need for the same for any of the purposes specified in paragraphs (a), (c) and (d) of Section 2 of these regulations.

Section 9. Whoever willfully violates any provision of this Executive Order or of these regulations or of any rule, regulation or license issued thereunder may be fined not more than $10,000, or, if a natural person, may be imprisoned for not more than ten years, or both, and any officer, director, or agent of any corporation who knowingly participates in any such violation may be punished by a like fine, imprisonment, or both.

This order and these regulations may be modified or revoked at any time.

God Judges Noble Prize for Economics

During 1997–98, the wicked rich continued to use derivatives to plunder the financial markets of the world. Much of this plunder took place in Russia, where they were using derivatives to prop up the ruble for the benefit of Moscow's stock and bond markets.

Most of this market manipulation came through a highflying hedge fund by the name of Long-Term Capital Management (LTCM). Unfortunately for LTCM and its creditors, the ruble continued to devalue, and they found themselves $3.5 billion short on their margin calls due Thursday morning September 24, 1998.

This brought sixteen of Wall Street's leading investment houses and commercial banks together in an emergency bail-out meeting the night before. Attendees included insider corporations such as Merrill Lynch, Goldman Sachs, Travelers Group, and J.P. Morgan & Co. Jon Corzine of Goldman Sachs told the group that the collapse of LTCM would pose a threat to the entire world's financial system. The bail-out was so urgent that William McDonough, president of the New York Fed, was forced to drop his work in London and hop a concord flight to New York in order to attend the meeting held in the Fed's Manhattan office.[184]

LTCM's collapse and consequential bailout, was a huge embarrassment for its brain trust of managing partners. The management team included John Meriwether, a famous "Masters of the Universe" trader from Salomon Brothers during the 1980s, and David Mullens Jr., former Vice Chairman of the Federal Reserve. Both are renowned financial insiders, and are masters at unrighteous wealth transfer.

Management also included Nobel laureates Myron Scholes and Robert Merton, who collaborated with Fischer Black (deceased) to create the "Black-Scholes Model For Options Trading." That's right! The very investment that broke LTCM was developed by two of its managing partners.[185]

God Scoffs at Them

I don't believe it was the elites' plan to collapse LTCM, because it was a major insider stronghold for manipulating the markets. I believe it was God making a statement in response to their conspiracy to award the Nobel Prize to a financial abomination like the Black-Scholes formula, while they were using it to financially ravage the nations. God simply collapsed the company of the men who developed it as a judgment against their dishonest gain.

King David was very clear about how God can and will deal with those that conspire against Him:

> "Why are the nations in an uproar, and the peoples devising a vain thing? The kings of the earth take their stand, and the rulers take counsel [*conspire*] together against the Lord and against His Anointed. 'Let us tear their fetters apart, and cast away their cords from us!' *He who sits in the heavens laughs, the Lord scoffs at them. Then He will speak to them in His anger and terrify them in His fury.* (PSALMS 2:1–4)

Through the collapse of LTCM, God was showing the wicked that He can intervene in their affairs and rattle their financial cage anytime He wants. In His mercy, I believe God was trying to open their eyes to the reality that even those who control the world's financial system will not escape the curse of dishonest gain.

Debt and America's Children

From cradle to grave, corporate America promotes the pursuit of material possessions and then provides consumers easy credit for acquiring them. On children alone, the retail industry spends $2 billion a year on advertisement that tells them they must have the latest toys in order to be cool and accepted by their peers.[186] In some instances, the establishment even gives them the credit to buy them with.

For example, three-year old Alessandra Scalise received a pre-approved credit card application in the mail. As a joke, Alessandra's mother, Antonia, truthfully filled out the application and returned it to Charter One Bank. Under occupation Anotonia put "pre-schooler." For income she put "nothing." She did not give any social security number, and jokingly wrote, "I'd like to have a credit card to buy some toys, but I'm only 3, and my mommy says no." In August 1999, Alessandra received her very own platinum credit card with a $5,000 limit, which was a higher limit than her mom and dad's credit card.[187]

Easy credit is also extended to college students, where 70% of undergrads own at least one credit card.[188] Average credit card balances soared 134% from $900 in 1990 to $2,100 in 1995, and are even higher today. For 5% of student debtors with balances over $7,000, the load is too much. Many have had to cut classes or drop out altogether and work a job to make their payments.

Some used student loans to pay off their credit cards, but that severely impacted their ability to pay for classes.[189]

Easy credit seems to have overcome their financial savvy. When asked how long it takes to pay off a $1,000 credit card balance at 18% interest making minimum monthly payments of 3%, only 20% guessed the answer of six years.[190] It seems to me that today's college students should have a required class on credit card debt. Better still, maybe they should read this book!

Landslide of Bankruptcies

During my April/May 2000 trip to Southeast Asia, Indonesia defaulted on a multi-billion dollar loan to the IMF. They had to call a special meeting between the government and the IMF to draw up a new agreement to roll the debt (principal and interest) over into a new loan. This confirmed that Asia's financial crisis was not over, and that the global debt problem had not been resolved. All the globalists can do is continue to extend the debt cliff that the entire world's financial system will eventually go crashing over.

When Indonesia defaulted on its loan, I heard the Spirit of God say, *"Bankruptcies! A landslide of personal and corporate bankruptcies is coming as a judgment for the sin of debt."*

As I prayed about this Word, the Lord gave me a vision of the landslide on May 28, 2000 that I shared with my church during the Sunday morning service. He fashioned it like unto the California mudslides, where people had built their homes in places with great views, but the ground was on sinking sand. When the rainstorms came, the foundations were washed away, and home after home slid over the edge, crashing down the mountainsides into the ravines below.

At this point, the Lord showed me how the sinking sand was the debt that most homes and businesses are built on. The rainstorms were the economic shakings that currently plague the financial world. These financial storms were causing the debt foundation of the world's financial system to collapse underneath them, sending millions of homes and businesses crashing over the edge into bankruptcy. The Lord spoke prophetically and said, *"This is not coming on the world only, but on many of My people. For many of My people have a great love of money and material possessions. They have used debt to acquire the material things that feed the lusts of their flesh."*

God made it clear that the coming bankruptcies were part of His discipline for the love of material possessions that had been accumulated through debt. He indicated that bankruptcy is simply the curse for trusting in debt, and that He was going to use it as a tool to get His people back on course with Him financially. He said:

"My people must repent of their love of money and the sin of trusting in debt instead of Me. Those who repent and come out from their debt, will be delivered. Those who do not will suffer the discipline of bankruptcy. This is because of My great love for them. For I discipline those whom I love. They will look like failures in the eyes of the world, but living on debt is failure in the eyes of the Lord."

The Lord also indicated that, because there was so little time left, He was going to do a quick work in the church. He said, *"My purifying fire is going to come more quickly than in times past. Rewards for obedience, and discipline for disobedience are going to manifest faster and faster as you move closer and closer to My coming.*" At this point the vision ended.

Day Trader Killings

On July 29, 1999, "day trader" Mark Barton, 44, went on a killing rampage that claimed the lives of his wife, his two children, and nine other traders at two different Atlanta brokerage houses.[191]

According to his father-in-law, Barton had lost over $150,000 of his own money and had started to raid his wife's accounts. When Leigh Ann, 26, confronted him about it, he killed her with a hammer and stuffed her body in the closet.

The next day he was barred from further transactions because his accounts did not have the necessary balances to continue trading. That was when he went home and killed his children Matthew, 11, and Michelle, 8, with the same hammer.

The next day, Barton walked into Momentum Securities carrying two handguns, a 9mm and a .45 caliber. He was heard saying, "I hope this doesn't ruin your trading day," after which he opened fire, killing five people. Then he crossed the street and killed four more people at All-Tech Investment group, another day trading firm.

The following is the text of Barton's suicide note found in his apartment along with the bodies of his wife, son and daughter, as released by Henry County, Georgia, police: [192]

July 29, 1999, 6:38 a.m.

To Whom It May Concern:

Leigh Ann is in the master bedroom closet under a blanket. I killed her on Tuesday night. I killed Matthew and Michelle Wednesday night.

There may be similarities between these deaths and the death of my first wife, Debra Spivey. However, I deny killing her and her mother. There's no reason for me to lie now. It just seemed like a quiet way to kill and a relatively painless way to die.

There was little pain. All of them were dead in less than five minutes. I hit them with a hammer in their sleep and then put them face down in a bathtub to make sure they did not wake up in pain. To make sure they were dead. I am so sorry. I wish I didn't. Words cannot tell the agony. Why did I?

I have been dying since October. I wake up at night so afraid, so terrified that I couldn't be that afraid while awake. It has taken its toll. I have come to hate this life and this *system of things*. I have come to have no hope.

I killed the children to exchange them for five minutes of pain for a lifetime of pain. I forced myself to do it to keep them from suffering so much later. No mother, no father, no relatives. The fear of the father is transferred to the son. It was from my father to me and from me to my son. He already had it and now to be left alone. I had to take him with me.

I killed Leigh Ann because she was one of the main reasons for my demise and I plan to kill the others. I really wish I hadn't killed her now. She really couldn't help it and I loved her so much anyway.

I know that Jehovah will take care of all of them in the next life. I'm sure the details don't matter. There is no excuse, no good reason. I am sure no one would understand. If they could, I wouldn't want them to. I just write these things to say why.

Please know that I love Leigh Ann, Matthew and Michelle with all of my heart. If Jehovah is willing, I would like to see all of them again in the resurrection, to have a second chance. I don't plan to live very much longer, just long enough to kill as many of the people that greedily sought my destruction.

You should kill me if you can.

Mark O. Barton

Mark Barton had a generational curse of fear that probably centered on not having enough. As a result, the spirit of fear fed his love of money and the desire to get rich quick, which fostered his lust for unjust gain through leveraged day trading. Although he had a knowledge of God, he was never taught about the destructive force of dishonest scales.

He tried to blame his demise on his wife and the brokerage firms, but it was his own greed that took him captive to sin. In the end, his love of money could not live with being financially wiped out, and the root of all evil led to the tragic deaths of thirteen people.

U.S. Banks Preparing for Collapse

The U.S. Federal Banking System has already begun to prepare for a system-wide collapse and the eventual run by depositors. The most profound evidence of this plan took place in a failed attempt by the Federal Deposit Insurance Corporation (FDIC) to limit depositor's insurance to $100,000 per person in the Bank Reform Act of 1991.

Originally, an individual could have any number of $100,000 accounts in an equal number of federal banks and be insured for the full amount deposited. This was clearly stated on the original seal of the FDIC system, which reads, "*Deposits* Federally Insured to $100,000" (see Figure 9 below). However, under the proposed 1991 legislation, depositors would only be insured for a total of $100,000 regardless of how many accounts they had in any number of banks.

Figure 9: *Original FDIC Seal*

This strategy surfaced again on January 26, 1993, when the FDIC board approved a proposal that would "seek ways to limit insured bank deposits to $100,000 per person." Six months later, depositors in Wisconsin began receiving notices in their banking statements that read:

> "Due to a change in federal regulations, beginning July 1, 1993, our funds availability policy is amended to permit exception holds to be placed on items such as cashier's, certified, teller, government, U.S. and government checks under certain circumstances."[193]

Whoever heard of anything as ridiculous as putting a hold on a cashier's check or a U.S. government check? The key is found in the wording, "exception holds" and "under certain circumstances." About the only "exception" or "circumstances" that would exist for putting a hold on a U.S. government check would be a collapse of our financial system and a government shut-down.

Another hint that banks are preparing for a run by depositors was a Texas BankOne notice, which said:

> "Texas and federal law says that all banks must notify customers with interest bearing checking accounts that the bank reserves the right to require at least seven days advance notice before you make a withdrawal."[194]

Checking accounts are *demand deposits* and money is supposed to be available to depositors on *demand*. Although banks are not currently requiring the 7 days' advance notice, "under certain circumstances" (like a run on the banking system), they can require it, thereby giving them a one-week advance notice of a run by depositors.

Figure 10: *Current FDIC Emblem*

Simply put, the FDIC is systematically passing legislation that will limit their liability when the collapse occurs. This is plain to see when you look at the current FDIC insignia the next time you are in the bank. It states: "Each *depositor* insured to $100,000" (see Figure 10 above).

The legislation is not even officially passed yet, but FDIC has already changed the words from *Deposits* to *Depositor*. They are preparing for a collapse, and so should we.

One reason that this limitation is not fully implemented yet is that the banking system has no way of keeping track of a single individual's numerous accounts. But, according to FDIC spokesman Alan Whitney, FDIC is currently in the process of constructing a computer program that will allow regulators to locate and monitor the "real time balances" of the multiple deposits a single individual might have anywhere in the U.S. banking system.[195] This is clearly a prelude to the antichrist's system of controlling and monitoring all financial activities (REVELATION 13:16–18).

End Time Josephs

There are many conflicting allegorical teachings concerning the end time Josephs. When applying Scripture allegorically to the last days, we must be very careful not to compromise the integrity of what the Word of God is saying.

End time allegories are generally stated within the Scriptures themselves. A good example of this is the parable of the tares among the wheat (MATTHEW 13:24–30, 36–43). There are many good allegorical teachings concerning this parable, but when using it to minister about the end time harvest, REVELATION 14:14–20 is the fulfillment. Any other application perverts the plan of God and causes believers to miss what God wants to do. Today, a host of inaccurate teachings about what the harvest is all about has churches trying to reap a harvest that does not exist.

End Time Anointings

The best way to allegorically apply Scripture to any time period is to apply Scriptural principle in the lives of the people living at the time. By doing this in the last days, those principles will manifest and work themselves out as end time anointings (divine enablements or gifts). In other words, there will not be an end time company of Josephs because the Scripture specifically calls for one, but because a group of individual believers will operate according to Joseph principles during the last days.

It will not be a structured network or a church organization, but anointed individuals flowing in the unity of God's Spirit under a Joseph anointing. Personally, I believe that all the anointings of God's servants of the past (Abraham, Joseph, Moses, David, Solomon, Elijah, Elisha, etc.) are designed by God to manifest in the lives of His people during the last days. It is part of the fullness of Christ and the restoration of all things.

The Joseph Anointing

When it comes to the Joseph anointing, there are a lot of confusing allegorical interpretations being applied to the end time church. Because the Joseph anointing has to do with wealth, there seems to be a tendency among some people to misapply Joseph's gifting in a way that best promotes their agenda (physical buildings, church programs, organizational networks, or business enterprises). This is generally caused by the love of money combined with the spirit of manipulation and control that permeates the church today.

We cannot allegorically twist the Scriptures to say whatever we want them to say in order to validate our program. This was actually one of the reasons why the church strayed so far from the Hebraic roots of God's Word after the second century.

Literally speaking, Joseph was ordained and anointed by God to warn Pharaoh and Egypt (leaders and their governments) that a famine was coming, and how they should physically prepare for it. Although he was ordained by God, he was empowered (authorized) by Pharaoh to do what he did. This was the same scenario that Daniel operated under in Babylon. God used both of them to affect the heart of the king so that God's purposes could be fulfilled. In both Joseph's and Daniel's case those plans were accomplished through the resources of Egypt and Babylon, i.e. the world system.

Some say that Josephs are called to set up a Christian financial system or network, which operates independent of the world system. However, Joseph's ministry did not have a system separate from Egypt's, but clearly operated within the Egyptian (world) system.

In truth, neither Joseph nor Daniel owned very much. They were predominantly managers of the government's resources. Nor did they do whatever they wanted to with those resources. In Joseph's case, both a goal and a plan were laid out before Pharaoh, and he empowered Joseph to carry them out (GENESIS 41:33–37).

Even though Joseph was given authority over all Egypt, there was no mistaking that the authority came from Pharaoh. Joseph may have manipulated Pharaoh a little, but he always understood that Pharaoh was in charge (GENESIS 46:33–47:6).

This does not mean that all end time Josephs have to work for the government, only that they must be operating within the world's system and submitted to the government's laws (ROMANS 13:1–6). Every attempt by Christians to set up some type of business organization or financial network that operates outside the world system has failed. That is because it is not part of the Joseph anointing or God's plan for the last days.

Many are confused at why Joseph would make the Egyptians store up their own grain during the "years of plenty" and then force them to buy it back during the "years of famine." Most ancient Rabbis understood that Joseph bought the grain for Pharaoh's storehouses during the seven years of plenty when prices were low. When the famine came, he simply sold grain to the Egyptian people and the nations of the world as a matter of conducting state business (GENESIS 41:56–57).

Sometimes Christians assume certain things that just don't make any sense in the real world. If Joseph would have forced the

Egyptians to buy back their own grain, they would have cursed him, but they did not. Even after they lost everything and became Pharaoh's slaves, they blessed Joseph for his forward-thinking that delivered them from death (GENESIS 47:20–26).

This principle was best expressed by Solomon when he said, "He who withholds grain, the people will curse him, *but blessing will come on the head of him who sells it*" (PROVERBS 11:26).

Joseph Was A Forerunner

Many teach that because Joseph was a type of Christ, those with his anointing will save God's people in the last days. However, when applied to the last days, Joseph fulfills more the role of a forerunner who was sent to help preserve life during the famine. This is clearly seen when Joseph says to his brothers, "And now do not be grieved or angry with yourselves, because you sold me here [to Egypt]; *for God sent me before you to preserve life*" (GENESIS 45:5).

My point is that the end time Joseph anointing is a prophetic forerunner ministry similar to that of Elijah's and Ezekiel's. In the last days, this anointing warns the people of the coming difficulties (famines, judgments, etc.) and then helps prepare them in spirit, soul and body for the day of Christ (LUKE 1:17; 1 THESSALONIANS 5:23). I believe we are quickly approaching the end of the age, and the season of the forerunner ministries is here.

Goshen

As a forerunner, the Joseph anointing provides a place that sustains the spiritual, mental and physical lives of God's people. In Egypt, this place was called Goshen. Goshen was the "best of the land," but it was also a somewhat isolated region. Joseph's purpose for putting Israel *in* Goshen was to sanctify them as far from Egyptian culture as possible. This way, they were *in* Egypt (the world) without being *of* it. This has always been God's way (JOHN 17:15).

Don't read more into this Scripture than is there. Some are teaching that Goshen literally means, "near to God" because of GENESIS 45:10, and that today Goshen represents a network, or a system, or a geographic location where large numbers of Christians will gather to be safe in the last days. Again, this type of reading into the Scripture is generally done in order to legitimize someone's program.

Goshen is the Hebrew word #1657 in the Strong's concordance, which is simply defined as: *"Goshen, the residence of the [Israeli's] in Egypt."* Goshen was given its name long before Joseph ever arrived in Egypt. It is important to note that Goshen is also called the "land of Rameses" (literally spelled Ra-ameses), which was a name given after the Egyptian sun god *Ra* (GENESIS 47:6–11).

When Joseph said he wanted Israel in Goshen, it was so the nation would be sanctified from Egypt and geographically near to him (Joseph), not Him (God). The Lord did not actually set Goshen apart and protect it until He started His judgment on Egypt through Moses' ministry (EXODUS 8:22–23). During that time, God referred to Goshen as the place where Israel was already living (v 22).

In fact, the real division was not between the land of Goshen and the land of Egypt, but between God's people, Israel, and Pharaoh's people, Egypt. Because Israel was living in Goshen, the land was protected also (v 23). God does not protect programs; He protects His people.

God's protection was supernatural and separate from any program or project. Even Joseph's God-ordained food storage was just a temporary natural project to help the people survive the famine. Although Israel eventually went into enslavement, the food storage allowed them to survive as a people until Moses brought deliverance through the blood of the Passover Lamb.

Likewise, today's Joseph projects[196] are temporary ministries designed to help God's people through the famine (difficult times) and prepare them for the Lord's coming. Eventually, a new Pharaoh will arise as the antichrist to enslave the world (EXODUS 1:8–11; REVELATION 13:7, 8, 16–18). I believe that God will supernaturally protect His people during the early stages of antichrist's rule just before the harvest, when he reaps (raptures) His people into the Kingdom of God and releases His wrath on Mystery Babylon (REVELATION 11:3–6; 14:14–20).

Therefore, today's Goshen is simply that place where God has individually called us to be. This pertains not only to our physical dwelling, but our job, our investments, our church, our spiritual growth, etc. In other words, God will provide a place where we can be sanctified *in* the world without being *of* the world, so we might disciple the nations (JOHN 17:15).

A Famine Of God's Word

A purely spiritual allegory that is very applicable for the end time church, would be that today's Josephs are called to preserve God's people during the spiritual famine of the last days. This famine is a famine of the true Word of God that seems to come during the inflationary collapse of the world's financial system (AMOS 8:4–11).

According to this allegorical application, end time Josephs are called to provide the necessary resources to teach, train, activate and release God's people to fulfill the New Covenant mandate of writing God's Torah (laws) on their hearts (JEREMIAH 31:31–33). This work is spearheaded by fulltime five-fold ministers (apostles, prophets, evangelists, pastors and teachers). However, in the home, fathers train and activate their children, and in the business world, elder marketplace ministers disciple those of like calling.

Beware Of The Nimrod Spirit

Over-spiritualizing Old Testament Scripture can be dangerous, because we might mistakenly believe that God will do something He has no intention of doing. However, being too literal can be almost as dangerous.

For example, believers who are overly literal about building any type of physical building, end time organization, or religious program run the risk of being seduced by the Nimrod spirit, which is always saying, *"Come, let us build for ourselves a city, and a tower whose top will reach into heaven, and let us make for ourselves a name; lest we be scattered abroad over the face of the whole earth"* (GENESIS 11:4).

This spirit always wants to build some religious program that becomes an idol that it can identify with. When that happens, the "builders" generally find themselves manipulating people, circumstances, money, and Scripture to keep their program (city and tower) going.

The Lord has shown me that much of the confusion in the church surrounding many of the different religious programs is coming from Him. It is the same confusion that He released on Nimrod's program at the tower of Babel, when they tried to build something that was not of God (GENESIS 11:7). It is also the same confusion that he allows to come on His people when they walk in rebellion to His commandments and execute a plan that is not His, to trust in Egypt (the world) for their safety (EZRA 9:7; ISAIAH 30:1–6 [KJV], 31:1–3).

Building the church is not about religious programs. It is about Jesus building the individual members of His body up into a temple made of living stones that are being transformed into His image (1 PETER 2:4–5; ROMANS 8:29; 2 CORINTHIANS 3:18).

Where Are All the Josephs?

Many times I hear rich people being referred to as Josephs. However, I don't believe that this is necessarily the case. Most of today's rich people are rich in debt: debt-based investments, leveraged stocks, mortgaged real estate, and empty paper promises called currency. Although they may have the image of prosperity, they are actually slaves to their lenders without even realizing it.

When the full shaking comes on the world's financial system, these will find themselves to be among the church of Laodicea, who think they are rich and wealthy and have need of nothing, but they are really poor and blind and wretched and miserable and naked (REVELATION 3:14–22). These are not the Josephs of the last days.

Joseph did not even know he was a Joseph until after his brothers came to Egypt (GENESIS 45:5–7). I believe that most end time Josephs are still in the pit or serving in Potiphar's house, where God's Word is testing them, just like it did Joseph before he came into the fullness of his ministry (PSALMS 105:16–19). When they are thoroughly tested and found to be faithful to God's ways in the small things, God will bring them out and give them charge over much (PSALMS 105:20–22; LUKE 12:35–44).

Some true end time Josephs are just beginning to emerge. Everyone who is working to build up the body of Christ and restore God's commandments in the marketplace during these last days, are end time Josephs. As we are faithful to study and teach and do God's Word (EZRA 7:10), He will send us Joseph projects that will be above all we can ask, hope or think possible.

A Delicate Balance

God is working in both the natural and the spiritual realm. Therefore, the allegorical application of any Old Testament anointings to God's people today must be done with the utmost care. I believe that there are six basic allegorical applications of the Joseph anointing that the end time church should expect to function in.

1 End time Josephs are forerunners who are called to warn government, church and business leaders that both a physical and spiritual famine are coming on the earth. This is only done as the Lord authorizes and opens the doors.

2 Joseph's primary anointing is to extract real wealth out of the world's system and judiciously channel it into the Kingdom of God as the Lord directs. The goal is to use the finances of the world system to deliver the message of the Gospel, which saves and sanctifies man from sin and the world and teaches him to obey God's commandments.

3   Josephs who are government officials influence their governments to legislate biblically based law. They also use their influence to persuade their legislature that it would be wise to build up the nation's food and other crisis supplies.

4   Josephs who are pastors of churches or one of the other five-fold ministries (EPHESIANS 4:12) are actively writing God's Torah on the hearts of the people in preparation for the spiritual famine that is coming. They also work closely with marketplace ministers to establish Joseph projects as the Lord leads. They teach their people the Joseph principle of having a physical storehouse in preparation for the physical famine and other crisis. If the Lord leads, they prepare a food storage project that will allow them to minister to their immediate community during the coming famines (ACTS 11:27–30).

5   Josephs who are marketplace ministers actively transfer the wealth of the world into the work of the Gospel. The Gospel of the Kingdom not only wins the lost, but also teaches, trains, activates and releases believers in the ways and purposes of God. In other words, they should be actively discipling others who are called as marketplace ministers and assist in financing other end time Joseph projects.

6   Individually, Josephs are writing the Torah indelibly on their own hearts, so they can spiritually feed their family and others during the coming spiritual famine. They aggressively seek the Holy Spirit for guidance on what church programs and Joseph projects to support. As the Lord leads and provides, they also provide a storehouse of natural food to sustain their families during the coming crises.

Conclusion

Being a Joseph is not a glamorous ministry like so many think it is. Most of the time you are either in the pit of preparation or battling the false accusations of Jezebel. There can be no love of money in you or any willingness to compromise God's Word. Only when you pass God's testing does He grant you this vital end time anointing.

The Woman on the Beast

The prophet Daniel says that when antichrist comes, he will worship "the god of fortresses," who is *Ala Moahozine* or "the *god* of fortifications" (DANIEL 10: 36–38). This is a direct reference to Nimrod's wife Semiramis, who ruled Babylon after his death and finished building its fortified cities.

As a result, she was deified and worshipped in a later Babylonian dynasty as Rhea, who was known as the "*goddess* of fortifications."[197] She was worshipped as Cybele in Asia, Artemis in Greece, and Diana in Rome. Diana wore a turret of the "tower of Babel" as her crown, which best reveals her origins (see Figure 11).[198]

In the last days, she is the "woman on the beast" (REVELATION 17:1–7), who symbolizes the satanic one-world religion, and her personal representative on the earth will be the "false prophet." This religious entity will support the man antichrist and work with him to complete the ancient mystery of Babylon that Nimrod started on the plains of Shinar.

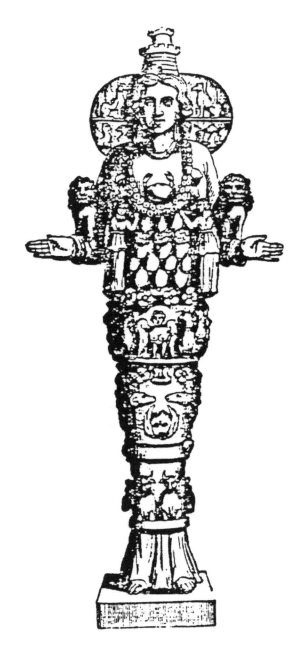

Figure 11: *Diana of Rome with tower of Babel crown;*
also Artemis of Epheseus (Acts 19:19–29)

Why the Wicked Prosper

Although the earth and everything in it belongs to the Lord, it is clear that Jehovah is not the author of our current world order of things. Remember, Jesus came to bring life, but Satan came to kill, steal and destroy, which is the hallmark of the NWO.

The Greek word for "world" is *cosmos*, and it literally refers to *the system or arrangement that is on the earth*. When Adam and Eve fell into sin, they surrendered their dominion to Satan, who began building his unrighteous political, financial and religious cosmos.

An example of Satan's authority over the world system came during the third temptation of Christ, when he offered Mystery Babylon to Jesus, if He would only bow down and worship him (MATTHEW 4:9–11). Noticeably, Jesus did not refute Satan's authority to offer it, because it was his to give. Later, Jesus confirmed this by referring to Satan as "the ruler of the world [cosmos]" (JOHN 14:30).

The "kingdom of this world" does not fully "become the Kingdom of our Lord and of His Christ" until the Mystery of God is finished and His wrath is poured out (REVELATION 10:5–7; 11:15–19). That is why the apostle Paul still refers to Satan as "the god of this world" (2 CORINTHIANS 4:4) even after Jesus had risen from the dead with all power and authority (MATTHEW 28:18). It is not that Jesus does not have sovereign authority over Satan, but that, in His sovereignty, Jesus has given Satan authority to build Mystery Babylon (REVELATION 13:2–7; 17:12–13, 17).

Therefore, until the day of the wrath of the Lord, with the exception of God's periodic sovereign interventions, Satan has the authority to use the world system to prosper and promote whoever will serve him. For example, David Rockefeller's wealth comes easy to him because he is among the financial elite who have sold out to Lucifer for a piece of the NWO pie. If Mr. Rockefeller fails to repent, his end is foreseen in the Scriptures.

King David says that this is something God's people must understand if we are ever going to stop fretting over material possessions and say, "No" to the love of money:

> "Do not fret because of him who prospers in his way, because of the man who carries out wicked schemes. … For evildoers will be cut off, but those who wait for the Lord, they will inherit the land. Yet a little while and the wicked man will be no more; and you will look carefully for his place, and he will not be there. … The wicked plots against the righteous, and gnashes at him with his teeth. *The Lord laughs at him; for He sees his day is coming.*" (PSALMS 37:7–13)

Don't worry about why the wicked prosper, but come away from the ways of the world so that you are not destroyed on the day when God judges the love of money in every man.

Mark of the Beast

In the early 1980s, globalists began applying identification and information technology to the banking process for the expressed purpose of creating a financial infrastructure that would be able to identify and track the economic transactions of everyone on planet earth. After ten years of trial and error, these two technologies came together to produce the "smart card."

More than just a credit card, smart card technology is destined to allow money (in the form of digital credits) to be stored on a computer chip embedded in the card. This system allows the amount of a purchase to be deducted immediately from the card/chip without the need for bank authorization. When balances run low, the chip can be recharged with additional funds from the holder's bank account or other sources. Funds can also be transferred back to a bank account or from one card to another at any system provider or remote station.[199]

The MARC

In August 1994, the U.S. DOD (Department of Defense) issued its new "MARC" (**M**ulti-technology **A**utomated **R**eader **C**ard) system to the 25th Infantry Division at PACOM in Oahu, Hawaii. According to an internal memo from the Pentagon, the MARC included a standard "3 of 9" bar code, magnetic strip, embossed data, printed information, an electronic (digitized) photograph, and an Integrated Circuit (IC) computer chip."[200]

Figure 12: *The MARC*

The MARC is a complete system that:

1   Serves as a meal card for all company-level dining facilities.

2   Replaces all handwritten medical records by allowing all medical information, evaluations and treatments to be read from or recorded to the MARC with a hand-held reader/ writer.

3   Records all newcomer processing, deployment orders and produces an electronic roster.

4   Provides troop manifests and monitors mobility processing and re-deployment of overseas transport.

5   Produces a cashless society on the base, where all pay and financial transactions are deposited to or subtracted from the MARC. In other words, *no one can buy or sell without their MARC.*[201]

Biometric Identification

In order to stop smart card fraud, an identification system employing the unique biology of the user had to be developed to work in connection with the smart card. This resulted in what is known as biometric identification, which was first introduced to the public in 1996 as MasterCard's fingerprint I.D. system.

In its promotion, MasterCard referred to the user's fingerprint I.D. as his "MARK," which required his hand (usually the right hand) to be scanned as part of the buying/selling process. Along the same line, most banks throughout the U.S. now require customers to provide fingerprint I.D. in order to cash two-party checks.

Another system in the growing field of biometric identification is IrisIdent developed by Sensar. According to *USA TODAY*, "IrisIdent" identifies people by unique variations in the iris, the colored ring of the eye. The iris is a reliable identifier because it does not change after age one and is even more distinctive than fingerprints, having some 400 identifying features such as contraction furrows, filaments, freckles, pits and rings.

Customers enroll in this biometric I.D. system by standing a few feet from a camera when they open a bank account. The camera takes about a minute to photograph the right iris (the left and right irises have different characteristics). The picture is converted to a digital code and is stored in the bank's computer along with the person's account number.

This type of iris scanning device uses military targeting technology that allows the camera to immediately zoom in on the right iris of any person approaching it. The camera shoots the iris several times, verifying in seconds that the pupil moves and thus it is a real eye rather than a photo. Within two seconds, the computer can compare that iris with up to 250 million data codes.

Biometric I.D. requiring people to put an eye several inches from its camera for security access control began hitting the market in 1996, and is commonplace at companies with high security protocols.[202]

Implantable Biochips

The next step toward the mark-of-the-beast system was the development of the implantable biochips for animals that are about the size of a grain of rice (see Figure 13). By injecting a biochip containing the name, address and phone number of its owner into

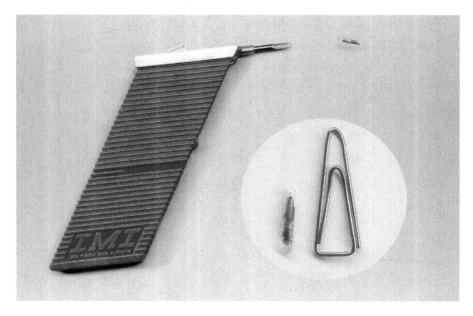

Figure 13: *Animal biochip and injector system*

an animal, the "dog catcher" could simply scan a lost pet with a Radio Frequency Identification (RF/ID) system to obtain the name of the pet's owner and reunite them.

Applying the same logic to lost or kidnapped children, biochip advocates now suggest that children be injected with human biochips that can be tracked by satellite. Many go on to argue that as long as we are putting it in, why not put all the individual's social, medical, scholastic, employment and financial information on it as well.

Ronald Kane, Vice President of Cubic Corp's "Automatic Revenue Collection Group," clearly expressed the spirit of the antichrist at work in this industry when he said, "if we had our way, we'd implant a chip behind everyone's ear in the maternity ward."[203] Believe it or not, this philosophy is catching on worldwide.

Cyborg Technology

On August 25, 1998, Professor Kevin Warwick of England's Reading University claimed to be the first person in the world to have a computer chip surgically implanted into his body. At a news conference, Warwick boasted, "cybernetics is all about humans and technology interacting. For a professor of cybernetics to become a true Cyborg—part man, part machine—is therefore rather appropriate."[204]

In the spring of 2000, researchers took cyborg technology to the next level by mating human cells with bionic chip circuitry. Although it is being promoted as a way to help man medically cure disease, this technology carries the potential of being able to genetically engineer a truly new race of cybernetic beings, which no longer exist in the likeness and image of Jehovah.

In other words, Lucifer is still trying to play God by creating a race of beings in his own image of rebellion and sin. Unfortunately, just like Adam in the garden, mankind continues to believe that he can also play God.

Patented Human Biochip

On October 30, 2000 (Halloween season), Applied Digital Solutions, Inc. (ADS), announced that it had obtained patent number 5,629,678 for its new sub-dermal implantable bio-microchip for use in human beings. It is called "Digital Angel," because it can "locate" and "monitor key body functions—like pulse and body temperature" of its users through the GPS (Global Positioning Satellite) system.[205]

ADS also said that Digital Angel will be "marketed as a means of verifying online consumer identity for the burgeoning e-commerce world."[206] This technology will eventually combine with the banking system to provide access to the user's financial assets when conducting e-commerce over the Internet.

The Rise of the Beast System

What we are witnessing is the creation of global financial transfer systems that will be the fulfillment of the mark of the beast. It will probably work very similar to the following scenario:

A person's financial information and account balances will ultimately be stored on a biochip implanted just under the skin of the right hand or the forehead. Personal identification will be determined by scanning the finger/handprint of a person's right hand or the iris of a person's right eye.

Those using finger/handprints as their personal I.D. systems will receive the implantable biochip in their right hand and buy and sell using a hand scanner that can read both the financial information and the personal I.D. simultaneously.

Those using the iris scan as their personal I.D. system will receive the implantable bio-chip in their forehead and buy and sell using a facial/head scanner that can read both the financial information and the personal I.D. simultaneously. When these two technologies are tied together, no one will be able to buy or sell without the mark of the beast (Revelation 13).

www.thebeast.com

Using this system when conducting international e-commerce and e-investing with e-cash over the World Wide Web (www) is also very significant as it relates to the mark of the beast. In fact, a sign that the World Wide Web is part of the beast system is evident in the log on letters www.

The Hebrew letter for "W" is the *vav*. It is the sixth letter of the Hebrew alphabet and carries the numerical value of six. Therefore, every time we log on to the Internet with www, we are requesting access using the numerical value 666 as it is calculated in the Hebrew language (REVELATION 13:16–18).

It's Closer Than You Think

The coming of the antichrist with his beast system is rapidly approaching, and the globalists are working over time to prepare for his arrival. I have it on good authority[207] that NWO leaders[208] are conducting high-level closed-door meetings with national leaders around the world, where they openly discuss plans to bring their nations under the control of the all-powerful NWO. These meetings are casual dress and so secret that no one is allowed to bring any recording equipment—not even pencil and paper.

Reliable sources within the international banking community[209] also tell me that there are six to eight international banks[210] that are currently forming a new global business and financial system. It is a closed "*intra*-net" system that only patrons of the banks are allowed access to. Although it is tied into the Internet (World Wide Web), it is a separate system with its own security to protect it from intruders.

It is called "Business-to-Business" and provides a complete array of standardized on-line business and financial tools to its members. To business operations, it provides what is called a "seamless system," which integrates marketing, price quotes, inventory control, billing, payment settlement, EFTs (Electronic Funds Transfers), accounting, shipping, and business analysis. It virtually does away with a company's back office, and allows an individual to run a substantial business operation from his personal computer.

On the financial side, it uses the same "seamless system" to connect personal and business operations to the global investment markets. It provides its members with worldwide banking, insurance and investment services. This system will be so powerful, that the rest of the financial and business community will be compelled to join in order to stay competitive.

Although there was no specific launch date mentioned, I believe this system will most likely be presented as the "antithesis" of the next international financial crisis.

God's Sovereignty Over Babylon

The best example of God's sovereignty over Babylon goes back to Satan's plans surrounding the ten horns of the beast. In REVELATION 17:12–17, John points out that God actually uses the NWO conspiracy as a piece of the puzzle for fulfilling His sovereign end time prophetic word:

> "And the ten horns which you saw are ten kings, who have not yet received a kingdom, but they receive authority as kings with the beast [antichrist] for one hour. These have one purpose and they give their power and authority to the beast ... *For God has put it in their hearts to execute His purpose by having a common purpose* [NWO conspiracy], *and by giving their kingdom to the beast, until the words of God should be fulfilled.*" (REVELATION 17:12–13, 17)

Right now you are probably asking how any part of the NWO conspiracy could possibly work into God's sovereign plan. I asked the Lord the same question, and He answered me with a vision.

In the vision, the conspirators appeared as puppeteers who were sitting above the earth. They were pulling the strings of men, markets, and governments as a way manipulating them in accordance with their plans. I told the Lord that I understood this part of it, but I wanted to know how His sovereign plan worked in all of it.

At that point, the Lord backed me off to where I got a wider view of the situation. From this vantage-point, I could see that the Lord was the master puppeteer seated above the conspirators, and He was pulling their strings. I could see that, although the conspirators thought they were in control, God was ultimately using their plans to fulfill His greater plan. In other words, the "Mystery of God" is greater than the "Mystery of Babylon."

Pray for Rulers and Those in Authority

All rulers are not corrupt, and even those who are, we do not curse them (EXODUS 22:28). We can confront and expose their unrighteousness, but then we are called to bless and pray for them, primarily because they need it most. Cursing them only makes things worse for them and for us. That is why Paul instructs Timothy:

> "First of all, then, I urge that entreaties and prayers, petitions and thanksgivings, be made on behalf of all men, for kings and all who are in authority, in order that we may lead a tranquil and quiet life in all godliness and dignity." (1 TIMOTHY 2:1–2)

Even though most rulers are part of the NWO and govern in a worldly fashion, believers are also commanded to submit to them (ROMANS 13:1–7). This principle was made crystal clear when Israel was taken captive back to Babylon. Through the prophet Jeremiah, God commanded them to submit to King Nebuchadnezzar and work to benefit the city:

> "And seek the welfare of the city [Babylon] where
> I have sent you into exile, and pray to the Lord on
> its behalf; for in its welfare you will have welfare."
> (JEREMIAH 29:7)

Just as ancient Babylon was raised up to deal with all the nations for their disobedience to God (JEREMIAH 27:1–17), so also Mystery Babylon is being raised up to deal with the rebellion of the nations in the last days. Even though we are not to be *of* today's Babylon, we are still *in* it, and, therefore, we must bless and not curse its leaders. This does not stop us from exposing its unrighteousness, nor does it hinder us from coming out from being *of* it. We just have to bless and pray for its rulers as we do.

The way of God's Kingdom is to love our enemies, bless those who curse us and pray for those who despisefully use us (MATTHEW 5:43–48). This releases the Kingdom of God in our lives, which brings the blessing of the Lord that makes rich and adds no sorrow.

How Wealth Does Not Transfer

There is a host of erroneous teachings about the end time transfer of wealth that has attacked the body of Christ. For example, *this wealth will not transfer all at once* like some teach, simply because the church is spiritually unprepared to handle it. Most of the church is still trying to prosper by going into debt to the beast system of fractional reserve banking and leveraged investing. Just think of how disastrous it would be if they were to all of a sudden receive massive amounts of the world's wealth.

Many have the concept that all the world's wealth is going to come into the church before Jesus returns. This misunderstanding has led many Christians to believe that every multi-billion dollar money scheme that comes along is part of God's end time transfer of wealth. As a result, they have been duped into scam after scam that promises huge sums for the work of the ministry.

The promise is always built around getting something for nothing, which feeds the love of money. Because it is supposedly ministry-based, Christians will throw Biblical principles on money and investments out the window. This unbiblical approach has actually led many believers into a myriad of get-rich-quick financial scams that are currently sweeping through the church. These schemes always promise huge amounts of money but ultimately require upfront money in the form of a processing fee or small percentage of the money to be paid in advance.

Some scams are even designed to pay off at first, which seduces the "mark" into putting more money into the scheme. Then they are encouraged to share it with others in the church as a proven wealth transfer program in order to get others involved.

These types of schemes always appeal to the desire for the large and immediate end time transfer of wealth and *never* pays off. As a result, Christian churches, businesses and individuals are being taken for millions of dollars each year, and the wealth of God's people is actually being transferred into the hands of the wicked.

Others teach that the end time transfer of wealth comes in direct proportion to the size of the offering that people sow into their ministry. Then they tell you that all you have to do is "confess" that you are prosperous. Unfortunately, kingdom prosperity does not come through confession; it comes through obedience to God's Word.

God is trying to reveal that the love of money and the desire to get rich quick is still alive in the body of Christ. In part, this is manifesting as the church of Laodicea. It is now time to repent and return to God's ways of prosperity.

False Hope From False Prophets

If Christians refuse to obey God's Word and give it time to work in their finances, they become prey for the get-rich-quick false prophets who have flooded the church. I recently heard of a well-known TV minister falsely prophesying that, if Christians who were in debt would send his ministry a $1,000 offering, God would get them out of debt.

This is the same kind of soulish prophecy that has plagued God's people for millennia (JEREMIAH 14:13–16; 2 PETER 2:1–3). You cannot give (bribe) your way out of debt by giving money to God through another man's ministry. The only way to get out of debt is to:

1   Repent for the lust of your flesh and the love of money that caused you to go into debt in the first place. Even if your debt were magically repaid, without repentance you will go right back into more debt. Some have already been through this scenario once or twice.

2   Repent for trusting in the world's debt system for your

provision instead of "Jehovah Jireh," who is the "Lord your Provider." Buying things with debt and credit is not about trusting in God; it is about trusting in the lender.

3   Start living *within* your means, even if you have to cut back on some non-essentials. Again, this calls for repentance from the lust of your flesh.

4   Start paying off your debt, even if you have to liquidate some of your assets to do it.

This is something I had to do to get out of debt myself. I sold my house and one car to pay off those loans. Then I started methodically paying off my other loans as fast as I could. As I said earlier, it took over seven years for me to get completely out of debt, but today I am the richest man I know, because I owe no man anything but to love him (ROMANS 13:8).

Missions and Financial Crisis

When Asia's currencies suddenly devalued, it caught everyone off-guard including the church. Dr. Met Castillo, Executive Director of Evangelical Fellowship of Asia Missions Commission, put it best in an article he wrote for the July/August 1998 edition of *BERITA*, a publication of the National Evangelical Christian Fellowship of Malaysia:

> "The current currency crunch that hit several countries in Asia came as a surprise, not only to the affected societies, but to the churches as well. ...
>
> "The financial crisis sneaked in like an unexpected guest, and it threw off balance the socio-economic life of many segments of society including the churches.

"As we take a look at the present situation of missions in our churches, we have a few observations to make. Some of these observations are real concern for prayer.

1 There is a marked slowing down in the momentum of sending out Asian missionaries. Owing to the drastic devaluation of the currencies of Korea and the Philippines, missionary support has become an acute problem. ...

2 As a result of the difficulty to sustain financial support, sending bodies (churches and mission organizations) are recalling home some of their missionaries. ... ."

Asia's financial crisis forced missionary organizations in the East to re-evaluate their approach to missions as a whole. Referring to something a Filippino missionary said, Dr. Castillo made an interesting and prophetic observation when he wrote:

"Perhaps, as a positive outcome of the crisis, certain sending-bodies and mission strategies are taking a serious look at the way they have been doing missions.

"'The way we do missions which is patterned after the West, and in some cases an exact copy of western systems, does not work for us any longer,' commented a Filippino mission leader. 'I refer to the support system in particular. Mission budgets are exact copy cats of western missions budgets. Budgets are prepared based on the US dollar economy, which makes it very difficult to sustain.'

"There is need to reconsider the missions financial support system. We have to take into account our Asian situation and the capabilities of our churches to sustain missions. …

"In times like these, we have to seek the presence and the mind of the Lord in prayer and in reflective study of the Word. We must be alert to how the Spirit of God will lead us to venture into new ways of doing missions in Asia."

Asia's financial collapse didn't stop the church's *desire* to give to missions. It stopped their *ability* to give to missions. I can confidently tell you that Christians in Asia were not exempt from the devastating effects of the currency devaluations. There was no supernatural protection for Christians who were invested in paper assets, and many were financially wiped out the same as everyone else.

God is not going to supernaturally protect our worldly investments when He has been warning us of an impending collapse for years. Those who want to continue the work of the great commission in spite of future economic crises, must begin to systematically come out of the debt-based paper system before God releases His full judgment on it (REVELATION 18:4).

Precious Metals in the Last Days

As a biblical response to the world's use of dishonest paper currencies, I want to stress the fact that gold and silver are mentioned 487 times in Scripture and are the only honest medium of exchange ever ordained by God for use as money.

It is clear that gold and silver are not the salvation of God, nor do they provide the spiritual riches that the Lord commands us to seek from Him. However, many times God will use the tangible assets of gold and silver when referring to the spiritual riches of His Kingdom and man's work in it (JOB 23:10; PSALMS 19:9–10; PROVERBS 8:12–21; 1 CORINTHIANS 3:12–15; REVELATION 3: 17–18).

God's message is that our spiritual walk and relationship with Him should be as pure as the honest weights of gold and silver. Therefore, I maintain that the spiritual truth behind the honest weights of precious metals is at war with the spiritual unrighteousness found in the dishonest weights of the world's debt-based paper currencies.

The acquisition of precious metals is simply the physical application of God's spiritual truth as it pertains to the investment world. My goal is not to substitute or pervert the spiritual application of the Scriptures noted above, but to apply their spiritual truths to the ongoing battle between righteous versus unrighteous mammon in the world's financial system.

World Leaders Favor Precious Metals

Even world leaders recognize the power of precious metals over paper. The best and most recent example took place during Iraq's invasion of Kuwait. When Saddam Hussein raided the Kuwaiti banks, he did not take their paper currency back to Iraq. Instead, he took their precious metals (gold, silver and platinum). That is because in times of war or financial crisis, paper money instantly becomes worthless, while precious metals maintain and/or increase in their value.

In the future, the true value of precious metals is also realized by the antichrist, who covets and eventually gains control over vast amounts of them during his reign as world dictator:

> "But he [antichrist] will gain control over the hidden treasures of gold and silver, and over all the precious things of Egypt [the world] ... ." (DANIEL 11:43)

In fact, all the wicked rich of the last days hoard gold and silver along with the antichrist, believing that it will satisfy their souls. The prophet Ezekiel points out that they do this right up to the day of the Lord's wrath, when all money including precious metals fail:

> "They shall cast their silver in the streets, and their gold shall be removed: *their silver and their gold shall not be able to deliver them in the day of the wrath of the Lord*: they shall not satisfy their souls, neither fill their bowels: because it [the love of money] is the stumblingblock of their iniquity." (EZEKIEL 7:19, KJV)

This corresponds with John's description of God's judgment of Mystery Babylon on the day of His wrath. On that day no one will be trading anything—not even gold and silver:

> "'Woe, woe, the great city, Babylon, the strong city! For in one hour your judgment has come.' And the merchants of the earth weep and mourn over her, because *no one buys their cargoes anymore; cargos of gold and silver* and precious stones and pearls and fine linen ..." (REVELATION 18:10–12a).

This is the day when *all money fails*, and the wicked rich are judged for all their unjust gain:

> "Come now you rich, weep and howl for your miseries which are coming upon you. Your riches have rotted and your garments have become moth-eaten. Your gold and your silver have rusted; and their rust will be a witness against you and will consume your flesh like fire. It is in the *last days* that you have stored up your treasure." (JAMES 5:1–3)

It is obvious that in the day of the Lord's wrath, even precious metals become worthless. The only question is: *Why do the wicked use their gold and silver in an effort to buy their deliverance up until then?* Obviously, it is because precious metals are the most valuable monetary assets on the planet during that time. In their delusion, they attempt to use money in the form of gold and silver to satisfy their souls. This becomes their ultimate stumbling block, because only Jesus can satisfy man's soul.

Precious Metals and the Love of Money

God's people must approach the ownership of precious metals according to their faith in God and His Word. For example, I keep a portion of my long-term savings in precious metals, not because I trust in the precious metals, but because I trust in the Lord who says that their honest weights won't fail during economic crises. Since a just weight is His delight, and He delights in the prosperity of His servants; I trust Him to bless my ownership of precious metals.

I also know that when the worldwide financial system collapses, that portion of my savings will be protected. As a result, my soul is at rest, and I am not watching the market every day, worried about whether the price of metals is up or down. I just continue to make wealth and consecrate it to establishing God's covenant among the nations and the rest will take care of itself (DEUTERONOMY 8:18).

However, many Christians have come to my meetings in search of just another way to make money. Once they hear the truths concerning the honest weights of precious metals, they go out and buy gold in an attempt to get rich, only to have the prices drop. Then they turn around and blame me because they lost money.

Unfortunately, they lost money because their love of money simply switched from paper investments to precious metals. Instead of manipulating the ways of the world's financial system to feed their lust for riches, they tried to manipulate the ways of God to get rich, and that will fail you every time.

Do Not Hoard Precious Metals

Although precious metals may very well produce huge profits in the face of a global economic meltdown, *please do not acquire precious metals as an investment for making money.*

Precious metals are simply the only *monetary* asset, where you can safely store wealth outside of the collapsing debt-based paper financial system.

Precious metals should be used as an insurance policy to hedge against your exposure to the world's financial system when it collapses. The goal is to preserve a portion of your savings so you can continue to finance the discipling of the nations in the midst of global economic chaos.

If you do acquire precious metals, I recommend that you follow the *Ten Rules of Precious Metals Acquisition* on page 276.

Ten Rules of Precious Metals Acquisition

by Warren Schoder[211]

Once you have decided that you are going to begin acquiring precious metals, you must evaluate your need for precious metals based on biblical truth, not on conventional economic understanding. It is important to understand that precious metals are money and not investments.

However, just like everything else, precious metals can be misrepresented, so wisdom must be exercised when purchasing them. There are ten basic rules for acquiring precious metals that will benefit you greatly:

1 Understand your objectives

Although price appreciation is probable, your primary objective for owning precious metals is asset-protection and wealth-preservation. They can be acquired easily and safely with a good basic understanding of coins and precious metals in general.

2 Acquire only low-end rare gold coins (MS-64 and below)

Because of the gold confiscation laws that exist in the U.S. and other countries, low-grade rare coins should be used as the primary form for holding gold. Although you should not look at precious metals as an investment, the confiscation laws consider them as such and exempt them from government confiscation.

Select coin grades that qualify as non-confiscatable, but do not have exorbitant rare coin premiums: AU, CU, BU, MS-61, MS-62, MS-63 and MS-64 (prices increase rapidly and dramatically above MS-64). These low-end coins not only protect your purchasing power, but are also highly liquid (marketable).

Always purchase common date coins. Don't be lured into date-specific coins with various mintmarks. These are only of concern and significance to professional collectors.

3 DO NOT acquire high-end rare gold coins (MS-65 and above)

Don't use high-end rare coins for wealth-preservation. These are investment-grade coins that focus on grade (quality) of coin plus rareness of date and mintmark. They are less liquid (marketable), and purchasing them requires a high degree of market skill that takes years to develop.

High-end rare coins have very thin markets, which sometimes makes it difficult to establish fair market value. Dishonest coin dealers can actually exercise a degree of control in these markets by buying up supplies and then setting their own prices.

4 DO NOT deplete all your cash

Our recommendation is that you limit your precious metals holdings to between 10%–40% of your monetary and investment assets. Don't put your short-term liquidity in precious metals. You don't want to be forced into selling your metals in case you need cash.

Since everyone's financial situation is different, each individual must consider the state of his own flock/ investment portfolio before acquiring precious metals or any other monetary/investment asset (PROVERBS 27:23).

5 Take direct possession of the metals

Never let the dealer safekeep metals for you and give you

a paper receipt. Getting out of paper promises and into a tangible monetary asset is why you are purchasing precious metals in the first place.

6 DO NOT place an order when you do not know the size and grade of your coins

Size and grade are critical factors in your purchase. The size dictates how much metal you are getting. The grade determines the relative value within the size.

7 DO NOT place a large order without a reliable recommendation

It just makes good sense to talk with someone who can attest to the broker's validity, pricing and service.

8 Ask about delivery time

Some companies take forever to deliver your coins. In a calm financial environment, two weeks should be the maximum time needed to complete the banking process and delivery of the metals.

However, during an economic crisis, demand for precious metals often exceeds supply. This most generally always extends the delivery times, which is why it is good to acquire them sooner rather than later.

9 Place a smaller order first

If you still have qualms about placing a larger order, place a smaller order first. By placing a smaller order, you have an opportunity to learn how the dealer operates. You also get to experience the process from placing the order to receiving the delivery.

10 Open packages upon receipt

Mistakes can be made. That is why it is necessary to open the packages immediately and verify the precious metals received against your order confirmation notice. NOTIFY THE DEALER IMMEDIATELY OF ANY DIFFERENCES. Adjustments should take place within a reasonable period following delivery. ⸺⸺⸺⸺

What Every Businessman Wishes He Could Tell His Pastor

"Dear Pastor, Please help me understand my ministry"
by Os Hillman[212]

Dear Pastor,

For some time now I have felt the need to write you this letter. Let me first say I want to thank you for what you do in helping me learn more about how I can grow in my relationship with Jesus. Your contributions to my spiritual life are so important and are greatly appreciated.

But, there are times I think that you and I may have a wrong view of each other. For instance, sometimes as a person in the workplace, I feel I may be valued only for the financial contributions I can make to the church, or the ministry position I should be filling "at church." Pastor, sometimes this makes me feel disconnected and de-valued. I know God has created me for a unique purpose, and like you, He has called me for a special ministry, but I don't always sense that it is a ministry "at church". I know God has given me Spiritual gifts and I enjoy making contributions to the church as well as to the broader Kingdom. Maybe it's just me, but sometimes I sense that my ministry at my workplace does not seem to fit the mission and philosophy of ministry in our church. And yet, I love our church and I really have a heart to serve. Can you help me understand how to reconcile these feelings? I want to give more than just money to the work of God. I want to understand and fulfill my purpose, my life ministry.

Sometimes I feel that the church spends more time equipping me to do *the church's* ministry instead of *my* ministry. God has begun to show me something very important. My work *is* my ministry. I feel that God has "called" me to this work and that I have been called as a minister in the workplace, in the same way He has called you to be a pastor. I really see it as an extension of your ministry and an extension of the ministry of our church. But, we don't often discuss ministry in this fashion. You see, I believe my ministry is in the workplace to my co-workers who have never been inside a church building. They don't really relate to anything about our church so our primary hope of reaching them is through people like me, ministering at work. I may be the only "Jesus" they ever see. Pastor, I wish you could see the people here at work. They are so open to talking about spiritual things.

As I read the Bible, it seems like Jesus spent most

of his time reaching people in the marketplace. It was obviously where he found most of the people. You have taught me to follow his example. I am finally beginning to understand what you have taught us from EPHESIANS 4: 11–12. "*And He Himself gave some to be ... pastors and teachers, for the equipping of the saints for the work of ministry*". I agree with you, that as my Pastor, God has assigned you the responsibility to equip *me* for "the work of the ministry." God has revealed to me that my greatest ministry is at work. I need your help. I need more training on my calling and on how to reach people at work. Maybe we could all use more biblical teaching about how everyone has been "called to minister" and how everyone is "on mission" at work.

Pastor, I read that many of the revivals and awakenings that have taken place started in the marketplace? Revivals such as the one that started in 1858 in New York that spread across the country began because of the faithfulness of a person in the marketplace. Near Wall Street, Jeremiah Lamphier started holding a noon-day prayer meeting in 1857. That was the beginning of the entire movement that resulted in the greatest spiritual awakening in America. Over one million people were saved. I discovered that this man's church equipped him and commissioned him to do this. Many believe the same thing is beginning today. Henry Blackaby recently wrote, "... in the Bible, most of the activity of God that changed society was done in the workplace and not in the church ... ."

I have realized that God knows the gifts He has given us, and that He wants to use them to build His Church. And Pastor, since we spend 70% of our waking hours in the workplace it is vital that we understand that God has called us to minister in the workplace. We must discern how God wants us to use all this time and workplace opportunity. We must have help understanding Biblical principles about our work and how we can relate to these spiritually hungry people in our workplace so that we can ultimately introduce these people to Jesus and to our local church. Would you consider teaching us about our "calling" in life, the purpose of work, and how faith and work cannot be separated? We need your help to understand our calling so we can all fulfill our ministries. Maybe you would even consider commissioning us for our ministries in the workplace. Wouldn't it be great if every member of our church would see themselves as "on mission" Christians in the workplace! Just think of the impact the members of our church could make.

Pastor, I know you have a desire to see our congregation reach more people. If we shared your vision and we were committed to reaching the largest mission field in the world—our workplaces—just think what could be done. Wow! What would God do through an army of excited, motivated workplace Christians accountable to the local church as missionaries? We might really begin to fulfill the great commission. Please pastor, train us and let us go! I love you and appreciate all that you do. I hope that together we can reach the people in my workplace.

Very truly yours,

Your church member

When God Allows Debt

In our financial relationship with non-believers (the world), the Lord says that His people shall be lenders and not borrowers (DEUTERONOMY 28:12). However, in relationship to believers, there is no commandment that says, "Thou shall not borrow." That's because there are certain instances where the Lord allows us to incur debt. The following is only a brief summary of the statutes and ordinaces that govern debt. Borrowing, lending and investing amoung believers will be covered in greater detail in a future book.

Lend to the Brethren Without Interest (EXODUS 22:25)

First of all, God commands that all loans among His people are to be interest free, because to charge interest makes the lender a creditor to the borrower. Ultimately all of a believer's assets are Kindom property, of which he is simply a steward. Therefore, lending to a fellow believer is like lending to the Lord, and you would never charge Jehovah interest. All who lend to the brethren interest free will be blessed by God (DEUTERONOMY 23:19-20), but all who lend at interest will be "shaken out" (NEHEMIAH 5:1-13).

Personal Loans to the Poor (DEUTERONOMY 15:1-11)

Since "the poor will never cease to be in the land," God makes provision, for those who are able, to not only give outright, but to also grant them pesonal loans (up to six years). In His sermon on the mount, Jesus refers to this statute when He conunands, "Give [outright] to him who asks of you, and do not turn away from him who wants [because of a need] to borrow" (MATTHEW 5:42).

Loans to Prevent Financial Failure (LEVITICUS 25:35-37)

When a fellow believer begins to falter, the highest form of brotherly love is for the community of believers to step in and help him from becoming destitute. The term "you shall sustian him" includes offering him a loan, investing (equity) in his business, offering him employment, and other assistance that will keep him from becoming impoverished. This is provided that his problems are not because of sin, lack of ability, etc.

Obadiah Projects (1 KINGS 18:1-15; 2 KINGS 4:1-7)

The prophet, who was the husband of the woman with the oil, was Obadiah who met Elijah on his way to see King Ahab. This Obadiah (not of the book of Obadiah) borrowed money to feed 100 prophets that he hid in caves to protect them from Jezebel. I call this an Obadiah project, and, although God released him to borrow the money, he and his family were still subject to the universal law that "the borower is slave to the lender." The way we know that God sanctioned the debt was the supernatural deliverance provided through Elisha. If God had not approved the debt there would have been no deliverance, and bankruptcy (slavery) would have been the result.

Prepare For War

"Proclaim this among the nations: Prepare a war;
rouse the mighty men! Let all the soldiers
draw near, let them come up!"
Joel 3:9

As the world heads into a global recession, it becomes increasingly likely that major wars will break out on the earth. Just as World War I, World War II, Vietnam, The Gulf War, etc. were designed, in part, to stimulate the world economy and move political boundaries, a global recession/depression would be excellent fodder for another series of global military conflicts. It would also destroy enough of the current world order so that a new world order would be the only solution for insuring mankind's recovery.

To better understand where I believe we are in relationship to the Scriptures, it is necessary to look at the first four seals of REVELATION CHAPTER 6. However, before we do this, let me say that end time Bible prophecy is never totally understood until after it happens, and sometimes not even then. We also know that no one man or ministry has the full understanding of this book. This is obvious because everyone seems to be teaching something different concerning it.

Having said this, the following are my prophetic insights into the first four seals, and why I believe that we are moving toward the fourth seal/horseman being fully opened upon the earth.

The First Seal

> "… I looked, and behold, a white horse, and he who sat on it had a bow; and a crown was given to him; and he went out conquering, and to conquer."
> (REVELATION 6:2)

The first seal releases the white horse of the spirit of antichrist, which prepares the way for the coming of the man antichrist. This is not the spirit of antichrist that has been in the world since the first century A.D. (1 JOHN 2:18), but the Nimrod/Babylonian-type antichrist. This antichrist is released at the end of the age to bring all men together under the rule of a one-world political, financial, military and religious new world order, i.e. Mystery Babylon (REVELATION 17).

This horseman could have been released as early as May 1, 1776, when Adam Weishaupt initiated the Illuminati's plan to bring about a NWO. Since then, the Illuminati has functioned unhindered within Freemasonry and numerous other secret societies, which have been behind every major war since its inception. Even the Boston Tea Party, which sparked the American Revolution, was carried out by a group of Freemasons on a break during a Masonic Lodge meeting.

As I pointed out in chapter five, the first modern day attempt at world government was through the League of Nations at the end of World War I. Having failed this, World War II followed close behind, with the more successful global government of the United Nations (UN) as the result. Since the 1990–91 Iraq War (JEREMIAH 50 & 51), the UN has risen to the forefront of political, financial and military rule on the earth. Everything points to the probability that the UN system will produce the one-world government that will be the throne of the man antichrist.

On the walkway leading up to the UN, there is even a rider on a horse with a crown on his head and an olive branch, shaped like a bow, in his left hand (see Figure 14 below). For these and many other reasons that time and space do not permit me to expand on, I believe that the first seal has already been opened and it is headquartered at the UN.

Figure 14: *Rider on a horse at the entrance of the UN Building, New York.*

The Second Seal

> "And when He broke the second seal, I heard the second living creature saying, 'Come.' And another, a red horse, went out; and to him who sat on it, it was granted to take peace from the earth, and that men should slay one another; and a great sword was given to him." (REVELATION 6:3–4)

The second seal releases the red horse of war. This is not the regular type of war, but planned wars since 1776 that have worked hand in hand with the spirit of antichrist of the first seal to bring the nations together under a Nimrod-type NWO.

As stated earlier, since the Iraq War, the UN has been dictating its new global policies to sovereign nations. Countries that resist suddenly experience a financial crisis or an internal civil war that only the UN Peacekeepers and the International Monetary Fund (IMF) can solve.

I also believe that the "*great sword*" carried by this horseman is speaking about the development of our modern day weapons of mass destruction (nuclear, chemical and biological). If this view is accurate, this seal could have been opened with the chemical weapons of World War I, but definitely refers to the nuclear bomb that was released on Japan at the end of World War II.

The Third Seal

> "And when He broke the third seal … I looked, and behold, a black horse; and he who sat on it had a pair of scales in his hand. And I heard as it were a voice in the center of the four living creatures saying, 'A quart of wheat for a denarius [a day's wages], and

three quarts of barley for a denarius; and do not harm the oil and the wine." (REVELATION 6:5–6)

The third seal releases the black horse of famine. Again, this is not referring to normal famines that are the result of war, plagues, drought or other natural disasters, but famines that are artificially induced according to the New World Order of things.

Note that this horseman emphasizes the use of scales in relationship to the high cost of food. In John's time, scales where used to measure out grain to determine the price that was paid for it. As I have already pointed out, if they were dishonest scales, it destroyed the value of the money, which raised, then collapsed the value of money along with the price of food.

Like the prophet Amos (AMOS 8:4–10), I believe this is what John saw in the scales carried by the third horseman. This is in harmony with the fact that the dishonest scales of today's FRB system have destroyed the value of the currencies in most of the crisis countries. In many of these countries, a day's wages is less than $2 U.S.

The Asian Development Bank just recently issued a report that described Asia's poverty problem as follows:

> "About *900 million people* in Asia—from Fiji in the south to Mongolia in the north and as far west as Kazakhstan—*live on less than $1 per day*, twice as many as in the rest of the developing world. Almost *two billion Asians live on less than $2 per day*."[213]

It is important to note that a quart of wheat contains 2,000 life-sustaining calories, and represents a one-day supply of food. Therefore, wages of $1 or $2 per day is just enough to buy one day's food supply, which would seem to be a manifestation of the third horseman.

I believe this horseman also refers to today's man-made famines in Africa and other places, which are not the result of food shortages. Ample food has been delivered to these countries, where it lies rotting on the docks, because the NWO's depopulation policies have kept it from being distributed to the people. Publicly stated NWO policy is to reduce the world's population by 1 to 2 billion people within the next ten years. Artificially induced famine would appear to be one of the tools that is being used to carry out this policy.

The Fourth Seal

> "And when He broke the fourth seal, I heard the voice of the fourth living creature saying, 'Come.' And I looked, and behold, an ashen horse; and he who sat on it had the name Death; and Hades was following with him. And authority was given to them over a fourth of the earth, to kill with sword and with famine and with pestilence and by the wild beasts of the earth."
> (REVELATION 6:7–8)

The fourth seal releases the ashen horse of Death, which produces Hades (Hell) on earth. This combination kills 25% (1.5 billion) of the world's population through sword, famine, pestilence, and wild beasts.

The sword is undoubtedly the "Sword of Islam" that moves beyond today's localized small-scale terrorism into large-scale international terrorism, and couples it with regional ethnic, religious and political wars. This is different than the red horse wars of the second seal, because they are not in a controlled theater, but are more widespread and random throughout many nations of the world.

For example, the "Sword of Islam" has carried out terrorist attacks throughout Israel and the West with threats of more and larger attacks in the future. This has put America on terrorist alert, where the FBI is currently conducting terrorist recognition and prevention training with local law enforcement of high-risk areas. The premise behind the training is not a matter of *if* terrorists will strike, but *when* terrorists will strike.[214]

Bio-chemical or nuclear terrorism against countries with nuclear weapons will most likely lead to a response in kind. For example, if Israel suffers a bio-chemical or nuclear terrorist attack that can be traced back to any of its Arab neighbors, it will undoubtedly respond with the full weight of its nuclear capabilities. This would undoubtedly lead to a regional nuclear and bio-chemical war in the Middle East, thus fulfilling the regional war(s) prophesied in JEREMIAH 49, EZEKIEL 25 and ISAIAH 17, in which Israel completely destroys her Arab enemies.

Other major hotspots capable of producing regional wars are Russia and the Muslim breakaway republics, the Yugoslavia region, India and Pakistan, China and Taiwan, and the Korean peninsula.

Famine will undoubtedly result from this type of large-scale terrorism and regional wars. This will be real famine as opposed to the artificially produced famines like those of the third seal. Currently, when a disaster happens, the nations come together and respond with food and other aid. However, when this seal is fully released throughout the nations, they will be so busy taking care of their own crisis that they would not be able to respond to each other's, and famine will be widespread.

Pestilence from widespread war and famine will produce contagious plagues that will be spread among the population. There is also planned pestilence, i.e. modern chemical weapons will be used to terrorize the civilian population as they were in the subways of Japan.

Wild Beasts are most likely not lions and tigers and bears, Oh my! During my spring 1999 Asia trip, I met with two high-ranking government officials from two different countries. I shared with both of them, in two separate meetings, about how I felt that the fourth seal was preparing to be opened more fully. When we discussed what the *wild beasts* might be, they both agreed that if lions and tigers and bears were roaming the streets attacking people, their military would simply shoot them. Therefore, we all concluded that these beasts had to be something else.

I explained that the Greek word for beast is *therion,* and it is defined as "a dangerous animal, hence a *little beast, little animal.*"[215] I explained how these "wild (little) beasts" are most probably the micro-viruses contained within today's man-made biological weapons as well as in the chemical weapons of mass destruction. When I shared this revelation, both of the Asian officials agreed that this was probably what the apostle John was talking about.

There is also much documented evidence that AIDS and Ebola are man-made viruses that evolved during cancer virus experiments in which monkeys were infected with viral genes from other animals. This produced a deadly effect that was exploited by the U.S. military complex to be used as biological weapons.

Tests of the short and long-term effects of the AIDS virus are currently being conducted throughout the populace of Africa and among the homosexual and drug addicts around the world.[216]

It is also interesting that numerous medical journals and news reports have actually projected that AIDS alone has the capacity of destroying a quarter of the world's population, just as the fourth seal prophesies.

[Author's post 9/11 note: This book was originally written and published before the 9/11 terrorist attack on the World Trade Center in New York. Consequently, 9/11 was most probably the opening of the fourth seal, where the "Sword of Islam" moved beyond the "localized small-scale terrorism into large-scale international terrorism" as predicted on pages 290-291. It is also interesting to note that the ensuing "War on Terrorism" engages nations that make up roughly one-fourth of the earth. If this is an accurate assessment, and I believe it is, then we have entered the days of the fourth seal, and the ashen horse of "Death and Hades" is now galloping among the nations.]

Birth Pains

Upon close examination, it appears that the seals of Revelation chapter 6 correspond with the events that Jesus said would take place just prior to His return (MATTHEW 24:3–8). He likened them to the birth pangs of a woman in labor, with the contractions coming more frequently and with greater intensity the closer she gets to the child (Messianic age) being born. This means that these events will continue to take place closer together and with greater intensity until they become like popcorn going off. Therefore, we must work with the Lord to sanctify ourselves in spirit, soul and body until the day of His coming, because "he who endures to the end shall be saved" (1 THESSALONIANS 5:23; MATTHEW 24:13).

Epilogue

"The Lord is not slow about His promise, as some
count slowness, but is patient toward you,
not wishing for any to perish but for
all to come to repentance."
2 PETER 3:9

I believe the evidence in this book makes it clear that there is no hope for the world system, and that the only hope for mankind is the literal, physical return of Jesus Christ as King of kings and Lord of lords. The only question is, are you spiritually prepared to stand before Him upon His return or at your death—whichever comes first?

You may be someone who has been financially devastated as a result of playing around in Commercial Babylon, and your life is in the dumps. If so, Jesus is the only one who can forgive you and restore you, but you must repent of your sins and submit to His Lordship.

Or, you may be someone who has been successful in your career and financial endeavors until now, but you can see the handwriting on the wall. You don't want to serve the beast anymore, but you don't know where to go from here. If you truly turn to Jesus and give your life to Him, He will show you the way, because He is the Way, the Truth and the Life (JOHN 14:6).

You may even be one of the wicked among the financial and political elite who have played a role in creating the NWO beast system. However, now you realize that the hope you once had in the world system is dust in the light of God's prophetic word. You want Jesus to save and deliver you, but you are afraid that your sin is so great that you can't be forgiven. Let me assure you that Jesus died specifically for you, and He has been waiting for you to turn from your ways and ask Him to come into your life for a long time.

It doesn't make any difference who you are or what you've done, because "God so loved *the world*, that He gave His only begotten Son, that whoever believes in Him should not perish, but have eternal life" (JOHN 3:16).

Because time is growing short, no one can afford to pass up an opportunity to receive Jesus Christ as their personal Savior. If you are not saved according to JOHN 3:3, but you want to be, then pray this prayer:

> Dear Jesus, I recognize that I am a sinner who is lost and does not know you. I realize that the wages of sin is death, and that forgiveness and salvation come only through faith in your atoning death on the cross. Therefore, by faith I receive your forgiveness and ask that you come into my life and save me at this very moment.

Now, according to Your Word, I believe that I am born again and have eternal life in You. I ask that You baptize me in your Holy Spirit and teach me your ways, and I will serve You for the rest of my life. In Jesus' Name, Amen.

Name:_____

Date:_____

If you prayed this prayer from your heart, you are now a child of God who has entered His Kingdom as a new creature in Christ. Your name is now written in the Book of Life, and all heaven is rejoicing over your salvation.

Just as it has been written in heaven, sign your name and the date of your salvation in the space provided above and save it as a memorial to you and your family.

Please, contact me through our website "ascensionministries. net" and tell me about your conversion so that I can rejoice with you.

Last Word

As you see the world getting worse and worse in terms of the fulfillment of Bible prophecy, do not be afraid. Just trust in the Lord with all your heart and remember that Jesus said:

> "These things I have spoken to you, that in Me you may have peace. In the world you have tribulation, but take courage; I have overcome the world." (JOHN 16:33)

Endnotes

1   Strong's Hebrew and Greek Concordance, Hebrew word #8636 *tarbiyth*, #7235 *rawbaw*.

2   Strong's Concordance, #3701 *keceph*.

3   U.S. Constitution, Article I, Sections 8 & 10.

4   Ibid.

5   Egon Caesar Corti, *The Rise of the House of Rothschild*, p 8.

6   James Wardner, *The Planned Destruction of America*, p 37.

7   Dr. Larry Bates, *The New Economic Disorder*, p 140–141.

8   Carroll Quigley, *Tragedy and Hope: The History of the World in Our Time*, pp 48–49.

9   J. A. Thauberger, *Billions for the Bankers*, pp 28–29.

10   Quigley, *Tragedy and Hope*, p 49.

11   Strong's Concordance, *neshek* 5392; *neshak* 5391.

12   My ability to do this was only by God's enabling grace through Jesus Christ and His death on the cross, but I had to say, "Yes" and commit myself to His ways.

13   *Webster's II New College Dictionary*.

14   Federal Reserve-Money Stock and Debt Measures, June 15, 2000.

15   Bates, *The New Economic Disorder*, p 141.

16   Quigley, *Tragedy and Hope*, p 51.

17   Gary Kah, *Enroute to Global Occupation*, p 107.

18   Adam Weishaupt quoted by Clarence Kelly in *Conspiracy Against God and Man*, p 200.

19   William Still, *New World Order: The Ancient Plan of Secret Societies*, p 81.

20   Ralph Epperson, *The New World Order*, p 106.

21   *Encyclopaedia Britannica*, 15th Edn, s.v. "Illuminati," quoted by William Still, *New World Order: The Ancient Plan of Secret Societies*, p 69.

22   Adam Weishaupt, quoted by John Robison, *Proofs of a Conspiracy*, p 123.

23   Winston Churchill, *Illustrated Sunday Herald*, February 8, 1920, quoted by Ralph Epperson, *The New World Order*, pp 104–105.

24   Adam Weishaupt, quoted by John Robison in *Proofs of a Conspiracy*, p 123.

25   Still, *New World Order*, p 74.

26   Quigley, *Tragedy and Hope,* p 950.

27   Robison, *Proofs of a Conspiracy*, p 91.

28   Quigley, *Tragedy and Hope*, p 950.

29   Cleon Skousen, *The Naked Capitalist*, pp 28–31; FYI: Bill Clinton is a Rhodes Scholar.

30   Quigley, *Tragedy and Hope*, p 950.

31   Ibid, p 952.

32   Council on Foreign Relations Handbook of 1936, reprinted by Kah, *Enroute to Global Occupation*, p 30.

33   Ibid.

34   Ibid, pp 30–31.

35   Ibid p 50.

36   Kah, *Enroute to Global Occupation*, pp 38–39.

37   Skousen, *The Naked Capitalist*, p 108.

38   Kah, *Enroute to Global Occupation*, pp 40–41.

39   Mihajlo Mesarovic and Eduard Pestel, *Mankind at the Turning Point,* pp 161–162; quoted by Kah, *Enroute to Global Occupation*, pp 40–41.

40   Kah, *Enroute to Global Occupation*, pp 44–49.

41   Skousen, *The Naked Capitalist*, p 1.

42   Ibid.

43   Ibid.

44   Quigley, *Tragedy and Hope*, p 954.

45   J. Edgar Hoover quoted in "The World in Collusion," *The Elijah Report*, March/April 1997, pp 1–11.

46   Adam Weishaupt, quoted by John Robison, *Proofs of a Conspiracy*, p 4.

47   Bates, *The New Economic Disorder*, p 59.

48   *Webster's II New College Dictionary*, "dialectic."

49   James P. Warburg quoted in *Monetary and Economic Review*, March 1993, p 1.

50   "State of the Union—Bush Seeks to Inspire Support for His Persian Gulf Mission," *Congressional Quarterly*, February 2, 1991, pp 308–310, quoted by Kah, *Enroute to Global Occupation*, p 63.

51   David Rockefeller speaking at the June 1991 Bilderberg meeting, quoted in *The Coming Wealth Transfer: Window to the 21st Century*, a World Research Report, p 104.

52   Quigley, *Tragedy and Hope*, p 324.

53   U.S. Constitution, Article I, Sections 8 & 10.

54   Skousen, *The Naked Capitalist*, pp 15–16.

55   G. Edward Griffin, *The Creature From Jekyll Island*, p 5.

56   Frank Vanderlip, "Farm Boy to Financier," *Saturday Evening Post*, February 9, 1935, p 25, quoted in *The Naked Capitalist*, p 17.

57   Skousen, *The Naked Capitalist*, p 21.

58   William Guy Car, "Pawns in the Game," p 155 quoted by James W. Wardner, *The Planned Destruction of America*, p 37.

59   Shearson-Lehman Brothers, *Dictionary of Financial Investment Terms*, p 152.

60   Ibid p 272.

61   *The McAlvany Intelligence Adviser,* December 1997.

62   Ibid, *Dictionary of Financial and Investment Terms*, p 146.

63   Beth Belton, *USA TODAY,* Financial Section, October 15, 1997.

64   Ibid.

65   "Beleaguered Giant: As Derivatives Losses Rise, The Huge Industry Fights to Avert Regulation," *The Wall Street Journal*, August 24, 1994, p A1.

66   *Monetary and Economic Review,* October 1994, pp 10–11.

67   Ibid.

68   *U.S. General Office of Accounting Monthly Report,* May 1994.

69   Ibid, "Beleaguered Giant: As Derivatives Losses Rise, The Huge Industry Fights
      to Avert Regulation," *The Wall Street Journal,* August 24, 1994.

70   Ibid.

71   "Derivatives Force First Closure of Money Fund," *The Wall Street Journal,*
      September 28, 1994.

72   "Thais learn hard lesson," *USA TODAY,* November 17, 1997, p B1.

73   "Bank of Montreal's Harris Unit Records $51.3 Million Loss From Derivatives,"
      The Wall Street Journal, June 27, 1994, p A4.

74   Ibid.

75   "Insurance Crisis Fallout," *Monetary and Economic Review,* August 1991, p
      12.

76   Ibid.

77   Ibid.

78   *Monetary and Economic Review,* October 1993, p 9.

79   Republican Jim Saxton (R., NJ) quoted in "A Raid on America's Pension Funds,"
      The Wall Street Journal, September 29, 1994.

80   CNN TV report quoted in *Monetary and Economic Review,* October 1993, p
      9.

81   "Nasdaq Falls to Nearly 50% Below Record," *The Wall Street Journal,*
      December 1, 2000, p C1.

82   "Web retailer eToys to file for bankruptcy with $274 million in liabilities," The
      Canadian Press via COMTEX Internet report, 02/26/01.

83   "When the Bubble Bursts," *The Wall Street Journal,* August 18, 1999, p A18.

84   *Encyclopaedia Britannica,* Volume 2, p 971.

85   Ibid p 962.

86   *The Travels of Morco Polo,* Book 2, Chapter 24.

87   Alan Greenspan, *The Objectivist,* quoted in *The McAlvany Intelligence Advisor,*
      p 1.

88   "Legal License to Steal," *Monetary and Economic Review,* March 1994, p 6.

89   Thomas Jefferson, quoted in *The Coming Wealth Ttransfer,* p 73.

90   Michel Chossudovsky, Professor of Economics at the University of Ottawa,
      paper entitled "The Global Financial Crisis" posted on the Internet.

91   "Sudden Targets: Foreigners Snap Up Mexican Companies; Impact Enormous,"
      The Wall Street Journal, September 30, 1997, p A1, A12.

92   *USA TODAY,* December 9, 1997, p 3B.

93   *Monetary and Economic Review,* March 1993, p 5.

94   *USA TODAY,* "For Malaysia, leaders' talk may not be cheap," October 8, 1997,
      p 5B.

95   Zbigniew Brezezinski at Mikhail Gorbachev's "State of the World Forum,"
      October 1996, quoted in "The World in Collusion," *The Elijah Report,* March/
      April 1997, pp 1–11.

96　Kah, *Enroute to Global Occupation*, pp 40–41.

97　Ibid.

98　Constitution for the Federation of Earth, Article II, Paragraphs 5 & 7.

99　"Deal will stop 'spread of financial devaluation,'" *USA TODAY*, February 1, 1995, p 2A.

100　Robert Rubin, quoted in *The Wall Street Journal*, February 6, 1995.

101　IRS Letter to a U.S. Corporations.

102　"A New North America," *The Los Angeles Times*, reprinted in *The Denver Post*, August 30, 1992, pp 22A–23A.

103　Ibid.

104　Ibid.

105　Ibid.

106　Ibid.

107　Ibid.

108　The goal of the CFR and other RTGs is best described by Admiral Chester Ward, a former Judge Advocate General (J.A.G.) for the Navy and member of the CFR for 16 years. It was his expert opinion that the CFR's sole existence was for the "… purpose of promoting disarmament and submergence of U.S. sovereignty and national independence into an all-powerful one-world government." He continued to say that, "this lust to surrender the sovereignty and independence of the United States is pervasive throughout most of the [CFR] membership … The majority visualize the utopian submergence of the United States as a subsidiary administrative unit of a global government … ." Notice that Admiral Ward points out that the CFR plans to bring the U.S. in "as a subsidiary administrative unit of a global government … ." This is called Regionalization, and it coincides with the plans of the other RTGs.

109　Members of ASEAN consist of Brunei, Cambodia, Indonesia, Laos, Malaysia, Myanmar, the Philippines, Singapore, Thailand and Vietnam.

110　"Coin of the Regional Realm: Welcome the 'Asian,'" *The Asian Wall Street Journal*, February 18, 1998.

111　Henry Morgenthau, quoted in *Monetary and Economic Review*, March 1993, p 1.

112　John Maynard Keynes, quoted in the *The McAlvany Intelligence Advisor*, April 2000, p 10.

113　"Under Boom Economy, Strain Over Debt," *The Wall Street Journal*, August 17, 1999; quoted in *The McAlvany Intelligence Advisor*, March, 2000, p 3.

114　SMR Research Corporation statistics reported in "Bankruptcy Pace For Individuals Is Accelerating," *The Wall Street Journal*, December 1, 2000, p B1.

115　*The McAlvany Intelligence Advisor*, February 2000, p 20.

116　Ibid.

117　"Debt, bankruptcies causing concerns about economy," *USA TODAY*, October 25, 2000, p 9A.

118 Ibid; See also "Credit Tightens, Posing A Risk to Weak Firms And Maybe Economy," *The Wall Street Journal*, December 1, 2000, p A1.

119 "Debt, bankruptcies causing concerns about economy," *USA TODAY*, October 25, 2000, p 9A.

120 *The Economist*, October 2000, p 65–68.

121 Glass-Steagall Act of 1933 authorized deposit insurance and forbid commercial FRB banks from owning insurance or securities companies. This prohibited commercial banks from participating in insurance and investment banking activities, i.e., underwriting insurance policies or investments securities (stocks, bonds, etc.). It was designed to separate the three major pools of money, so in case one experienced a crisis like 1929 the others would be insulated. In the mid-1980s, banks began to challenge Glass-Steagall by creating holding companies that owned all three. This allowed banks to market insurance and investments offered by the other companies within the holding company. Today, the majority of Glass-Steagall has been repealed, which means we are right back in the same situation we were in 1929.

122 *The McAlvany Intelligence Advisor*, March, 2000, p 7.

123 "As Japan Economy Sags, Many Favor Collapse," *Washington Post Foreign Service*, March 9, 2001, p A01.

124 Ibid.

125 Ibid.

126 "Japan may sell bonds," *The Wall Street Journal*, June 24, 1997, p C1.

127 Treasury Department website at "www.publicdebt.treas.gov/opd/opdpdpdt. htm"; *The McAlvany Intelligence Advisor*, March 2000, p 3.

128 Martin Khor, "Baring and the Search for a Rogue Culprit," World Economics, No. 108, 1–15 March 1995, p 10, quoted by Michel Chossudovsky, paper entitled "The Global Financial Crisis" posted on the Internet.

129 *The McAlvany Intelligence Advisor*, March 2000, p 5.

130 Ibid.

131 Interest rate swaps are the simultaneous buying and selling (swap) of interest rate sensitive securities on margin. One order is generally contingent on the other, and a change in interest rates is stipulated as the condition to execute the order.

132 *Dictionary of Finance and Investment Terms*, Barron's Educational Series, Inc.; Federal Reserve-Money Stock and Debt Measures, June 15, 2000.

133 *United Nations Report* on Debt-Equity Swaps and Development, March 1993, p 1.

134 John Daunton, *The New York Times*, "In Decolonized, Destitute Africa, Bankers Are the New Overlords," June 20, 1995.

135 "Foreigners Snap Up Mexican Companies; Impact Is Enormous," *The Wall Street Journal*, September 30, 1997, p A1.

136 Ibid.

137   "The Asian Crisis: How it started, what happens next," *USA TODAY*, December 9, 1997, p 3B.
138   "Banks may profit from Asia's woes," *USA TODAY*, November 28, 1997, p B1.
139   David Morgan, *The Ashville Tribune*, Special Report on the EPA including quotes from a WTZY radio interview posted on the Internet.
140   Ibid.
141   "War on People," *Monetary and Economic Review*, May 1996, p 15.
142   Ibid, *The Ashville Tribune*.
143   "Public Land Statistics 1992," U.S. Department of the Interior, Bureau of Land Management, Volume 177, September 1993, p 55, quoted by William Perry Pendley, *War on the West: Government Tyranny on America's Great Frontier*, pp 124–125, 273. Pendley also notes the number of ACECs and their total acres are as follows: CA: 112 areas– 937,714 acres; UT: 41 areas–911,420 acres; OR: 104 areas–514, 325 acres; ID: 65 areas–505,438 acres; WY: 31 areas–493,860 acres; CO: 41 areas–387,780 acres; AZ: 33 areas–305,581 acres; NM: 58 areas–258,906 acres; NV: 7 areas–134,236 acres; and MT: 5 areas–38,328 acres.
144   Ibid.
145   Ibid, "Public Land Statistics 1992," U.S. Department of the Interior, Bureau of Land Management, p 5, quoted by Wlliam Perry Pendley, *War on the West: Government Tyranny on America's Great Frontier*, pp 8, 234. Pendley notes that by 1992, Uncle Sam had come to own more than 80% of Nevada; over 60% of Idaho and Utah; as much as 50% of Oregon, Wyoming, Arizona, and California; over 33% of Colorado and New Mexico; and 25% of Washington and Montana. On the county level, the government has virtually taken over 97% of Teton County, Wyoming, 84% of Kane County, Utah, 84% of Coconino County, Arizona and 78% of Lincoln County, Montana.
146   Ibid, Pendley, *War on the West: Government Tyranny on America's Great Frontier*, p 68.
147   "Clinton's designation of monuments are likely to stand," *The Washington Post National Weekly Edition*, February 26–March 4, 2001.
148   Ibid, *The Ashville Tribune*.
149   "War on People," *Monetary and Economic Review*, May 1996, p 15.
150   "Biodiversity Treaty: Blue print for the 'Green War,'" *Monetary and Economic Review*, January 1996, p 6.
151   "The Reorganization of Society," *eco•logic Magazine*, September/October 1995, p 4, reported in "The War on People," *Monetary and Economic Review*, May 1996, p 15.
152   Jan Tinbergen, "Global Governance for the 21st Century," *The UN's 1994 Human Development Report*, p 88.
153   Ibid, p 6.
154   Ibid, Tinbergen, *1994 Human Development Report*, p 88.

155 The New World Central Bank will most likely be a revamped IMF that merges with today's World Bank.

156 *1994 Human Development Report*, p 84.

157 Ibid.

158 "World financial crises could become common," *The Los Angeles Times*, reprinted in the Ft. Collins, Coloradoan, February 3, 1995.

159 "Financial system is at fault, says Soros," *The Business Times*, November 11, 1998, p 14. Also see December 31, 1997 Reuters report which states: "Financier George Soros said Wednesday the international financial system was suffering a systemic breakdown thanks to the crisis in Southeast Asia ... the financial community should grab the opportunity to set up a new global authority to guarantee international loans for a fee. What started out as a minor imbalance (in Asia) has become a much bigger one that threatens to engulf not only international credit but also international trade."

160 Ibid.

161 "Sakakibara suggests new world monetary system," *Reuters Wire Service*, March 2, 1998.

162 CNN TV news report, November 5, 1998.

163 CNN TV news report, November 2, 1998.

164 The WCPA's plan for an "Earth Financial Credit Corporation," p 1; see also the WCPA's Constitution for the Federation of Earth (Article 8, Section G "The World Financial Administration") p 15.

165 Ibid.

166 *Webster's* defines "inflation" as "the increase in the quantity of money or credit or both that causes a sharp and sudden drop in its value and a rise in prices."

167 Global Resource Bank General Prospectus. Address: 126 SE 3 St., Hallandale, FL 33009 USA; Global Resource Bank advertisement in *The Economist*, April 30–May 6, 1994 Edition.

168 Global Resource Bank Charter, Article 3.

169 Global Resource Bank General Prospectus.

170 *1994 UN Human Development Report*, p 18.

171 *Bio-Science Report*, quoted in *The Ithaca Journal* and reprinted in *USA TODAY*. Copy of article only; dates unavailable.

172 Not specifically proposed by the GRB, but is part of the U.N.'s plan. When all the different proposals are merged into one, private property will be abolished.

173 Ibid, General Prospectus of the Global Resource Bank; Global Resource Bank advertisement in *The Economist*, April 30–May 6, 1994 Edition.

174 Antichrist's role primarily has to do with bringing the spiritual and political sides of Mystery Babylon together, which will be the subject of a future book.

175 "Halim Considers Delisting Renong," *The Asian Wall Street Journal*, October 25, 2000, p 1.

176 Within the parable of the talents there is a biblical investment strategy we call an "Initial Kingdom Offering" (IKO) that will be discussed in a future book.

177 Alan Greenspan, "Gold and Economic Freedom," quoted in "Toward Global Financial Turmoil: The War on Gold," *The McAlvany Intelligence Advisor*, January 1998, p 1.

178 Strong's Hebrew and Greek Concordance, Hebrew word #779 *awrar*.

179 Also note that in Malachi chapter 3 God sends the forerunner anointing of Elijah to purify the sons of Levi, so that "they will present to the Lord offerings in righteousness."

180 Strong's Hebrew and Greek Concordance, Hebrew word #2742 *charuwts*, Greek word #4710 *spoude*.

181 Strong's Hebrew and Greek Concordance and the Online Bible Thayer's Greek Lexicon and Brown Driver & Briggs Hebrew Lexicon. Hebrew word #4399 *mel-aw-kaw*; from the same as OT: 4397; properly, deputyship, i.e. ministry; generally, employment (never servile) or work (abstractly or concretely); also property (as the result of labor): KJV—business, + cattle, + industrious, occupation, (+~pied), + officer, thing (made), use, (manner of) work ([~man], ~manship). Occupation, work, business, property, work (something done or made), workmanship, service, use, public business, political, religious.

182 Strong's Hebrew and Greek Concordance Hebrew word #4397 *mal'ak*; from an unused root meaning to despatch as a deputy; a messenger; specifically, of God, i.e. an angel (also a prophet, priest or teacher): KJV—ambassador, angel, king, messenger.

183 *The McAlvany Intelligence Advisor*, December 1997, p 6.

184 "A Hedge Fund Falters, So Fed Persuades Banks to Ante Up," *The Wall Street Journal*, September 24, 1998.

185 Ibid.

186 *CBS Morning Show*, August 8, 1999.

187 *Democrat and Chronicle*, Rochester New York, "Bank gives tot $5,000 credit limit: Mom sends in pre-approveed application as a joke, but 3 year-old gets Visa card," August 9, 1999, p 1.

188 1999 Consumer Federation of America Study, reported by *USA TODAY*, "Students binge on credit," September 14, 2000, p 26A.

189 Claritas Market Research, reported by *USA TODAY*, "Students binge on credit," September 14, 2000, p 26A.

190 Nellie Mae Student Loan Corporation, reported by *USA TODAY*, "Students binge on credit," September 14, 2000, p 26A.

191 James Pierpoint, "Alanta shooter had $150,000 market lose report," *Reuters Wire Report*, July 31, 1999.

192 "Text Of Atlanta Ginman's Notes," *Associated Press Report*, Atlanta, July 31, 1999.

193 Given to me verbally over the phone by a Wisconsin resident.

194 Houston Texas BankOne notice, October 7 to November 4, 1993.

195 This information was acquired during a personal conversation with Alan Whitney of the FDIC during a phone interview with First American Monetary Consultants during my tenure there as a senior economist.

196 The difference between a Joseph project and a religious program is that a Joseph project is a Spirit empowered campaign that produces the fruit of God's Kingdom for a specific time and purpose, while a religious program is a work of the flesh, which becomes an Icon that goes nowhere and never seems to end.

197 Hislop, *The Two Babylons*, pp 20, 29–30.

198 Ibid.

199 *The European*, August 1996, p 17.

200 Unclassified January 1995 DOD information paper from Major C. A. Kirscher/ J4(MRD)/35104/6 provided to me by well-known Christian researcher Terry Cook.

201 Ibid

202 *USA TODAY*, May 28, 1996, p 6B.

203 Phil Patton, "e-money," *Popular Science*, July 1995, p 74.

204 Neil Wilson, *Science and Technology* correspondent, "Professor claims to receive first chip implant," *Reuters Internet News*, August 25, 1998.

205 *ADSX News* (Applied Digital Systems Press Release), October 30, 2000.

206 "Digital Angel unveiled: Human-tracking subdermal implant technology makes debut," *WorldNetDaily*, exnews 20001101, November 1, 2000.

207 Confidential sources within the international banking community.

208 Ibid, Henry Kissinger and Zbigniew Brezezinski, just to name two.

209 Ibid.

210 Ibid, headed by Citicorp (Rockefeller).

211 Warren Schoder heads Royal Bounty Financial; "www.royalbounty.com".

212 Os Hillman heads Marketplace Leaders in Cumming, Georgia: "www.marketplaceleaders.org"

213 "Indian Economy Is Set To Beat China," *The Asian Wall Street Journal*, April 27, 2000, p 3

214 Confidential sources inside the law enforcement community.

215 Strong's Concordance, Greek word #2342.

216 *Emerging Viruses: AIDS and Ebola: Nature, Accident or Intentional Conspiracy?* by Leonard G. Horowitz, MD and W. John Martin, MD, is a flawlessly documented exposé on the plans and purposes of the AIDS and Ebola viruses.

Distribution Information

International Sales and Distribution

Ascension Ministries International
PO Box 19426
Denver, CO 80219
USA
www.AscensionMinistries.net